Poet of Hope

'you will be my people, and I will be your God.'
Jeremiah 30:22

Selwyn Hughes
Revised and updated by Mick Brooks
FURTHER STUDY: IAN SEWTER

© CWR 2014. Dated text previously published as *Every Day with Jesus: The Pursuit of Excellence* (July/August 1996) by CWR. This edition revised and updated for 2014 by Mick Brooks.

CWR, Waverley Abbey House, Waverley Lane, Farnham, Surrey GU9 8EP, UK
Tel: 01252 784700 Email: mail@cwr.org.uk
Registered Charity No. 294387. Registered Limited Company No. 1990308.

Unless otherwise indicated, all Scripture references are from the Holy Bible: New International Version (NIV), Copyright © 1979, 1984 by Biblica (formerly International Bible Society). Used by permission of Hodder & Stoughton Publishers, an Hachette UK company. All rights reserved. 'NIV' is a registered trademark of Biblica (formerly International Bible Society). UK trademark number 1448790. Other versions used: *The Message*: Scripture taken from THE MESSAGE. Copyright © 1993, 1994, 1995, 1996, 2000, 2001, 2002. Used by permission of NavPress Publishing Group. TLB: *The Living Bible*, © 1971, 1994, Tyndale House Publishers

Cover image: Linh Nguyen
Quiet Time image: Fotosearch
Printed in England by Linney Print

A word of introduction ...

Jeremiah, often referred to as the 'weeping prophet', is probably not the first book that comes to mind for summer reading! And there is no doubt it can be hard to follow, possibly even appearing disorganised as it bounces back and forth between poetry, biography, arresting visions and metaphors. But above all, I have found it to be a book of contrasts. Jeremiah has been typecast as the doom and gloom merchant, offering a tirade of judgment and condemnation. The narrative does bounce back and forth, not just between literary styles but more importantly between dark, difficult times and hope. It reveals to us the nature of God's relationship with His people and between Jeremiah and Himself. Their exchanges can only be described as real, heartfelt and honest. The whole range of emotions is expressed and experienced; it's certainly not been doctored or given spin for those of a gentle disposition. It paints for us God's amazing invitation for a genuine, passionate, intimate relationship with Himself; a relationship in which we can be our messy, confused selves, without fear of rejection and where He can be Himself - loving, compassionate, 'slow to anger and quick to forgive'. I hope that as you spend time with Jeremiah and God you will be able to enter into that rich authentic relationship, and that if you feel overrun by circumstances, you will know the hope on offer and, as did the Old Testament theologian Walter Brueggeman, that you will discover in Jeremiah not a weeping prophet but 'profoundly a poet of hope'.

Mick

Mick Brooks, Consulting Editor

Free small group resources to accompany this issue can be found at www.cwr.org.uk/extra. The *EDWJ* Facebook community is growing! To join the conversation visit www.facebook.com/edwjpage **f**

What's in a name?

TUE
1 JUL

FOR READING & MEDITATION - JEREMIAH 1:1-3
'The words of Jeremiah son of Hilkiah' (v1)

Today we begin our doctrinal study of one of the most profound and spiritually productive books of the Old Testament – the prophecy of Jeremiah. Time and space prevent a verse by verse exposition of what is the longest book of the Old Testament, so we must content ourselves by looking at some of its key passages.

Jeremiah lived approximately 600 years before Christ and was called to minister to Judah during the reign of its last five kings: Josiah, Jehoahaz, Jehoiakim, Jehoiachin, and Zedekiah. He lived for a period of about sixty years, most of which he spent conveying God's Word to the people. In some ways, his ministry is reflected in his name; it means 'the Lord hurls'. We read that the 'word of the LORD came to him in the thirteenth year of the reign of Josiah' (v2). But it not only came to him; it came out of him. He never failed to pass on what God had given him – sometimes hurling it into the midst of an obstinate nation with all the force of a thunderbolt.

Nowhere does Scripture reveal more clearly a model of spiritual faithfulness than in the life of Jeremiah. He kept true to the Word of God: despite the setbacks and struggles he was faithful and he endured. There were times when the fiery darts of doubt pierced his heart but they were always quenched when, through open and honest prayer, he allowed God's presence to flow into his soul. If you feel stretched as you try to live for God in difficult circumstances, or if you are plagued with doubts and uncertainties concerning the path to which God has called you, then Jeremiah is the book for you. The greatest thing anyone can do in this life is to fulfil their spiritual destiny. Jeremiah shows us how.

FURTHER STUDY

2 Cor. 1:3-11;
4:7-18

1. What difficulties did Paul endure?

2. What was the key to his faithfulness?

Loving Father, I live in difficult times. Help me to hold tight to the fact that You never call me or lead me where You cannot help me. Teach me to trust myself less and You more. In Jesus' name. Amen.

The larger story

FOR READING & MEDITATION – JEREMIAH 1:4-5

'Before I formed you in the womb I knew you' (v5)

Jeremiah would have been encouraged to learn that before he became interested in God, God was interested in him. 'Before I formed you in the womb,' God says, '*I knew you.*' This statement is intended to help Jeremiah understand that he is part of a larger story. It is not (as some commentators have claimed) an attempt by God to get Jeremiah to think about issues such as predestination, election, the relationship of time to eternity, and the connection between human choices and divine purposes.

It is rather God's reassurance that Jeremiah had always been known. It is a statement designed to warm his heart, not to satisfy his intellect. God is saying in effect: 'Jeremiah, you have always been known and always will be known. You are not an accident of birth. You are part of a much bigger story. I appointed you as a prophet before you were ever formed in your mother's womb.'

FURTHER STUDY

Psa. 139:11-16;
Eph. 1:3-14

1. What was the psalmist's conviction?

2. When did God choose you?

We do not discover our identity as persons when we know ourselves but when we realise that we are known by someone else. We don't know who we are until we know whose we are. We were known by God before our parents even knew we were on the way. Keep hold of this thought and you will never have an identity crisis.

Derek Kidner suggests in his commentary that this first word of God to Jeremiah gives the prophet a centre of gravity not in himself or his circumstances but in his Creator. Jeremiah was a prescription baby – made for the task which God had foreseen he could best accomplish. And so are you. You too have been chosen for something important that God is doing in this generation. It is something that nobody other than you can do.

Father, help me to understand that my destiny is not to be a spectator but a participant in Your eternal purposes. Make even clearer to me the work You want me to do. Then enable me to do it, as You did for Jeremiah. In Christ's name. Amen.

Not my ability but His

'Then the LORD ... said to me, "Now, I have put my words
in your mouth."' (v9)

The Bible is full of examples of people who, whenever they were asked by God to do something for Him, started pleading their inadequacy. Moses did it. Isaiah did it. Gideon did it. And as we see in this passage, Jeremiah did it. We are all good at rationalising reasons why God should let us off the hook: 'I am too young and inexperienced. I have never had a university education. I find it difficult to get up in front of people. I am tied up with many other things at the moment. It's a little bit more than I can manage.' God must sometimes 'smile' at our responses! The truth is that each of us is utterly inadequate for the tasks God asks us to do for Him. We are not bright enough, smart enough, or efficient enough to do the tasks He asks of us. God has to have a part in our lives if His work is to be accomplished through us. And it must be the *greater* part. God assures Jeremiah that He will be with him, then He touches his mouth and puts into his mind the very words He wanted him to speak. The God who made his mouth could provide him with the words to speak.

It is not wrong to feel inadequate. But we must be careful not to let those feelings lead us to despair. Rather they lead us to a deeper dependency on God the Father. I know that everything I have ever accomplished for God was done not out of a sense of adequacy but of inadequacy. It's not our ability but our response to His ability that is the key to service. 'God does not send us into the dangerous and exacting life of faith because we are qualified,' said Eugene Peterson. 'He chooses us in order to qualify us for what He wants us to be and do.'

FURTHER STUDY

Exod. 3:7-12; 4:10-17; Acts 7:20-22

1. Was Moses right to feel inadequate?

2. What was God's response to his excuses?

Father, I do not want to escape the tasks You have for me by pleading my own inadequacy. The issue is not what I decide but what You decide. Help me to understand that where Your finger points Your hand always provides. In Jesus' name. Amen.

Shaped by a vision

FOR READING & MEDITATION – JEREMIAH 1:11-19
'Today I have made you a fortified city, an iron pillar and
a bronze wall' (v18)

Jeremiah is pictured by God as a strong fortified city, as immovable as an iron pillar, and as impregnable as heavy gates of brass (v18). How did he change from lacking confidence to being secure in God? It came about through two remarkable visions.

In the first, he saw a rod of almond. The almond is one of the earliest trees to bloom in Israel. When the land is still chilled by winter the blossoming almond tree shows that spring is on the way. It showed Jeremiah that just as surely as spring follows winter, God is watching over His word to fulfil it; the words for 'almond' and 'watch' are similar in Hebrew. Next he sees a pot of boiling water that was tipped; its scalding waters were spilling towards the south. Both the village of Anathoth where Jeremiah had been brought up and the city of Jerusalem (an hour's walk from Anathoth) were directly in its path. The boiling water cascading down to the holy city represented enemy armies that were poised to invade. Judgment was coming because of their broken covenant and wilfulness.

FURTHER STUDY

Exod. 14:10-31

1. Contrast the responses of Moses and the Israelites.

2. How was God's power released?

These two visions, the blossoming almond branch and the pot of boiling water, have been described by one writer as 'Jeremiah's Oxford and Cambridge' – in other words, his core curriculum. He was learning never to underestimate God and never to overestimate evil. We too, if we are to stand strong as iron pillars in difficult situations, must learn the same lesson. God never goes back on His Word and evil will not triumph. When we are shaped by that vision we will have the strength and courage to pursue the path that God has planned for us.

O God, as Jeremiah was shaped by this vision, shape me by it too. Help me never to underestimate You and never to overestimate evil. Grant that I might always be gripped and guided by this vision. In Jesus' name I ask it. Amen.

How problems develop

FOR READING & MEDITATION - JEREMIAH 2:1-18

'My people have ... forsaken me ... and have dug their own cisterns'
(v13)

This was probably Jeremiah's first ever sermon. But perhaps the word 'sermon' is hardly the one to describe it. It is more of a 'case for the prosecution'. Jeremiah, using highly charged metaphors as he speaks, issues a powerful indictment of the people of Israel, accusing them of spiritual promiscuity. Like an expert prosecutor he challenges them to answer some sharp and incisive questions. What fault have you found in me? Has any other nation ever changed its gods? And where are the gods you made for yourselves? The challenges ring out one after the other.

Then in one of the most powerful statements in the whole of Scripture, Jeremiah sums up their spiritual condition. It consists of two great evils: first, forsaking the spring of living water and second, digging their own water-storage cisterns. This illustrates, I believe, the root cause of many of our problems. I often use this verse to demonstrate to people from a biblical perspective how problems develop in the human personality.

FURTHER STUDY

Isa. 53:6; 55:1-6

1. What is our tendency?

2. What does God offer?

When we dig our way beneath the layers of psychological symptoms ultimately we come to a *person*. This person refuses to satisfy their thirst in God, preferring instead to find stagnant water in a 'cistern' of their own making – money, power, status, and so on.

But why would anyone choose a stagnant cistern over a fresh spring? There is only one explanation. We like to feel we hold the resources for our well-being in our own hands. We don't like feeling *dependent*; we prefer to feel *independent*. And this attitude of independence is the energy which makes many of our emotional and psychological problems grow.

O Father, I sense that even though I belong to You this stubborn commitment to my independence is still in my heart. Teach me how to depend more on You, not merely at some times, but at all times. And in all things. For Jesus' sake. Amen.

Stop!

FOR READING & MEDITATION - JEREMIAH 2:19-32

'You are a swift she-camel running here and there' (v23)

One wonders how anyone listening to this shockingly authentic and impassioned complaint about Judah's spiritual condition could have remained unrepentant. But clearly the people had become complacent – one of the most devastating and debilitating diseases that can afflict anyone. One of the seven churches in the book of Revelation was in this condition. When addressing the Christians in Laodicea, Jesus threatened to 'spit you out of my mouth' (Rev. 3:16). Why does He use such uncharacteristic, even shocking, language? Because complacent people sometimes need to be stopped in their tracks. Perhaps this is why He chooses these vivid and unflattering word pictures to describe the condition into which Judah had fallen.

FURTHER STUDY

1 John 2:15-17; Rev. 3:14-22

1. How may God's love be squeezed out?

2. What did the Laodiceans think?

One graphic metaphor after another illustrates their spiritual decline: a degenerate vine (v21), ineffective ablutions (v22), a wild ass on heat (v24), a disgraced thief (v26) and a forgetful bride (v32). And in the verse I have highlighted for today, which if it wasn't so serious would border on the comical, God described them as: 'a swift she-camel running here and there'.

God was saying in effect: 'You are like a camel in heat, racing up and down the desert looking for sexual satisfaction from a mate.' The metaphor implies that Judah is actively engaged in seeking out idolatrous experiences like a camel sniffing at the wind to detect a mate's scent. When God's people desire the things that lie outside of God's will so much so that they will do anything to get them, then it is a sure sign of a lost direction that needs to be firmly arrested and put back on course.

O God, help me to examine myself today to see if the debilitating disease of complacency has taken root in my soul. If it has, perform whatever surgery or treatment is necessary to rid me of it. In Christ's precious name I pray. Amen.

CWR Ministry Events

PLEASE PRAY FOR THE TEAM

E	EVENT	PLACE	PRESENTER(S)
Jul	Teaching the Bible: Communicating Well to All Ages	Waverley Abbey House	Andy Peck
Jul	Seniors' Summer Holiday	Pilgrim Hall	
1	Prayer Breakfast	PH	
l	Women's Summer Day: Give Me an Undivided Heart	WAH	Jennifer Rees Larcombe
ul	Bible Discovery: Great Chapters of the Bible - John 17	WAH	Philip Greenslade
ul	Insight into Depression	WAH	Chris Ledger
ul	Understanding Yourself, Understanding Others	PH	Lynn & Andrew Penson
Aug	Introduction to Biblical Care and Counselling	WAH	Angie Coombes & team
3 Aug	Family Summer Holiday	PH	Jon & Sarah Stannard, Ben & Laura West
ug	Study Skills	WAH	Kathy Overton & John Munt
0 Aug	Developing an Integrative Christian Approach to Counselling	WAH	Sarah Lloyd

ase also pray for students and tutors on our ongoing **BA in Counselling** programme
Waverley and Pilgrim Hall and our **Certificate and Diploma of Christian Counselling** and
 in Integrative Psychotherapy held at London School of Theology.

 further details and a full list of CWR's courses, phone +44 (0)1252 784719
visit the CWR website at **www.cwr.org.uk** Pilgrim Hall: **www.pilgrimhall.com**

Pride breaks God's heart

FOR READING & MEDITATION - JEREMIAH 3:1-25

'"Return, faithless Israel," declares the LORD, "I will frown on you
no longer"' (v12)

At times, complacent people need a reality check, so
Jeremiah adds another arresting statement. Continuing
the analogy of a broken marriage (2:2) he reminds them
of the law given to Moses that forbade a divorced couple
to be reunited to each other (v1; Deut. 24:1-4). The purpose
of this law was to maintain a high view of marriage and
to protect relationships from being degraded to the casual
level in which a man could divorce his wife and have her
back whenever he felt like it. A society that has a low view
of marriage inevitably becomes unstable (v1).

**FURTHER
STUDY**

Gen. 6:5-6;
Micah 7:18-20

1. How does sin
affect God?

2. In what does
God delight?

Unless any society maintains a high view of
marriage social infrastuctures become shaky
and insecure. God is illustrating here that Judah's
spiritual adultery and breaking of her covenant
has put her in danger of being separated from
God. And if that happens, then she might not be
able to return. They are startling words. God then
compares the southern kingdom of Judah to her
northern sister Israel (vv6-11). He describes how
Israel had defected from God and had suffered
the consequences of being destroyed while Judah had also
sinned but pretended to repent (v10).

During this discourse God's tone suddenly changes. He
turns from warning and arresting them to wooing and
winning them. Passionately and plaintively God cries out:
'Return ... I will cure you of backsliding' (v22). If you listen
to this cry from the heart of God you will see in a new way
how sin affects God – in a way that perhaps we as human
beings can never conceive or understand. But it might help
us to understand if we keep in mind that the most awful
thing about proud resistance is not simply that it breaks
God's design, but that it breaks His *heart*.

**O Father, it gives me a new awareness of sin when I see how it
affects You in the deepest part of Your being. It is an offence not
against a principle but against You as a person. Help me never to
forget this. In Christ's name I pray. Amen.**

The next move is ours

FOR READING & MEDITATION - JEREMIAH 4:1-4

'the LORD says ... "Break up your unploughed ground and do not
sow among thorns"' (v3)

We need to keep in mind that whenever we move away from our relationship with God either through commission or omission, *the only way back is the way of repentance*. But what does it mean to repent? Is it merely a matter of kissing and making up? No, I don't believe so. Repentance, as a little boy once put it, is not merely being sorry about sin, but being sorry enough to quit.

The opening words of this chapter reveal God's real concern, expressed through Jeremiah, for the repentance of His people to be genuine and lasting. Acts of idolatry and independence are to be given up. The people are told through God's illustration that as a plough breaks up the rocky soil, so they can break up the hardness of their hearts in the same way. The seeds of repentance can only be sown in prepared soil. Unless there is a complete breaking with sin, there is little hope of the spiritual life ever flourishing in the way that is possible.

I have met many Christians who have been involved in unhelpful and wrong behaviour and who have excused themselves by saying, 'I don't feel convicted about what I am doing. When or if God convicts me, then I will give it up.' That is a very dangerous and deceptive way of thinking. Enough is said in Scripture to show us what is right and what is wrong. Jeremiah reminded the people that they needed to remove the sin that hardened their heart before the good seed of God's Word could take root. If we say to God, 'Restore me and then I will give up my sin,' the result is stalemate. God has made the first move. We must now respond.

FURTHER STUDY

Hosea 10:12-13;
14:1-3;
Luke 3:1-14

1. When would Israel receive God's love and forgiveness?

2. What was John's message?

Father, I see that I must be willing to remove any heart-hardening if Your Word is to take root and grow in my life. Help me to be ever ready to make the next move if and whenever my relationship with You needs to be improved. Amen.

Are you listening?

FOR READING & MEDITATION - JEREMIAH 5:18-31
'Hear this, you ... have eyes but do not see ... ears but do not hear'
(v21)

The section of Jeremiah's prophecy from 4:5 to 6:26 is a vivid and poetic description of the judgment that is to come upon the people because of their refusal to listen and respond. Babylonian armies would come from the north to destroy them. Language is stretched to its limits to describe the catastrophic consequences of the refusal of God's people to turn back to Him. The picture is so black and vivid that in places it almost resembles apocalyptic language.

The verse I have selected for comment reveals the degree of their spiritual deafness and blindness. They refused to hear or see God's message. There is a saying that 'there are none so deaf as those who do not wish to hear, none so blind as those who do not wish to see.' How do you feel when you find yourself talking to someone about something serious or important only to realise that they have not heard a single word you have said? You probably feel frustrated and ignored. Imagine how God must have felt as He pleaded with the people to turn from the impending disaster that was coming upon them only to find them tuning Him out.

FURTHER STUDY

Matt. 15:1-9;
Acts 7:51-60

1. Why may people not hear God?

2. What could be the result?

Jesus made the same observation of some of the people of His day: 'You will be ever hearing but never understanding; you will be ever seeing but never perceiving' (Matt. 13:14). Nothing can be more spiritually damaging than to tune God out when He is speaking. Those who think that the problem in their spiritual life is that God doesn't speak to them may find that the problem is rather that they are not listening to a God who is always trying to speak.

O God, can it be that You are speaking and I am not listening? Forgive me if so. Help me to tune my spiritual ear, and to focus my spiritual perception so that I hear and see all that You want me to hear and see. In Jesus' name. Amen.

Healing wounds 'lightly'

FOR READING & MEDITATION - JEREMIAH 6:1-15

'They dress the wound of my people as though it were not serious'
(v14)

One of the great tragedies in Jeremiah's day was the fact that the priests were as insensitive to God's warnings as were the people. Treachery, fraud and deception were part and parcel of their daily lives. Following Jeremiah's stinging statements about the people's lifestyle, one would have hoped that the priests would have gone into mourning and pleaded with God to withhold His justice. But they did not.

Instead they set about trying to heal the serious rupture between the people and the Almighty with superficial remedies that were no more effective than putting a band-aid on a huge gaping wound. They dressed the wound of the people 'lightly' by saying that all was well when it wasn't. This was about as helpful as a doctor telling a patient with a brain tumour to take a couple of aspirin each day in the hope that it will disappear. The priests adopted the common attitude that if they ignored the problem it would go away. They didn't even know how to blush.

This same attitude can be seen in many parts of the church today. People who are called by God to apply spiritual remedies to serious matters do so in a way that only heals the wound 'lightly'. Ministers, leaders, counsellors and others who offer spiritual direction do the people of God a disservice when they deal only with symptoms instead of dealing with, for example, the issues of sin in a person's life when sin is the root of their problem. Just as a doctor who would suggest treating lung cancer with cough medicine deserves to be struck off the medical register, so Christians who treat sin lightly deserve no recognition as spiritual leaders.

FURTHER STUDY

Ezek. 13:8-23;
Luke 11:37-46

1. How does God feel about people making false promises?

2. How did Jesus expose false leaders?

My Father and my God, thank You for reminding me that sin is never removed by denying its existence. Give us leaders who, without going on witch hunts for sin, will lovingly confront it. In Jesus' name. Amen.

The past is important

FOR READING & MEDITATION - JEREMIAH 6:16-30

'Stand at the crossroads and look; ask for the ancient paths' (v16)

Jeremiah is often depicted as the prophet of doom and gloom, but in many of his prophecies there is also a great deal of light and hope. Take today's text for example. There *are* ancient paths, he says, which people have trodden through the centuries. They are well marked, clearly defined, and all one has to do is to look for them and travel along them. They lead to a life that is good and pleasing to God.

What are these paths? Without question Jeremiah is talking about the principles laid down in the written Word of God. He may be referring to the scroll of Deuteronomy which recently had been discovered in a corner of the Temple and given great publicity and prominence by King Josiah (2 Chron. 34). The word given to the people by Jeremiah is a word that needs to be repeated boldly in our churches today. There is a crisis of confidence amongst many in relation to the ancient Scriptures and some are asking whether the Bible is as relevant in contemporary culture as it was in the past.

Occasionally I get letters taking me to task for my strong stand on the authority of the Scriptures and the standards laid down in them. Some tell me my views are so Victorian and that I should come into the twenty-first century. My response is that when we talk about truth and morality we are not dealing with Victorian, Edwardian, or even the modern Elizabethan values. We are dealing with the living and timeless God. To live successfully in the present and the future we must listen to the past. And what does the past tell us? That there *are* ancient paths marked out for us by God. To stray from them is to put our lives in peril.

FURTHER STUDY

Deut. 32:7-15;
Isa. 35:8-10

1. Why should we remember the past?

2. What paths do God's people walk?

Heavenly Father, I am so thankful that You have given me in Your Word some clear directions for making my way through the world. Help me to heed and obey them. In Jesus' name I pray. Amen.

Deceptive words

FOR READING & MEDITATION - JEREMIAH 7:1-11

'But look, you are trusting in deceptive words that are worthless.'
(v8)

The entrance to the Temple in Jerusalem was an excellent setting for one of Jeremiah's most powerful sermons. Undoubtedly he had watched many times as the people entered the beautiful courtyards and cried out 'The temple of the Lord! The temple of the Lord! The temple of the Lord!' But the prophet saw right through their deception and hypocrisy. He saw, sadly, that the words were nothing more than a religious cliché.

Deep down in their hearts they believed that though God might let the state of Judah fall, He would never allow His Temple to be destroyed. They believed, wrongly, that the presence of the Temple and its rituals in their city would protect them. 'You are deceiving yourselves,' cries the prophet. 'You are in the right place, saying all the right things, but you yourselves are not right. You use the Lord's house as a robbers' den. The Temple and its traditions are meaningless unless your behaviour matches your words.'

We need to live life as a whole, showing consistency in our words and in our deeds. Someone once observed that though Christians may not *say* lies in church, they often *sing* them. For example, we sing words like 'I've got a love song in my heart', 'Make my life a prayer to You' and 'Send revival, start with me'. Do we really mean what we sing? Or do we convince ourselves into thinking that the more religious phrases we use the safer we are spiritually? One person put it like this: 'Standing in a church worshipping doesn't make us holy any more than standing in a barn and neighing makes us a horse.' It's not so much what we say but who we are that's important.

FURTHER STUDY

Matt. 23:13-28; John 2:12-17

1. How did the Pharisees deceive people?

2. How did Jesus respond to those in the temple?

My Father and my God, save me from the kind of self-deception and hypocrisy that I have read about today. Let there be no dissonance in my spiritual life, but may my behaviour always match my words. In Christ's name I ask it. Amen.

'I am sorry!'

FOR READING & MEDITATION - JEREMIAH 8:1-21
'When men fall down, do they not get up?' (v4)

It is very strange that in our relationship with God we sometimes act in ways that are diametrically opposite to our natural inclinations. When we fall down physically, we immediately try to get up. If we discover that we have lost our way on a journey we immediately try to find the right road. How is it then that we do not apply these same correctives to our spiritual condition? Why is it that when we fall spiritually or move away from a close relationship with God we do not seek to correct it immediately?

Why is it that spiritually we don't like admitting that we have lost our way? I read recently of research which discovered that out of a long list of statements people found difficult to say, the one they found *most* difficult was: 'I am sorry'. There is a madness in us that can only be explained by the fact of blinding pride and independence. As Jeremiah points out, we can easily go off in the wrong direction like galloping horses (v6) or pretend we know better than God (v8).

FURTHER STUDY

Luke 13:1-5;
15:11-24

1. What did Jesus emphasise?

2. When did the son repent?

If we remain stubborn and independent then consequences follow. In Judah's case it came as a failure of the harvest (v13). God's justice concerning our sinfulness may seem harsh and hard but we must, however, remember that it is prompted by love and not indignation. He loves us as we are, but He loves us too much to let us stay as we are. Permit me to ask you two pointed and personal questions. Are you aware that you might have lost your way and strayed from the path spiritually? And what are you doing to get back on the right path? The first step to moving in the right direction begins with the words 'I am sorry'.

Father, thank You for reminding me that when I have strayed it is not enough just to seek to get back on the right path; I must also admit my failure. Help me acknowledge that true repentance begins when I say, 'Sorry'. In Jesus' name. Amen.

The bread of life, with love ...

... from you, to Christians in need at home and overseas, who seek – like you – the sustenance of biblically-based guidance, teaching and resources.

In Galilee, Jesus told the crowd of over 4,000 to sit down, 'Then he took the seven loaves and the fish, and when he had given thanks, he broke them and gave them to the disciples, and they in turn to the people. They all ate and were satisfied' (Matt. 15:36–37).

With your help, the ministry of CWR can feed the faith of many.

Please fill in the 'Gift to CWR' section on the order form at the back of this publication, completing the Gift Aid declaration if appropriate.

When did you last weep?

FOR READING & MEDITATION - JEREMIAH 9:1-26

'Oh, that my head were a spring of water and my eyes a fountain of tears!' (v1)

The verse I have chosen as our text for today, together with the last few verses of the previous chapter, provides a vivid picture of what is happening in Jeremiah's heart as he watches the nation reject God. This sensitive prophet is in tears as he contemplates the plight of his people. He had mixed emotions. He felt intense anger with them concerning their rebellious resistance, but he also felt deep compassion towards them too – a compassion born out of godly concern. He thinks for a few moments of leaving them and quitting his task as a prophet (v2) but as he spells out once more the consequences that are to fall upon the nation for its rebellious attitude towards God, he knows that he is unable to give up. This chapter describes in graphic and vivid detail the anguish Judah will feel when the invading armies are allowed by God to take control of the land.

FURTHER STUDY

Exod. 32:7-14; 30-32

1. Why did the Lord not punish sin?

2. To what lengths did Moses' intercession extend?

Jeremiah's godly concern for his people leads us to ask, how do we feel about the occasional state of the Church and the world? Does it drive us to our knees in heartfelt intercessory prayer? When did we last weep over the condition of both the world and the Church? I confess I have to hang my head in shame as I face those challenging questions. How about you?

But however ashamed we might feel we must not leave it there. We ask God to forgive our lack of compassion and invite Him to reveal His heart for the world He so deeply loves. Godly concern is not something that can be manufactured. It comes only as we are willing to press our hearts against His. And it is the source of true prayer.

O God, help me feel some of the compassion You feel for a world that is lost. Pull my heart into close proximity to Your own, so that I might share Your concerns. In Christ's name I ask it. Amen.

We *must* worship

FOR READING & MEDITATION - JEREMIAH 10:1-16
'No-one is like you, O LORD'(v6)

Nowhere in Scripture (with the possible exception of Isaiah 44) will you find such a scathing denunciation of idolatry as there is in this chapter. The picture of relying on idols that you have to hold up or fix to the wall, rather than being held up by them, would be laughable if it wasn't so sad.

Why did the people of God in Old Testament times allow themselves to be allured into worshipping idols? I think it is because we were designed by our Creator to worship Him. That is not because He is egotistical and likes to be affirmed, but because in the act of worshipping God we complete ourselves. Every part of us is drawn to wholeness when we worship the true God. Worship makes it possible for God to enter our lives and to be to us all that He promises to be. However, we cannot truly worship God without at the same time obeying Him. And there, as they say, is the rub.

If we are not willing to bow the knee to the true God then we are unable to worship Him, and a part of our soul shuts down, suppressed because it is unexpressed. An idol helps us express our need to worship without the necessity for inward change. That is why idolatry is so appealing. We can express our need to worship without any accountability, forgetting that in worship of God true transformation takes place. Those who do not worship the true God will worship something else, for they *must* worship. The people of Judah worshipped the stars as well as gods of wood and stone. They substituted the unreal for the real. A little boy was asked to define the word 'idol'. He said it was 'something that doesn't work'. He was thinking of the world 'idle'. But he was not far wrong.

FURTHER STUDY

Isa. 44:9-23;
Col. 3:1-5

1. Why are those who worship idols unthinking?

2. What is a modern form of idolatry?

O God, now that I see more clearly the motive behind idolatry may the old hymn writer's words be my constant theme: 'The dearest idol I have known, help me to tear it from thy throne.' In Jesus' name I ask it. Amen.

Unfaithful in marriage

FOR READING & MEDITATION – JEREMIAH 11:1-17

'Both the house of Israel and the house of Judah have broken the covenant I made with their forefathers.' (v10)

It was bad enough that the people of Jeremiah's day had turned from their Creator to worship idols. But an even more serious consequence results from their idolatry: they have broken the covenant which God had made with them when He brought them out of Egypt. He tells Jeremiah to remind them of the historic agreement made and sealed centuries earlier at Sinai in which God promised to supply all the needs of His chosen people in return for their relationship, worship and obedience.

FURTHER STUDY

Isa. 54:1-8;
Hosea 3:1-3

1. How did God relate to Israel?
2. How did Israel relate to God?

That covenant was similar to a marriage. God committed Himself to the nation of Israel in the same way that a man commits himself to his wife at a wedding. The Almighty refers to His people as His 'beloved' (v15); with the marital relationship in mind He reminds them of their spiritual adultery. In turning to other gods the people had become unfaithful. They had broken their marriage vows to God and had gone chasing after idols. Because of their broken covenant, consequences must follow.

Such is the pain that pulses in the heart of God that He instructs Jeremiah to stop praying for the people and to tell them that He will not listen to them when they pray (v14). Think over those staggering words. A time comes when God must inevitably judge sinful behaviour. There are consequences to all of our actions. Remember that there is no point in asking God to bless our lives when we are engaged in wilful sin; accountability is not unreasonable. Thankfully He does not wipe us out every time we err. He is incredibly patient with our frailties. The justice of God is not unreasonable but it is inevitable.

O God, help me to grasp that I am part of Your Church that is described in Your Word as the bride of Christ. Do whatever is necessary to keep me and all your people free from idolatry and forever faithful to you. In Christ's name. Amen.

Dealing with doubts

THURS
17 JUL

FOR READING & MEDITATION - JEREMIAH 11:18 - 12:4

'You are always righteous, O Lord, when I bring a case before you.'
(12:1)

Jeremiah must have been greatly shocked when God told him that the people of his own village of Anathoth were planning to kill him. Anathoth, about six kilometres from Jerusalem, was known as a 'priestly village' (see Joshua 21:18 and I Kings 2:26). Some of the priests who lived there were probably incensed at Jeremiah's continuous indictment of them for their spiritual failures, and shared in plotting his assassination. How does Jeremiah react to the news that his life is in danger?

First, he expresses surprise and astonishment at such a revelation. 'I didn't know they were planning to kill me. I had been as unsuspecting as a lamb or an ox on the way to slaughter,' he says (v19 TLB). Then as the full impact of the news hits him he turns to God and pours out his frightened feelings in passionate prayer. Many have been puzzled by Jeremiah's strong reaction as he changes from being a confident prophet to a man seemingly plagued with doubts. Is he guilty, they have asked, of leading a double life? Was he a hero when standing before a crowd, but a coward in private? I don't believe so. His reaction is that of any normal person in such circumstances. There is nothing wrong with having doubts; it is what we do with those doubts which is important. Doubt is best dealt with in prayer before God, not peddled in public. A minister whose sermons were often filled with doubts was told by one of his congregations, 'I have enough doubts of my own. When I come to church I come to hear convictions'. I rarely share my doubts in *Every Day with Jesus*. I deal with them in the best possible place – before God in prayer. I invite you to take yours to the same place.

FURTHER STUDY

Luke 22:39-46;
John 20:24-29

1. What did Jesus do with His doubts?

2. How did Jesus respond to Thomas' doubts?

Father, I cannot stop doubts entering my heart but I can stop them residing there. Help me to bring my doubts to You, dear Lord, and to leave the place of prayer, as Jeremiah did, with doubts turned into convictions. In Jesus' name. Amen.

Struggling well

FOR READING & MEDITATION - JEREMIAH 12:1-4

'Yet I would speak with you about your justice: Why does the way of the wicked prosper?' (v1)

As I put together these meditations on Jeremiah two questions kept coming to my mind: why is it that he seems so rocklike on the outside but so prone to discouragement on the inside? And did he ever arrive at a place in his life where he never had another moment of discouragement? Let me try to answer both. Being a servant of God does not mean that you will never again face and feel discouragement. Some Christians believe that you can be so filled with God's life that discouragement can find no room to lodge in you. But that is unrealistic. Some of the finest Christian men and women I have known confess to feeling discouraged at times. They do not indulge themselves in it, but they do admit it. And that's the difference between a realistic and an unrealistic Christian. The realistic Christian says, 'I am discouraged and I will bring it to God in heartfelt prayer.' The unrealistic Christian says 'God is on the throne, and because of that I can never be discouraged.' Being honest with one's feelings is a mark of maturity, not of immaturity.

FURTHER STUDY

2 Cor. 11:22-33; 12:7-10

1. How did Paul struggle well?

2. What was the key to his strength?

And did Jeremiah ever come to a place in his life where he never had another moment of discouragement? I do not think so. The first section of his prophecy (chapters 1-20) focuses on his inner sufferings while the second part focuses on his outer sufferings. I believe his struggles continued for most of his life, but he learned to struggle well. That means relying not on our own strength of character but on the strength of God's righteous character, whose justice is real even if it is not always obvious as we struggle against the situations which discourage us.

Father, I see that I shall never be exempt from struggles. So help me I pray, as You helped Jeremiah, to struggle well. May Your unfailing grace and power be my constant strength. In Christ's name I ask it. Amen.

Running with horses

SAT
19 JUL

FOR READING & MEDITATION – JEREMIAH 12:1-17

'If you have raced with men on foot and they have worn you out,
how can you compete with horses?' (v5)

If God is good, why does He allow evil to flourish? That very modern question was often on the lips of the Old Testament prophets, especially when they faced hard and difficult situations. Jeremiah asks it here. Why does God allow miscarriages of justice? Why does He allow the wicked to get away with so much? Jeremiah knew that God's justice will ultimately be seen to be done and like many of us, he wants to see it *now*.

Have you noticed that God never answers the vexed question of why there are so many apparent miscarriages of justice in His world? Instead He questions us, re-directs us, or reassures us. Job never got his questions answered but he did get a richer experience of God. God is not in the business of explaining things (which we probably wouldn't understand anyway) but He is ultimately relational and wants us to trust Him. He deals with us not as a philosopher or as a pastor but as a perfect Father.

Job 13:13-15;
2 Pet. 3:1-10

1. How did Job view death?

2. Why might the Lord delay justice?

Jeremiah was in danger of sliding into self-pity and the remedy is not a doctrinal statement but a challenge. God gives him a bracing reply: *If you raced with men on foot and they have worn you out how can you compete with horses?* He turns the light back on Jeremiah himself rather than on his complaint. His problems with the wicked now were nothing compared with the difficulties he would face in the future. If he can't trust God in the still darkness how will he trust Him in a raging storm? What was Jeremiah's response to this challenging question? His biography from here on leaves us in no doubt. He responded not by argument but by action. He rose to the challenge. *He ran with the horses.*

Father, I see that Your greatest concern is to help me to live by faith – to take You on trust. Help me come to the point at which the absence of explanations makes no difference to my trust and confidence in You. In Jesus' name. Amen.

Looking for free counselling advice or referral?

Curious but not convicted

FOR READING & MEDITATION - JEREMIAH 13:1-14

'For as a belt is bound round a man's waist, so I bound the
whole house of ... Judah to me' (v11)

God called Jeremiah to be what today we might describe
as a 'visual-aid preacher'. Actions often speak louder
than words. In today's passage Jeremiah is being instructed
by God to buy a linen belt, to wear it for a length of time
around his waist without washing it, and then to bury it
in Perath. 'Many days later' he is commanded to dig it up
only to discover, as he expected, that it was 'ruined and
completely useless' (v7).

Jeremiah used this incident as a parable to point out to the
people that just as the linen belt was ruined by its contact
with the earth so the people would be corrupted
by their idolatrous behaviour and thus would no
longer be fit to be part of the divine purposes. A
linen belt (or loincloth) was an intimate garment
and God told Jeremiah to use this example to
challenge the people about the way they covered
up their spiritual nakedness with a superstitious
and unproductive devotion to pagan deities.

**FURTHER
STUDY**

Luke 23:8-12;
Acts 17:16-34

1. How did
Herod respond
to Jesus?

2. What was
the reaction of
the Athenians
to Paul?

In the second parable Jeremiah used the picture
of wine jars. He is commanded to tell the people:
'Every wineskin should be filled with wine,' a
popular saying of the day. When they gave the
usual response, 'I agree,' Jeremiah was to tell
them: 'That's not what I mean ... everyone living in this
land will be filled with helpless bewilderment' (v13 TLB). In
other words, unless you act on what God is saying, one day
you will stagger like drunken men spiritually and socially
lost and confused. Such words and actions aroused the
people's curiosity, but sadly did nothing to change their
minds. Persistent resistance to God can so dull and deaden
our conscience that no matter what God does we cannot
hear Him and see no need to turn back to Him.

**O God, the thought that I might become desensitised to Your
Spirit's convictions concerns me deeply. Save me from such a
predicament. Help me put away all that hinders. In Jesus' name.
Amen.**

God - an unhurried judge

FOR READING & MEDITATION - JEREMIAH 13:15-27

'Can the Ethiopian change his skin or the leopard its spots?' (v23)

In yesterday's reading we saw how Jeremiah used parables to bring God's message home to the people. The message contained clear warnings and in the rest of the chapter, three more spiritual alerts are given. In one (vv15-17) he describes the people as travellers, overtaken by darkness and stumbling in the gathering gloom as they try to make it safely to their destination. In another (vv18-19) he calls on both the youthful king Jehoiachin and his mother Nehushta (see 2 Kings 24:8) to leave the throne because they were unfit to rule God's people and they had ignored God's warnings. The final picture (vv20-27) is one of a flock that must be mourned because its shepherds have failed to look after the sheep entrusted to their care. Godlessness had so gripped the people that it was now a lifestyle they could not change, any more than an Ethiopian could change the colour of his skin or a leopard its spots.

FURTHER STUDY

Luke 13:6-9;
1 Tim. 1:12-17

1. Why might God not hurry to judge us?

2. What was Paul's experience?

All of this raises the question: why were so many warnings given and why did God take so long to act? Certainly God seems an unhurried judge in the chapters we have read so far. Is He not as concerned as He appears to be, or is He more longsuffering than we can imagine?

Clearly, it is not because of lack of concern. It is rather as the apostle Peter puts it; He does not want anyone to perish but wants all to come to repentance (2 Pet. 3:9). God's unhurried ways might encourage us to think casually about cause and effect. If we do, then we think wrongly. Praise Him for His patience which waited for you, but don't try His patience with wilful stubbornness.

Father, help me not to mistakenly think that because Your justice is slow it is not sure. You will not overlook sin, but You will look over it - to Calvary. May my attitude be one of continuous repentance. In Jesus' name. Amen.

God has feelings too

FOR READING & MEDITATION - JEREMIAH 14:1-21

'Let my eyes overflow with tears night and day without ceasing;
for ... my people ... suffered a grievous wound' (v17)

It is difficult to imagine any suffering worse than that which is triggered by drought. In his commentary, Derek Kidner points out that the word translated *drought* is in the plural 'indicating a series of such disasters, each one leaving the survivors less able to face the next'. Following the graphic picture of the suffering caused by drought (vv2–6), Jeremiah is seen rising to the challenge with a powerful prayer of penitence and intercession (vv7–9). He uses similar language to that of many of the other great intercessors of the Old Testament – Abraham, for example – but his intercession has no effect on the Almighty.

Jeremiah is told to stop praying as God's mind is already made up (v11). A further argument by Jeremiah that the people can surely be excused because they are the victims of false prophets is firmly rebutted by the Lord. It was the responsibility of all who lived in Israel to discern a false prophet. All they had to do was to evaluate his words in the light of God's written revelation. Jeremiah is to be commended for his desire to intercede for his people, but he is out of touch with their stubborn commitment to independence.

How does God feel about all this? In verse 17 we get a glimpse into God's personal feelings. The Almighty is heartbroken. It's sad that so often we are more concerned about our own anguish than the anguish of God. Never forget – God has feelings too. It breaks His heart to see the waywardness and obstinacy of His people. How different our lives would be if we could see that sin is not just a collision with the divine will but a wound in the divine heart.

FURTHER STUDY

Psa. 78:35-41;
Eph. 4:29-32

1. What were the results of Israel's unfaithfulness?

2. What did Paul warn against?

O God, help me never to forget that You have feelings too. May I learn the vital lesson that whenever I sin I do not just break a commandment - I wound Your loving and sensitive heart. Give me this perspective always. In Jesus' name. Amen.

Spiritual stalemate

FOR READING & MEDITATION - JEREMIAH 14:22 & 15:1-4

'Even if Moses and Samuel were to stand before me, my heart would not go out to this people.' (15:1)

Having foreseen the terrible drought that will fall upon unrepentant Israel, the prophet is moved to intercede for them. And what a powerful prayer it is (14:7-9). But yet again God tells Jeremiah not to pray for the people (v11). Later the Lord tells the prophet (in our text for today) that even if Moses and Samuel were to stand before Him and plead for the people's wellbeing He would not listen. Moses and Samuel were considered two of God's greatest prophets and like Jeremiah they had interceded between God and the people (Exod. 17:11-13; 1 Sam. 7:7-9).

FURTHER STUDY

2 Chron. 7:11-22;
1 Kings 11:1-13

1. What were God's conditions of blessing?

2. Why was Solomon not wise?

Intercession is a vital part of the Christian life but what should one do when God says 'Stop praying'? Because it is important to remember that when Moses and Samuel prayed, the people displayed a readiness to repent. The nation at the time of Jeremiah, however, was stubborn, obstinate and defiant. Jeremiah's intercessions, though sincere and well meaning, did not reflect the true mood of the people. They paid lip service to the faith that had been handed down to them by their predecessors, but their hearts were set on idolatry and pagan rituals.

Although in previous times God had responded to the voice of a single intercessor, here the situation was different. The people knew that God wanted to bless them and they knew that they could receive that blessing only if they returned to Him. They wanted God to do His part, but they were not prepared to do theirs. Hence, they were locked in spiritual stalemate and could not move forward with God. God's blessings are there to be taken, but they are never to be taken for granted.

Gracious and loving heavenly Father, help me never to take Your blessings for granted but with gratitude. This I ask in Christ's peerless and precious name. Amen.

'My wound is grievous'

'Why is my pain unending and my wound grievous
and incurable?' (v18)

Several times we catch glimpses of Jeremiah at prayer. Sometimes he prays for the people but other prayers are what some of the Bible commentators call 'confessionals' (honest complaints). There are seven of them in the book (8:18-9:3; 11:18-23; 12:1-6; 15:10-12, 15:15-21; 17:14-18; 18:18-23; 20:7-8). Today's passage includes one of them. In each of the confessionals all his emotions come to the surface as he wrestles with his feelings in the presence of God. His inner life is exposed for all to see. He is scared, lonely, angry and hurt.

All his fear, loneliness, hurt and anger are poured out into God's ear. Some people think of prayer as a time of quiet and calm solitude before God, but it can be a time of great personal struggle also. I know some of you might say, 'But such prayers are not right. They show no respect or faith in the Almighty.' I have discovered that God will never be against us for honest praying. He would far rather that you identify what is going on within you and that you talk to Him about it than to push it down inside you and pretend you do not feel that way.

In God's presence we need pretend about nothing, because God sees and knows us as we really are – we cannot surprise God. And He understands our feelings of hurt and anger. It is not sinful to feel such things; the real danger is that they may lead us to sin if we don't share them with God. Permit me to ask if you ever experience the feelings Jeremiah talks about here – fear, loneliness, anger and hurt? You do? Can I encourage you, like Jeremiah, to talk to and place them before your Father in heaven?

FURTHER STUDY

Psa. 13:1-6; 88:1-18

1. How did David express his feelings in prayer?

2. How is despair mixed with faith?

Gracious God, I realise that no one alive is a stranger to the feelings I have read about today. Help me whenever I next feel scared, lonely, hurt or angry to do more than just bear it. Help me to pray about it. In Jesus' name. Amen.

Renewed and restored

FOR READING & MEDITATION – JEREMIAH 15:19-21

'If you repent, I will restore you' (v19)

How does God respond to Jeremiah's bold and honest prayer? Does He enfold him in His arms in the same way a mother would take a hurt or lonely child and utter soothing words of comfort? He says something that at first seems strange and insensitive – *'repent'*. This was one of the key words in Jeremiah's message to the nation.

This does not mean that God was oblivious to the hurt and pain that Jeremiah was experiencing. God knew full well the anguish the prophet was going through but He would not let him stay there. One commentator suggests

FURTHER STUDY

Acts 2:36-41; 3:17-21

1. What was Peter's response to seekers of God?

2. What would follow repentance?

that there was quite a lot of self-pity circulating in Jeremiah's heart at this stage, hence he needed this bracing reply. So what was the reason behind God's response that Jeremiah should repent? As it implies, some sin has been committed. Of what sin was the prophet guilty? In all of Jeremiah's strife and conflict, he had a promise from God: 'I will be with you', so it was the sin of misplaced dependency. Sin, you see, is subtle as well as obvious. Deep down in his heart the prophet was failing to trust the word that God had given him in the beginning.

Whenever we sin or walk away, there is *only* one way back to God. And that is through the door of repentance. Admit your misplaced dependency, God is saying. If you repent of it you will be restored and renewed. You will stand on your feet once again. God doesn't change, neither does His Word change. But we do. And when doubt and fear cause us temporarily to lose our bearings, if we are willing to admit it and repent of it then God delights to restore us and confirm afresh the work to which He has called us.

Father, I see that though Your call does not change and Your Word does not change, the relationship between You and me is under constant assault. Help me to talk to You constantly. And I know You will always talk to me. Amen.

Whose side are you on?

FOR READING & MEDITATION - JEREMIAH 15:19-21

'Let this people turn to you, but you must not turn to them.' (v19)

I want to consider once more the passage we looked at yesterday. The statement made by God in today's text is so important that it cries out for comment. Jeremiah was a faithful preacher of righteousness. Whenever he preached he stood firmly on God's side, telling the people everything that God told him to say. However, in the prayer recorded earlier in this chapter he seems to have moved from God's side to the side of the people.

Now in one sense that is quite understandable. Many of the Old Testament intercessors, Moses and Abraham for example, identified themselves with the people and interceded for them. But here the situation is quite different. The people are stubborn and obstinate and there is not much room to excuse their human fallibility. Because Jeremiah is wavering God lovingly uses these rather direct words: 'Let your words change *them*. Don't change your words to suit them' (v19 *The Message*).

Christians involved in pastoral ministry, such as counsellors, ministers and church workers, can at times easily find themselves taking the side of the people against God, rather than standing on the side of the Almighty. This is not to say that we lose our compassion for people, or fail in our responsibility to intercede for them. But where resistance and rebellion remain in the heart, no matter what the extenuating circumstances, God's perspective and the consequences of their actions are made clear. Those who minister to others must ask themselves often: whose side am I on? When it comes to a matter of independence, there is only one side – God's side.

FURTHER STUDY

Exod. 32:19-29;
1 Cor. 15:33;
2 Cor. 6:14-7:1

1. How did the Levites single themselves out?

2. Why should we take sides?

Heavenly Father, help me when I minister to others to be more influenced by You than I am by them. I do not want to lose my compassion but I want it always to be known that it is Your side I am on. In Jesus' name. Amen.

Calling

FOR READING & MEDITATION - JEREMIAH 16:1-21

'You must not marry and have sons or daughters in this place.' (v2)

At first sight it seems rather harsh and demanding of God to require Jeremiah to remain celibate all his life. Celibacy was rare in that culture. Having children not only provided a retirement plan but it was also a way of preserving one's family name indefinitely. In an earlier chapter the animosity of his enemies focused on this point when they said: 'Let us cut him off from the land of the living, that his name be remembered no more' (11:19). Keep in mind too that Jeremiah had already lost his brothers (12:6) and now he is allowed no family to replace them. But God asks even more.

FURTHER STUDY

Matt. 10:37-39;
1 Cor. 7:26-38;
Eph. 6:1-2

1. How should we regard our families?

2. What pressures do families bring?

He is not even to join in the normal community experiences of births, marriages and deaths; he is forbidden to weep with those who weep or laugh with those who laugh (vv5-9).

Why should God demand that Jeremiah have no private life? It could be that God was saving Jeremiah from overwhelming heartbreak because the next generation of children would be devastated by disease and famine. It could also be that a wife and family might have distracted him from his single-minded ministry.

The chief reason, I believe, was that Jeremiah's personal life was to be an object lesson, an acted parable, about Judah's condition. His calling was to speak about 'tearing down and building up'. Planting and building his calling was very specific to this time. Compared to the serious spiritual condition into which Israel had fallen, and the devastation that was to come upon them because of that, *the loneliness which came from being without a wife and family was as nothing*. And like Jeremiah, our time, money and relationships all belong to Him. This is deeply challenging – is God calling you for a specific work today?

O Father, this is a question I am not sure I want to answer. Help me think this through and hear and evaluate your calling anew. In Jesus' name I pray. Amen.

Keeping Sunday special

FOR READING & MEDITATION - JEREMIAH 17:19-27

'keep the Sabbath day holy, as I commanded your forefathers.' (v22)

The theme of this chapter is sin and its consequences. Unless Judah repents she will pay the consequences of her continued rebellion against the Lord. There is a special reference in today's verse to the Sabbath. Sabbath keeping had always been taken as a sign of loyalty to God ever since it was laid down at Sinai (Exod. 31:12–17). Those who sought to keep it showed signs of spiritual health; those who flouted it showed signs of spiritual ill-health. The Sabbath was usually the first thing to be disregarded when the people began to drift away from God.

What is your view about keeping the Sabbath, the day which most Christians call Sunday? We can, like some do, become legalists who see the keeping of the Sabbath as essential to salvation. Or we can, as others do, become liberationists who see it as unnecessary and unimportant. But I am not comfortable with either of these positions. In Jeremiah's day the people were liberationists; in Christ's day they were legalists.

FURTHER STUDY

Luke 4:14-19;
Rom. 14:1-8

1. What was the habit of Jesus?

2. Should Sunday be special?

The true attitude, I believe, is to see Sunday (or the Sabbath) as a gift from God – a gift that gives us more freedom than usual to focus on Him, to worship Him, and to enjoy fellowship with others who also love and serve Him. Derek Kidner puts it helpfully when he says that the Sabbath should not be flooded with the mundane nor frozen by the forbidden. Whatever the world thinks of the Sabbath, the Church should think of it as special. You might find it helpful to list the things you do on a typical Sunday, and then to ask: Is there too much? Could some things be done on another day? Does God get the time He deserves from me?

Father, I do not want to become legalistic on the one hand or liberationist on the other. Help me to be balanced on this matter and give Your day the honour and respect it deserves. In Jesus' name I pray. Amen.

The potter's house

FOR READING & MEDITATION - JEREMIAH 18:1-12

'so the potter formed it into another pot, shaping it as seemed best to him.' (v4)

It has been said that the mind makes its richest movements by drawing analogies. Watch as Jeremiah draws an intriguing analogy between what he sees in a potter's house and what God is doing with the people of Judah. The prophet is directed by God to go into a potter's house to watch him at his work. Jeremiah sees him place a formless lump of clay on his wheel and stands entranced as under the potter's skilful touch a beautiful pot begins to take shape. But suddenly – disaster. There is a flaw in the clay and the vessel becomes misshapen. Now what will the potter do? Toss it aside and begin with a new lump of clay? No. His original intention frustrated, he begins again to shape a new vessel. It is not the one he originally intended, but it is a beautiful one nevertheless.

FURTHER STUDY

Luke 22:54-62;
John 21:15-17

1. How did Peter mess up?

2. How did Jesus regard him?

Jeremiah gets the point. The clay may hinder the purposes of the divine potter and prevent Him achieving His original intention, but even so He will not discard it. Justice will happen and the people will experience the consequences of their actions, but God will pursue them with infinite patience and persistence.

We can be encouraged and humbled by the fact that when we mess up God's original purposes for our lives by our own stubbornness, He nevertheless pursues His purposes with us still. He completely remodels us. His skill and power make something of us beyond what we dare imagine or even deserve. If by your actions or failure you have frustrated God's original purpose but have repented and come back to God, take heart. Through your frail humanity, He is able to achieve His original purpose and He will make something beautiful of you still.

O Father, I am so thankful that You do not toss me aside when I frustrate Your purposes by my actions and failures. You are ready to make me again. My gratitude knows no bounds. Thank You dear Father. Amen.

A ministers' conference

FOR READING & MEDITATION - JEREMIAH 19:1-15

'I will smash this nation and this city just as this potter's jar is smashed' (v11)

Fresh from the insights gained in the potter's house and ready to obey God's instructions Jeremiah arranges a conference of some of the religious leaders of Jerusalem. These men were actively engaged in the Temple worship but they were slow to respond to God and were sadly nothing less than blind leaders of the blind. The site he chose was a few hundred yards south of the Temple in the valley of Hinnon, also called Topheth. It was the garbage dump for the city. Here child sacrifices had been carried out and were still being done in secret (7:31). What a place for a ministers' conference! Jeremiah knew that no religious community ever rises higher than its leaders, so if his message is to get through then it must be aimed first at those who led the people in worship.

As he speaks to them he holds a clay jug under his arm which he has purchased from one of the potters. And after a blistering rebuff he raises the jug above his head and hurls it at their feet where it shatters into a dozen different pieces. The point he was making was that whereas a spoiled vessel on a potter's wheel could be reshaped, once it had hardened it was beyond reshaping and was fit only for breaking. Judgment is coming, says Jeremiah, and you had better face up to it.

I wonder what would happen if a modern-day ministers' conference had a visit from Jeremiah, especially where leaders have lost their confidence in the Scriptures and closed their eyes to wandering and waywardness. Many a church might profit from a few jugs being broken in the middle of a service to bring home to the congregation the inevitable consequences of continually turning away from God.

FURTHER STUDY

1 Kings 18:16-40

1. What conference did Elijah host?

2. What was the result?

Father, desperate situations need desperate measures. Forgive us for any indolence, lethargy and lukewarmness. We need to be shaken up, dear Lord. Send some Jeremiahs into our midst to do just that. In Jesus' name. Amen.

What screams the loudest?

FOR READING & MEDITATION - JEREMIAH 20:1-13

'Sing to the LORD! Give praise to the LORD!' (v13)

Jeremiah's scathing condemnation of the leaders and his prediction of what's going to happen next is met with a prompt response from Pashhur, the Temple overseer. The prophet is beaten and put in the stocks. Jeremiah responds to this humiliation by predicting Pashhur's downfall and giving him a nickname *Magor-Missabib* which means 'terror on every side'. This is a name that not only stuck to Pashhur for the rest of his life but has come down the centuries and is still in use today. In the South Wales village where I was brought up I often heard people say of someone, 'He is a real *Magor-Missabib*' – meaning 'he is a real pain in the neck'.

FURTHER STUDY

Hab. 3:16-19;
Acts 16:22-34

1. What screamed loudest in the prophet?

2. How did Paul respond to inner screams of pain and praise?

As a result of the beating and the humiliation Jeremiah plunges into the depths of despair. He accuses God of deceiving him, of failing him and of bullying him. The prophet has been discouraged before but he has never quite spoken like this. His words sound like high treason. Will God let him get away with it?

God does not respond. As Jeremiah reflects on the clear call that came to him in his youth and the Word that God gave him to speak, something begins to burn within him. It is the message that God gave him. His hurt and confused feelings scream out within him, but God's Word screams louder. He had allowed God's Word to penetrate his being to such an extent that in the moment of overwhelming test it was the divine Word that cried out the loudest. If we allow God's Word to so live and take root within us, when our hurts and frustrations scream within, God's Word will burn in us with His warming love, and we will hear His message above the storm.

My Father and my God, let Your Word so penetrate and permeate my being that when my emotions scream within me Your voice will scream the loudest. I ask this in and through Your precious name. Amen.

Swinging emotions

FOR READING & MEDITATION - JEREMIAH 20:14-18

'Why did I ever come out of the womb to see trouble and sorrow?'
(v18)

Yesterday we left Jeremiah rejoicing that the Word which God had given him when he was a youth still burned within him. His dampened and depressed spirit rises in praise and gratitude to God (v13). But his words of confidence, expectation and praise do not last long. Within the space of a few verses he descends once again into the depths of despair. He wonders why his mother did not abort him when he was in the womb.

I heard a psychiatrist on one occasion refer to Jeremiah as bipolar. He based his diagnosis on these verses in which Jeremiah swings from the heights of spiritual ecstasy to the depths of pessimism and gloom. 'If I had been treating him,' he said, 'I would have recommended that he be put on medication used in the treatment of this condition.' But is Jeremiah suffering a physiological mood swing or is there an emotional battle going on in his soul? I think it was the latter.

FURTHER STUDY

1 Kings 19:1-9;
Mark 9:17-27

1. What swinging emotions did Elijah experience?

2. How did the father express his swinging emotions?

Faith and doubt are locked together within him and he finds it difficult to endure the strain of that tension. How can he at one and the same time claim that God is within like a mighty warrior (v11) and then in the next breath curse the day he was born (v14)? And why did he write it down? Those who have battled with discouragement and despair will understand. Jesus would have understood. In Gethsemane He broke down under the tension, sweating blood and begging to be released from His mission – yet remained willing to obey His Father's wishes. Whatever is going on must not be denied. Tell God honestly how you feel. In His presence no anguish need be stifled or repressed.

God, I am thankful for the honest reporting of the Scriptures. You let me see Your servants under all conditions. Help me understand that I can share my negative feelings with You without being rejected. What relief this gives me. Amen.

The new shoot

FOR READING & MEDITATION - JEREMIAH 23:1-8

'The days are coming ... when I will raise up ... a righteous Branch'
(v5)

The next section of Jeremiah (chapters 21–52) at first might appear confusing. Many of the chapters follow no clear chronological order. Be alert to this fact, so that you do not become disoriented. The events in chapter 21, for example, took place twenty years after the events listed in chapter 20, and it better fits with chapters 32, 34 and 37 to 39. It is important to keep in mind that the book of Jeremiah is a collection of prophecies, not a diary of events; bearing this in mind hopefully will not inhibit our devotional study of the prophet's life.

FURTHER STUDY

Isa. 11:1-12;
1 Cor. 1:26-31

1. What were the qualities of the sons of Jesse?

2. What is our boast?

In today's passage Jeremiah contrasts the present corrupt kings and priests with the coming Messiah who is to be a perfect King and Priest. The only real hope for Judah's future is found in none other than the Son of God, our Lord Jesus Christ. The prophet is given a glimpse into the future where he sees that one day someone from King David's own line will come to reign over Israel with true justice and power.

'The shoot is that which sprouts from the roots of a fallen tree,' comments R. K. Harrison. 'New life will thus spring forth from the fallen dynasty.' The name given to the future Saviour indicates His true character – *the Lord Our Righteousness* (v6). The 'shoot' that will emerge – Jesus Christ – will impart to people a righteousness, which is not earned by works but given through grace. The high ideals commanded at Sinai which people felt were utterly beyond them will at last become realisable through a new covenant sealed in Christ's blood. Jesus not only imputes righteousness to our spiritual account, He also imparts it to our daily lives.

Father, I am so thankful that in Jesus the demands of the law are not brought down to my level, but that through the Saviour's power and grace I am brought up to their level. I give honour and glory to His wonderful name. Amen.

False teachers

FOR READING & MEDITATION - JEREMIAH 23:9-40

'My heart is broken within me ... because of the LORD and his
holy words.' (v9)

There are many reasons why the people of Jeremiah's
day became corrupt, but one of the contributing factors
was the way in which the teachers lulled the people into
a false sense of security. These men had a large and
enthusiastic audience. They were charismatic characters
and very popular with the people because they told them
what they wanted to hear.

People often ask how we can tell the difference between
true and false prophets. There are at least four evidences.
First, false teachers may appear to live according to God's
design but in fact they do not. Second, they tamper
with God's message, put a spin on it, and make it
more palatable. Third, they encourage their listeners
(usually subtly) to risk displeasing God. And fourth,
there is a tendency to arrogance, self-serving and
being more interested in pleasing people than in
pleasing God. Some would add a fifth difference –
the words of a false teacher would not be fulfilled
(unless coincidentally), whereas the words of a true
teacher would in God's time become fact.

FURTHER STUDY

2 Pet. 2:1-3,
12-19

1. What are
the marks of a
false prophet?

2. What will
happen to
them?

But be careful that you don't write someone off
as a false teacher or leader just because of their
over-enthusiasm. I have often seen sincere but misguided
Christians who, swept along by the emotion of the moment,
have made statements and predictions which never came
true. Many of them were later embarrassed and felt
deeply ashamed. They were not false teachers, just over-
enthusiastic ones. A false prophet would feel no shame or
embarrassment. There are more false prophets in the church
of today than we might imagine. Thankfully God has given
us the Bible – a more sure word of prophecy – by which to
test all other prophecies and teaching. Be sure to use it.

**Father, thank You that I have Your own eternal, errorless Word
as a judgment bar to which I can bring all prophecies. Help me
to test all things by the Bible without becoming over-critical of
what others say. In Jesus' name. Amen.**

Thank God for trouble

FOR READING & MEDITATION - JEREMIAH 24:1-10

'The good [figs] are very good, but the poor ones ...
cannot be eaten.' (v3)

This incident took place after Nebuchadnezzar had captured and enslaved Jerusalem. In order to fully integrate and assimilate the conquered nation, they often brought back the society's elite to their capital city. So the king of Babylon had sent his crack troops across the desert and marched the cream of Judah's society back to Babylon – the carpenters, the skilled tradesmen, the blacksmiths and so on. You might assume that those who had been taken into captivity were like bad figs, fit only to be thrown away. And that those who remained in Jerusalem were like good figs, worth keeping. But the opposite was true.

FURTHER STUDY

Deut. 8:1-5;
Heb. 12:5-13

1. Why does God discipline us?

2. Contrast discipline with no discipline.

In the vision Jeremiah, a true prophet as distinct from the false prophets, reveals that appearances can be deceptive. As far as God was concerned the people who were carried away were the good figs, and the ones who remained were the bad figs. This was because the future lay not with those who had remained and who lived under the treacherous regime of Zedekiah and the politicians who manipulated him, but with those who had been carried into captivity in Babylon. The exiles would be so shocked by their change of circumstances that their hearts would respond readily to God's Word, whereas those who remained in Jerusalem would continue to be stubborn and obstinate.

It's a sad fact that sometimes God has to corner us before we admit that His way is best. Trouble is often a blessing in disguise. Where would you and I be now I wonder if God had not loved us enough to chastise us at certain periods in our lives? We would be like bad figs, fit only to be thrown out.

Thank You, my Father, that You love me enough to help me grow. Circumstances hurt but they always turn to my good. Hence I can truly say thank You for them. They yield more than they cost. I am so grateful. Amen.

Twenty-three years!

FOR READING & MEDITATION – JEREMIAH 25:1-14

'For twenty-three years ... the word of the LORD has come to me
and I have spoken to you' (v3)

We are now at the middle of the book of Jeremiah and
the prophet is at the mid-point of his 'calling'. The
opening verses of this chapter fix the date as the fourth year
of Jehoiakim's reign – 605 BC. It is now twenty-three years
since Jeremiah began preaching to the people. Imagine
that! For twenty-three years he has been proclaiming the
Word of God faithfully, calling on the people to repent, but
they still have not listened. Now God explains that they
are going to endure a seventy-year captivity in Babylon
because the consequences of walking outside of God's will
can no longer be held back.

How was it possible for Jeremiah to keep
preaching the same message for twenty-
three years while continually being harassed,
ridiculed and rejected? Well, as we have seen
(and will continue to see) he had times of great
discouragement and came close to giving up – but
he never did. There is a great contrast between him
and the people of his time. They were vacillating
people whose interests and commitments changed
from one day to another. In John Fowles' book *The
Ebony Tower* there is a character who wanted to climb
Everest in a day, but if it took two days he just wasn't
interested. Jeremiah wasn't like that. He lived for God the
only way – one day at a time.

Jeremiah, I believe contritely, returned to the task
God had for him, and we, too, also need to continually
remind ourselves to do the same. It might sound dull and
boring doing the same thing day after day but if God has
commanded it, it is never the same thing. Nothing can be
greater than to do whatever God wants us to do. We will
never be bored by it.

FURTHER STUDY

Luke 18:1-8;
Heb. 12:1-4

1. What
did Jesus
emphasise?

2. How can we
keep going?

**O Father, whatever discouragements may come my way grant
that I, like Jeremiah, might never give up. Reveal Yourself in all I
do. In Jesus' name. Amen.**

Never give up!

'the LORD ... said to me: "Take from my hand this cup"' (v15)

I feel drawn to continue yesterday's theme – Jeremiah's commitment never to give up – perhaps because you are about to quit something God has called you to do. You have been labouring faithfully at the task for many years, but there don't seem to be many positive results. Life is hard for you and nobody seems to appreciate you.

If Jeremiah was there with you he would probably say, 'I understand how that feels.' For twenty-three years he got up day after day preaching the same message which God had given him – apparently to no avail. But Jeremiah was persistent. In today's passage, we meet him yet again carrying the message of God wherever the Lord sent him. Paul tells us in I Corinthians 4:2 'it is required that those who have been given a trust must prove faithful'. Note he says *faithful*, not successful. It would be nice to be successful but that is not what is required of us.

FURTHER STUDY

Gal. 6:7-10;
2 Tim. 4:6-8

1. What is necessary for harvest?

2. What could Paul declare?

When God gives us a task He wants us to stick to it no matter what happens. Perseverance is not a popular idea today. But it is one which carries great weight in heaven. When Sir Winston Churchill was an old man he was invited to give a speech to the students graduating from a university. He arrived very late and after making his way to the platform learned that the diplomas had been given out. Out of courtesy to the great man the organisers asked him if he would like to say a few concluding words. He rose to his feet, fixed the audience with his gaze and said: 'Never give up. Never, *never* give up. Never, never, *never* give up.' That was all. He sat down to a standing ovation. Jeremiah says that to us. He knew God never gives out impossible or fruitless tasks, and He never gives up on us.

My Father and my God, help me persevere on this pilgrim journey, not thinking about the long road that lies ahead but just the task You have given me for this day. And may I never, never, *never* give up. In Jesus' name. Amen.

Thank God for the laity

THURS
7 AUG

FOR READING & MEDITATION - JEREMIAH 26:1-24

'I will make this house like Shiloh and this city an object of cursing'
(v6)

The situation we have read about in this chapter is thought by some commentators to be the same as that described by Jeremiah in chapter 7. But here we have more information about the consequences. Imagine someone getting up in the middle of a Sunday morning service in Westminster Abbey and saying: 'This great building, beautiful though it may be, will be demolished. God will not hesitate to destroy it no matter how sacred you think it is.' Can you picture what a furore such an action would cause, not just in Christian circles but in the news media also? So it is not surprising that after making the statement Jeremiah's life is threatened, especially as in those times to say anything against the Temple was regarded as treason.

FURTHER
STUDY

Rom. 12:1-8;
Eph. 4:7-13

1. What is the ministry of the laity?

2. Who perform works of service?

Jeremiah is called to appear before the officials and rulers to give account of himself, but so authoritative, authentic and moving is his presentation and defence that many of his hearers come over to his side. Interestingly, some of the people who were called to judge Jeremiah were laymen not ordained into the priesthood, but they seemed to know more about Scripture than some of the priests.

I am deeply thankful for the ministry of the laity: the body of men and women who though 'untrained' at a seminary or Bible College level immerse themselves in the Word of God and are experienced in applying it to their lives in the world. Without such people we would lose a perspective on the Scriptures which the best Bible College in the world may be unable to convey to trainee ministers. Think of lay people whose ministry God has used to bless you; thank Him for them, and thank them, too!

O God my Father, I am grateful that You have drawn me, along with millions of other people, to search the Scriptures daily. This builds beneath my feet a solid foundation on which I can stand faithfully for You. Amen.

WAVERLEY ABBEY
COLLEGE

As we come to celebrate the 50th anniversary of CWR, we will be launching Waverley Abbey College, a development announced by Selwyn Hughes almost 40 years ago. This education arm of our ministry will focus on supporting key professions, with its main campus at Pilgrim Hall, but using Waverley Abbey House and even Singapore as its other campuses.*

Our Counselling Faculty will expand its qualifying BA and MA programmes with a second MA for qualified and experienced counsellors who wish to develop their knowledge and understanding. In autumn 2014 we are planning to set up an Education Faculty, and as we move into the future other faculties will be developed.

Our desire is to equip and support individuals to apply God's Word in their professional lives. With its unique Christian framework, the College will be a place of learning that offers a nurturing environment, high quality programmes, first class teaching and an overall transformational learning experience. This is a bold development: we look forward to inviting individuals and groups to study at Waverley Abbey College. We hope you will be part of our future.

Dr Coleen R Jackson
Consultant Principal

Interested? For more information, go to the
Waverley Abbey College website **waverleyabbeycollege.ac.uk**
or request a prospectus by calling 01252 784731.

*All existing activities at Waverley Abbey House and Pilgrim Hall
  will continue alongside the college programmes.

Under God's yoke

FOR READING & MEDITATION - JEREMIAH 27:1-22

'Bow your neck under the yoke of the king of Babylon' (v12)

Here Jeremiah is instructed by God to make a yoke (the wooden beam that was used to join oxen or other animals together to enable them to pull together on a load) and to fasten it on his neck with leather thongs 'as you would strap a yoke on a plough-ox' (v2 TLB). Then he was told to send messages to the heads of the surrounding nations, through their ambassadors in Jerusalem, that it was futile to fight against the Babylonian armies, because they would all have to accept the 'yoke' of service to Babylon. Jeremiah does as God says and he goes about his daily tasks carrying the yoke and illustrating the message that had come to him from God.

FURTHER STUDY

Matt. 11:27-30; Rom. 9:17-24

1. What is Jesus' invitation?

2. In what sense did Pharaoh serve God's purposes?

There is a phrase in this section which at first is difficult to understand. The Almighty refers to Nebuchadnezzar as 'my servant' (v6). Nebuchadnezzar was one of the most ruthless, despotic and godless men who has ever walked the face of the earth. How could he be described as God's 'servant'? Isaiah says something similar of Cyrus, king of the Persians, when he declared that the purposes of the Almighty lay behind all Cyrus's empire-building. It is in this sense, I believe, that God refers to Nebuchadnezzar as His servant. Without realising it, Nebuchadnezzar was being used to advance the purposes of God, even though he was a worshipper of idols.

God is not limited to working through His own people. He has the whole world and its peoples in His hand. They are under His yoke. We may find events baffling, bewildering and mysterious, and often wonder what God is doing. Jeremiah reminds us that God is doing something, even if we don't understand it.

Gracious Father, thank You that You are a sovereign God and that all peoples are ultimately within Your power. Help me to trust You when events seem inexplicable. In Jesus' name. Amen.

Prophet against prophet

FOR READING & MEDITATION - JEREMIAH 28:1-17
'At this, the prophet Jeremiah went on his way.' (v11)

It is very sad when people prefer to listen to comforting lies rather than to the painful truth. But that is exactly what is happening here. Jeremiah had prophesied that Jerusalem would fall and that it was futile to fight the Babylonians, but Hananiah (a false prophet) disagreed as he stood toe to toe with Jeremiah in the Temple and dismissed his prophecy with these words: 'This is what the LORD Almighty, the God of Israel, says: "I will break the yoke of the king of Babylon. Within two years I will bring back to this place all the articles of the LORD's house that Nebuchadnezzar king of Babylon removed from here"' (vv2-3).

Jeremiah's reply shows how secure he was in God. 'Amen! May the LORD do so' (v6). In other words: 'It would be wonderful if the disaster could be avoided, but I am afraid it will not be.' Jeremiah knew without any doubt that his words had come from God. So confident was he, that when Hananiah broke the symbolic yoke and separated it from Jeremiah's body the prophet simply walked away from the situation. He would not enter the debate unless he had a fresh word from the Lord and that did not come immediately (vv12-14).

FURTHER STUDY

2 Tim. 2:22-26; Titus 3:9-11

1. What might debate produce?

2. How should we respond to foolish arguments?

How different life would be for many of us if we were secure enough in God to walk away from unnecessary arguments instead of exchanging words to no avail. Jeremiah was not afraid of debate or discussion, but he was not drawn into one simply for the sake of it, *even though he knew that he was right!* He felt no need to defend himself; he was content to let time tell who spoke truly. It's an example that we, too, can follow.

O Father, give me the courage to present what I believe with conviction. Help me to know, without arrogance but with love and compassion, when to walk away. And give me the wisdom to know when to do one or the other. In Jesus' name. Amen.

Dear exiles, I love you

FOR READING & MEDITATION - JEREMIAH 29:1-32

'This is what the LORD Almighty ... says to all those I carried
into exile' (v4)

At this stage in Jeremiah's life many of the people who once occupied the city of Jerusalem and its environs are now in exile in Babylon. Nebuchadnezzar had taken several thousand of Jerusalem's key people into captivity. In Babylon things were vastly different. All that was familiar had gone. Naturally the exiles were downcast and depressed. Some religious leaders, sensing the discontent, began to prophesy that soon the exile would be over and they would return to their land.

FURTHER STUDY

Hosea 6:1-3; 10:12

1. What was Hosea's conviction about the Lord?

2. What time is it?

Jeremiah, hearing of these false reports and hopes felt that he was to warn the people against such delusion. So he writes this letter. They are in captivity, he says, because they have rejected the Word of God and it will be a long long time before they return home. Hence it is better to renounce false hope and settle down to make the best of the situation.

Jeremiah knows that the exile had put the people in a position where their inner emptiness could be exposed, and now was the time for them to seek the Lord (v13). They hadn't done so when they were in freedom; perhaps now they were in captivity things would be different. Notice how tenderly He deals with the exiles. He doesn't say, 'Serves you right! Stew there for a while!' He reassures them of His good plans and that one day He will restore them (vv11,14). Sometimes God has to upset us in order to set us up. Are you in 'exile' at the moment? Has your world been turned upside down? Then this is the time to seek the Lord. Search for Him with all your heart and I promise that you will find Him. Because He still loves you dearly.

O Father, why is it that sometimes You have to put me on my back before I will look up into Your face? Once again I want to record my gratitude. Help me to realise all that You have for me. Thank You my Father. Amen.

A book of hope

FOR READING & MEDITATION – JEREMIAH 30:1-24
'you will be my people, and I will be your God.' (v22)

Chapters 30 to 33 have been described by commentators as 'the book of hope'. Jeremiah reaches heights of eloquence that seem at times to surpass even that of the silver-tongued Isaiah. There is good reason; he is looking forward to the restoration of his people from exile. No one reading these chapters can think of Jeremiah simply as a prophet of doom. He is a prophet of hope too.

After the pruning process and the consequences of an obstinate people not following God's way and guidance, there is to come a time of restoration and great blessing. God will make a new covenant with them to replace the one they symbolically tore up. Once they walked away and refused to listen; one day they will repent and obey. I have only selected one of these chapters, but I suggest you read chapter 31 also. The rewards will be well worth the effort.

FURTHER STUDY

Ezek. 36:22-38;
1 Pet. 2:9-10

1. What was Israel's hope?

2. How could Jeremiah's prophecy apply to us?

Like Isaiah, Jeremiah associates events in the near future with those in the distant future. The prophecies he makes here have been compared to a range of mountain peaks. From a distance they look as if they are close to one another but actually they are great distances apart. He talks of events as if they will all happen together, but in fact there will be enormous time differences between them. He sees the end of the exile but he also sees the day when Christ will come as King and reign for ever. The key verse I have selected for our devotions sums up God's longings since the day He decided to form His human creation: You will be my people and I will be your God. Could anything be more beautiful? It applies as much to you and me as it did to Jeremiah's listeners.

O Father, how amazing it is to see Your heart so beautifully captured in one statement. You long that I might be one of Your family, and I long that You might be my God. Our longings meet together. I am so glad. Amen.

Invest in the future

FOR READING & MEDITATION - JEREMIAH 32:1-15

'Jeremiah said, "The word of the LORD came to me"' (v6)

It's one thing to say you have faith and confidence that God will bring about what He has promised; it's another thing to put that faith into operation. We often refer to this as 'walking the talk' or 'putting your money where your mouth is'. This is exactly what we see Jeremiah doing in this passage.

The prophet has been put in prison by King Zedekiah who was infuriated by Jeremiah's advice to surrender to the Babylonians. One of Jeremiah's cousins visits him with what seems an insensitive and untimely proposition to sell him a field in Anathoth. At that moment it was occupied by the invading Babylonians. It was hardly a safe or good investment! But God has already prepared Jeremiah for his cousin's proposition and he clinches the deal immediately by handing over the agreed price of seventeen shekels of silver. To buy land that was occupied by the enemy and take such elaborate care with the title deeds shows a tremendous faith in the future that says 'Things might look dark at the moment but God is and will be true to His Word'.

FURTHER STUDY

Prov. 3:1-8;
Heb. 11:1-6

1. Why can we not understand how to trust in the Lord?

2. How are faith and hope related?

Trust does not come easily. It probably wasn't easy for Jeremiah publicly to buy the land. But he believed that although God was discipling His people because of their covenant, the last word would not be judgment but restoration. Are the promises of God under attack in your life at the moment? Are the enemies of your faith hammering on the door and intimidating you? Does the thing He has promised to do for you look as if it might never happen? Remember God may delay His promises but He will never deny them. Perhaps to act with confidence is the very step of faith God is wanting you to take.

Father, I see that hope is buying into what I believe. Forgive me for doubting so much of what You have told me. I know that none of Your precious promises can fail. Help me now to walk Your talk. In Jesus' name. Amen.

God is merciful

FOR READING & MEDITATION - JEREMIAH 32:16-44

'Ah, Sovereign LORD ... Nothing is too hard for you.' (v17)

We saw yesterday how Jeremiah purchased a field in Anathoth – an act that to some might have looked foolhardy and impractical. But he did it, not on the advice of a broker but on the prompting of God. And by doing so he gave clear evidence to the people of his belief in and commitment to the continuity of God's promises. But once again his humanity came to the surface and he couldn't help but *feel* somewhat foolish.

How do we deal with negative feelings when they seem to contradict what our minds tell us, namely that we have done the right thing? We bring our whole being, will, thoughts, feelings to God and seek to re-centre and realign them in importunate prayer. Many Bible commentators point out that the prayer of Jeremiah here is a good model of how to pray in a difficult or desperate situation. Consider carefully how he prays because you may be called upon to pray such a prayer in the near future. First he focuses on the creative power of God (v17), then on His faithfulness and justice (v18). Next he concentrates on God's great redemptive acts (vv20–22). He concludes by referring to the sins and failing of the past (v23), the difficulties being experienced in the present (v24), and the mystery of the future (v25).

FURTHER STUDY

2 Kings 19:9-19, 35-37

1. How did Hezekiah pray for God's mercy?

2. What was the result?

How does God respond to such a prayer? He announces that though judgment is at hand His last word is not judgment, but mercy. God is justice. He cannot be any other and still remain God, but the delight of His heart is to restore, to forgive, and to pour out His blessings on His people. We must hold fast to this. There is always justice. But the joy of His heart is to forgive.

Father, I am so grateful that I do not have to wrest mercy from You. You delight to dispense it. Given my repentant heart all heaven bends down to lift and restore me. I am eternally grateful. Amen.

Turn your face to God

FOR READING & MEDITATION - JEREMIAH 33:1-26

'Call to me and I will answer you and tell you great and unsearchable things you do not know.' (v3)

It should not surprise us that God continues to encourage Jeremiah with promises that help him develop a clear picture of how God will restore the fortunes of His people (vII). It is one of the Father's characteristics to strengthen His servants in their darkest and most discouraging moments.

The key verse in this chapter is without doubt the one I have selected as our text for today: 'Call to me and I will answer you and tell you great and unsearchable things you do not know.' This is probably my favourite text in the Old Testament. Whenever anyone asks me to write a text on the flyleaf of their Bible this is the one I invariably choose. What a reassuring and encouraging word it is! God is saying that to those who seek His face He will reveal things they could never know by natural means.

FURTHER STUDY

Deut. 30:1-10;
1 Cor. 2:9-15

1. How do we turn to the Lord?

2. How does God reveal things to us?

Why is it that when we need help, guidance or encouragement, so often the very last person we call upon is the Lord? Pascal, the great French Christian and philosopher, said: 'It ought to be the soul's habit whenever discouraged or in need of guidance to first call out to the Lord before calling out to anyone else.' It is not wrong to seek help from others but our first port of call ought to be the Lord – it could save us considerable pain and anxiety. God can make Himself heard and known of course without us calling on Him. The whole of the Bible is evidence of that. But what He longs for is a true relationship with us. We prefer to talk to a person's face than their back. God does too. Turn your face to Him now, however you feel; perhaps in this chapter there are encouragements for you.

O God my Father, forgive me that so often I choose to rely more on human help than I do on Yours. I am grateful for the encouragement I get from my friends but help me make You my first port of call. Amen.

Permanent or temporary?

FOR READING & MEDITATION - JEREMIAH 34:1-21

'Recently you repented ... But now you have turned round' (vv15-16)

Jeremiah is faced with another tough task. He is commanded by God to go and tell King Zedekiah that Jerusalem is about to fall and that he personally will be exiled to Babylon. In the light of this prediction Zedekiah tries to think of some way to change God's mind. He hits on the idea of encouraging slave owners to give liberty to their slaves as the law required every seven years, in the hope that this might persuade the Lord to turn back the Babylonian armies.

The slave owners respond to Zedekiah's request but not long after they hear that the Egyptian army is on its way to assist them. The intervention appears to be miraculous, and the slave owners, thinking the threat is now over, revoke their earlier decisions and take their slaves back into captivity. This of course was an act of betrayal – a breach of faith – and brought from Jeremiah a blunt and scathing response.

FURTHER STUDY

Hosea 6:4-5; John 6:60-69

1. What was God's rebuke?

2. What was Jesus' experience?

Let's pause for a moment and ask ourselves if we might be guilty of a similar attitude. What do we do when we are in a tight spot? Do we panic and bargain with God, promising that if He delivers us we will be more faithful in prayer, reading the Scriptures and giving to His work? Then when the difficulty has passed do we soon forget our promises and go back to living the way we did before? I confess I have done this sometimes and I am sure most of us have done so too. Nothing sharpens up our spiritual lives like a threat to our welfare. But when the threat is over we go right back to living the way we lived before. God looks for permanent heart changes, not temporary mind changes.

O God, forgive me that my promises are so often pledged under pressure but not kept. I want to be the kind of person You want me to be. Help me dear Lord. In Jesus' name. Amen.

Recabite resolve

FOR READING & MEDITATION - JEREMIAH 35:1-19
'Go to the Recabite family ... and give them wine to drink!' (v2)

Even the most casual reader of the book of Jeremiah cannot help but be struck by the fact that God uses every means possible to bring home to His people the reality of their circumstance and spiritual condition. Here we see Jeremiah being commanded by God to invite the Recabite family into one of the side rooms of the Temple and ply them with wine.

The Recabites were a group of nomads who travelled through the land like gypsies performing tasks like sharpening knives, making chariot wheels, straightening bent javelins, and so on. They traced their ancestry back over a period of more than 200 years to a man called Jonadab (Jehonadab, a supporter of King Jehu in 2 Kings 10:15,23), the son of Recab, who zealously committed himself and his family to total abstinence. Jonadab's descendants had faithfully followed in his footsteps and were widely known for their refusal to drink alcohol.

FURTHER STUDY

Luke 4:1-12;
Gal. 4:8-11

1. How did Jesus show resolve and refuse the easy path?

2. What did Paul fear?

Why then would God, through Jeremiah, invite them to break their pledge and to drink wine? God knew that they would not yield to the temptation. He wanted to use this incident to show that here was a group of people committed to the word of a man who lived centuries ago, while Judah's people generally refused to commit themselves to the Word that God was speaking to them now. It must have grieved God to see this group more committed to the keeping of a custom than His own people were to the keeping of their covenant commandments. Is it possible that we, the present people of God, are more loyal to customs than the law of God? It can happen very easily, but we can see it only with difficulty.

O God, show me what customs I am putting before Your commandments, or what laws of the land before the laws of God. Help me to see this, and to remedy it with your grace. In Jesus' name. Amen.

God can't be stopped

FOR READING & MEDITATION - JEREMIAH 36:1-32

'Take another scroll and write on it all the words that were on
the first scroll' (v28)

We have had to wait a long time to learn how Jeremiah's
prophecies were written down. But now we see how
it was done. God commands Jeremiah to write down all
the messages he has been given, and he recruits a scribe
named Baruch to help him. Soon after the task is finished
the Babylonian armies are reported to be close to the land
of Judah. The people of Jerusalem, feeling their lives are
under threat, are deeply concerned. A fast is proclaimed
but because Jeremiah is out of favour with King Jehoiakim
he is not allowed to speak in public. So he appoints Baruch
to read to the assembled people the words which
had been recorded.

There seems to be no general reaction from the
crowd but a man named Micaiah is deeply touched.
He speaks to his father Gemariah, a government
official, about what he has heard. Gemariah
arranges for a second reading for himself and
a few other government officials. They too are
affected and know that the king must hear these
words. But they know too that the king will be
incensed by what he hears so they advise Baruch
and Jeremiah to hide. When eventually the king
hears the scroll being read, he takes a knife, cuts
the scroll into pieces and throws it into the fire.

FURTHER STUDY

Esth. 6:1-14;
7:10;
Psa. 27:1-3

1. What did
Haman's
advisers
acknowledge?

2. What was
the psalmist's
testimony?

This is the first record of the Word of God being
destroyed. God responds by commanding Jeremiah to
compile a new scroll. He and Baruch went back to work
again. But this time it came out more strongly. It is ill-
conceived to think anyone can outmanoeuvre God. He can
turn every reverse into a forward direction. The Almighty
is never stymied. Remember this incident next time you
face opposition or setbacks.

**Father, I rest my confidence in Your ability to outmanoeuvre
everything that is against You. You turn setbacks into
springboards, obstacles into opportunities. I am so grateful that
I am Your servant. My trust is in You, Lord. Amen.**

Who should change?

FOR READING & MEDITATION - JEREMIAH 37:1-21

'King Zedekiah ... asked ... "Is there any word from the LORD?"' (v17)

Today's incident is almost twenty years later than yesterday's. The Babylonians have temporarily lifted the blockade against Jerusalem, and King Zedekiah asks Jeremiah to pray that God will turn the situation around. But Jeremiah had already been told to stop praying against defeat (7:16; 14:11). It was a fruitless exercise as the die had already been cast. Jeremiah informs the king that the siege would be resumed eventually and that Jerusalem, as he had predicted many times, would fall into enemy hands.

FURTHER STUDY

Ezek. 11:19-21;
Eph. 4:17-32

1. What change does God make?

2. What changes should we make?

When the siege is lifted, Jeremiah tries to leave the city so as to claim some property that was his by right. But he is seen by one of the sentries, Irijah, who believes he is defecting to the enemy and so arrests him. When Jeremiah is brought before the officials they refuse to believe his story and he is severely beaten and thrown into prison. After a long time Zedekiah sends for Jeremiah and enquires of him: 'Is there any word from the LORD?' (v16). Did the king, I wonder, hope that Jeremiah's long incarceration had changed his mind about praying for the deliverance of Israel?

The prophet shows himself to be as faithful as ever to the Word of God and repeats his previous prediction concerning the king's fate. Only then, after he has given him God's Word, does he plead for better conditions. The king grants his request and moves him to the palace stockade. Zedekiah wanted God to change but he himself didn't want to change. This is typical of human nature. We plead for God to change His mind so that we will not have to change ours. May He forgive our selfishness and arrogance.

O God, forgive me if I seem more concerned about changing Your mind than changing my own. Help me to recognise that no matter what happens or how my life works out, Your original design is always best. In Jesus' name I pray. Amen.

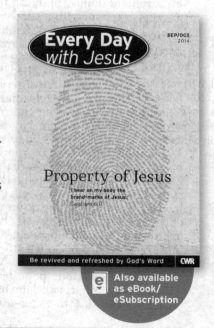

Standing for justice

FOR READING & MEDITATION - JEREMIAH 38:1-13

'these men have acted wickedly in all they have done to Jeremiah the prophet.' (v9)

Jeremiah's freedom may be restricted but that does not stop him telling everyone with whom he comes in contact what God has given him. Some of the officials hear that Jeremiah is telling people to surrender to the Babylonians (v2) and they demand that the king executes him. The king permits them to arrest Jeremiah and they throw him into an underground storage cistern. Although the cistern is not full of water it is full of mud. As soon as Jeremiah is lowered into it he begins to sink. Clearly he is in imminent danger of dying through either suffocation or exposure. This surely has to be the low point.

FURTHER STUDY

Isa. 59:9-21;
1 John 2:1-2

1. Why was the Lord appalled?

2. How does Jesus intervene on our behalf?

One of the officials, Ebed-Melech, an African from Ethiopia, hears of Jeremiah's plight and pleads with the king to let him save Jeremiah. The king agrees so Ebed-Melech gets ropes and rags, and with thirty others sets out to rescue Jeremiah. He instructs Jeremiah to put the rags under his armpits so that the ropes would not cut into his flesh, and then they pull him to the surface.

I think it is safe to say that Ebed-Melech feared God more than man. He alone among all the palace officials stood against the murder plot. It is both interesting and noteworthy that because of this he was spared when Jerusalem fell (39:15-18). How many of us have the courage to speak up when we see injustice being done? Someone has said all that needs to happen for evil to flourish is for good people to do nothing. Do we slink into the shadows or do we stand up for God and for right? Perhaps you can be an Ebed-Melech to someone today. It may not increase our popularity, but Jesus promised we will not lose our reward in heaven because we do such things for Him (Matt. 25:34-40).

O God, make me an Ebed-Melech to someone today. Forgive me that so often bad things flourish around me because I do nothing. Help me stand up for You, and for truth and justice, in our Lord's name I pray. Amen.

FOR READING & MEDITATION - JEREMIAH 38:14-28

'King Zedekiah said ... "I am afraid of the Jews who have gone over to the Babylonians"' (v19)

Jeremiah has been rescued from the cistern and is back in the courtyard of the guard where he is to remain until the fall of Jerusalem. Once more Zedekiah arranges for a secret rendezvous with the prophet, this time not in his palace but in the Temple.

His question is the same as before – what is the shape of the future and what is going to happen to me? Jeremiah is afraid that if he tells the king once more what God has told him about Zedekiah's destiny his life will again be in danger. But assured by the king this will not be so he spells out the clear alternatives. 'If you surrender,' he says, 'your life will be spared, and the city will not be burned down. If you will not surrender, the city will be destroyed and your life will be in danger.' Zedekiah commands Jeremiah not to divulge their conversation to anyone – on pain of death.

What a spineless and characterless person Zedekiah was. And how different from Jeremiah. Eugene Peterson describes Zedekiah as 'a marshmallow'. Character has been defined as what a person is like on the inside. Reputation is what other people think of you. Character is what you are in the depth of your being. Zedekiah had no stomach for facing reality. He wanted changes on the outside without being prepared to change on the inside. Zedekiah was soft like a marshmallow, and Jeremiah was firm like a rock. One pursued self-interest; the other pursued God. Every day we face a choice – living for ourselves and listening to others' opinions or living for God and standing firm on His truth. Which will it be for you and me today?

FURTHER STUDY

Col. 3:1-17;
Titus 2:11-12

1. Where do we set our hearts and how does that affect us?

2. What does God's grace teach us?

O God, with all my heart I want to live not for myself but for You. But sometimes it's not easy. Give me Your grace to rise to every challenge that faces me today and to live this and every other day to Your praise and glory. Amen.

The fall of Jerusalem

FOR READING & MEDITATION - JEREMIAH 39:1-18

'Take him and look after him; don't harm him but do for him whatever he asks.' (v12)

This chapter is a study in contrasts. Zedekiah, son of King Josiah and last king of Judah, ruled eleven years from 597 to 586 BC. Prior to Zedekiah the kingdom had been ruled by his two older brothers Jehoahaz and Jehoiakim, and by his nephew Coniah (also called Jehoiachin). When Coniah was exiled to Babylon Nebuchadnezzar made twenty-one-year-old Mattaniah the king and changed his name to Zedekiah (2 Kings 24:15-17). Zedekiah rebelled against Nebuchadnezzar who captured him, killed his sons before his eyes, then blinded him and took him to Babylon where he later died. Note, however, that Jeremiah was treated with respect, even admiration, by the Babylonians. Some commentators suggest that the superstitious Babylonians, who respected magicians and soothsayers, put Jeremiah in this category and treated him as a seer. No doubt they also knew that he had counselled co-operation with Babylon and had predicted a Babylonian victory.

FURTHER STUDY

Matt. 5:10-12;
James 1:1-12

1. How may we be like Jeremiah?

2. What is God's promise if we remain faithful?

What a difference there is between the fates of Zedekiah and Jeremiah. One was saved by faith; the other was destroyed by fear. One was filled with self-interest, the other with compassion for his people. One was treated with contempt, the other with respect. Note too that Ebed-Melech (who risked his life to save Jeremiah) is blessed by God and protected from the Babylonians. A life of commitment to the Lord can sometimes be tough, but God often has special blessings or compensations for His faithful people. He allows us to be tempted, but He promises also to make a way of escape. He allows us to suffer, but He promises to support us and bring good out of evil.

O Father, I am grateful for those miraculous interventions that are so beautifully timed by You. When my back is against the wall, You have a way of turning the situation around. My hope and trust is in You today, Lord. Amen.

The choice

FOR READING & MEDITATION - JEREMIAH 40:1-16

'So Jeremiah ... stayed ... among the people who were left behind
in the land.' (v6)

This is an amazing moment in Jeremiah's life which takes place after the fall of Jerusalem. The city is now in Babylonian hands just as Jeremiah had predicted; the lies of the false prophets have been exposed. It is decided to take Jeremiah to Babylon with the other exiles but when they are about five miles out from Jerusalem Nebuzaradan, the captain of the guard, gives the prophet the choice of going to Babylon with the exiles or returning to his native Jerusalem.

This is how *The Message* paraphrases his remarks: 'If you'd like to come to Babylon with me, come along. I'll take good care of you. But if you don't want to come to Babylon with me, that's just fine, too. Look, the whole land stretches out before you. Do what you like' (v4). What a choice! The prophet can go to Babylon where he will be given special treatment – no chains, no imprisonment, no deprivation. Or he can return to Jerusalem, a city now in ruins, and be part of the tiny remnant left behind.

Jeremiah is being offered a chance to retire in Babylon. He was about sixty-five at the time so the offer would have had its attractions. If anyone deserved a life of ease with special facilities, it was Jeremiah. But the prophet was not yet ready for retirement so it didn't take him long to make up his mind. He chose to return to Jerusalem and live as he had always lived, trusting God and confident in His purposes. Jeremiah's choice that day at Rama was typical of how he had lived all his life. He chose to be where the Almighty had enshrined His name – Jerusalem, the city of God. His choices were comfort or service. The same choice faces us daily, not just at life's big crossroads.

FURTHER STUDY

Ruth 1:8-18;
Josh. 24:14-27

1. Contrast the attitudes of Ruth and Orpah.

2. What choice did Joshua give?

Father, I face many choices in life and sometimes attractive choices. But no matter what choices I am faced with help me to always make the choice that is in line with Yours. In Jesus' name I pray. Amen.

Easy way or God's way?

FOR READING & MEDITATION - JEREMIAH 41:1-18
'They were afraid of them because Ishmael ... had killed Gedaliah'
(v18)

Before the Babylonians marched the exiles off to Babylon they had appointed Gedaliah, a life-long friend of Jeremiah, to be the governor of Jerusalem. But not long after his appointment a terrorist outlaw called Ishmael, accompanied by a small group of associates, murdered him and many of the Jewish officials and the Babylonian soldiers. The next day when a large group of people from the surrounding areas approached Jerusalem to worship at the Temple, Ishmael inveigled them inside the city and slaughtered them, throwing their bodies into a huge cistern.

FURTHER STUDY

Matt. 7:13-14;
Heb. 11:24-28

1. What did Jesus explain?

2. Why did Jesus choose to be ill-treated?

His murderous action was countered by Johanan who organised the people of Mizpah into a formidable band and chased Ishmael and his companions out of the country. Johanan, then fearing reprisals from Babylon over the assassination of Gedaliah, decided to move down into Egypt. The question arises, why Egypt? God had clearly told His people that they ought not to align themselves with Egypt (Isa. 30:1-3; Jer. 2:36) yet here a group is bent on settling there.

Egypt represented safety and security – a much more appealing alternative than staying in Jerusalem and depending on God to direct their lives. Jerusalem, with its city reduced to rubble and its economy in ruins, was a hard option. Egypt was an easier one. Many of us when faced with the choice between trusting the invisible God or putting our faith in the things we can see prefer to do the equivalent of living in Egypt. Trusting God is not easy, especially where there is an escape route that leads to more tangible things. But sadly they may prove unable to support us.

My Father and my God, Your Word keeps on finding me out. Yet I would rather be challenged by You than be lulled by the world into a false sense of security. Help me spurn all escape routes and trust only in You. In Jesus' name. Amen.

Keep an open mind

SUN
24 AUG

FOR READING & MEDITATION - JEREMIAH 42:1-22

'I have told you today, but you still have not obeyed the
LORD your God' (v21)

You could be forgiven for thinking that Jeremiah's
decision to return to Jerusalem meant that there, in
the city of God, he would end his days. However, it was not
to be. He ended his days in the place he had told his people
not to go to – Egypt. This is how it happened.

When Johanan decided to escape to Egypt he asked
Jeremiah to pray for God's guidance. Jeremiah did so and
later passed on God's response: 'If you are ready to stick
it out in this land, I will build you up and not drag you
down ... You don't have to fear the King of Babylon. Your
fears are for nothing. I'm on your side, ready to
save and deliver you from anything he might do
... If what's left of Judah is ... determined to go to
Egypt and make that your home, then the very
wars you fear will catch up with you in Egypt
and the starvation you dread will track you down'
(vv10–16, *The Message*). God could not have put
the issue more clearly – but Johanan ignored the
advice given by God and set off for Egypt, taking
Jeremiah and his friend Baruch with him.

FURTHER
STUDY

Psa. 143:7-12;
John 9:13-24

1. What was
the psalmist's
request?

2. How were
the Pharisees
minds closed?

It is clear that Johanan, in asking Jeremiah to
pray for God's guidance, had already made his
mind up. He didn't want guidance; he wanted confirmation.
It is a problem many of us face in our prayer lives. We
are not truly open to God; we don't take seriously the
possibility that He might say something that doesn't fit
with our preconceived ideas. Did Jeremiah and Baruch go
willingly? I cannot say. It is the supreme irony of Jeremiah's
life that he ended his days in Egypt. I have no doubt myself
that although little is recorded about Jeremiah's last days
he would have ended them as he began – magnificently,
honourably, loyally and courageously.

**Father, can it be that even though I pray for guidance I am
more interested in getting confirmation? Help me dear Father
to examine my heart. Help me when I pray to have a truly open
mind. In Jesus' name. Amen.**

Egypt - no refuge

FOR READING & MEDITATION - JEREMIAH 43:1-13

'The LORD our God has not sent you to say, "You must not go to Egypt to settle there."' (v2)

We saw yesterday that when Johanan and his associates asked Jeremiah to pray for God's guidance they really wanted God's confirmation of their plans to go down to Egypt. This is a problem many of us face for if we are honest we are more interested in getting God's approval for our own plans than seeking Him for His. An old Christian friend told me many years ago: never make any plans unless you are willing to have God change them, and never pray unless you are willing to accept God's answer. They are challenging words.

FURTHER STUDY

Psa. 118:6-9;
1 Tim. 6:6-19

1. Where is a safe refuge?

2. How may our securities hurt us?

Johanan and his companions, fearful of staying in Jerusalem and resisting God, make sure that Jeremiah is with them. I raised the question yesterday whether Jeremiah and his companion Baruch went willingly. Scripture does not say, but my own guess is that they were pressured, perhaps even forced, to go because Johanan thought that if the prophet was with them then God would spare them and allow none of the things to happen to them that he had predicted.

When Jeremiah arrived in Egypt his first action was to bury some paving stones at the entrance to Pharaoh's palace and announce that Nebuchadnezzar of Babylon would one day set up his throne on the stones that he, Jeremiah, had buried. He did. Nebuchadnezzar actually invaded Egypt in 568-567 BC and overthrew the nation. So much for the great empire on which Johanan and his companions had pledged their hopes. It is an object lesson for us. The things or people we trust may seem strong, but if they are not chosen by God they will end up letting us down. It's sad, but so often true.

O Father, with all my heart I ask You to help me to deepen my confidence and trust in You. Please help me in all that I do today. In Jesus' name. Amen.

Jeremiah's last sermon

FOR READING & MEDITATION - JEREMIAH 44:1-30

'This word came to Jeremiah concerning all the Jews living
in Lower Egypt' (v1)

This is now the last recorded scene in Jeremiah's life. And it shows him doing what he had done for most of his life – speaking God's Word to an antagonistic and rambunctious people. This encounter no doubt took place some months after their arrival in Egypt. His talk is a blistering attack on their refusal to listen to the current guidance of God, and he reminds them that their previous behaviour had brought destruction on the land. Jeremiah tells them that they will never return to Judah because they had gone against God's advice when they travelled to Egypt.

But these people, like the others of their generation, were unwilling to hear what Jeremiah was saying. Only those who repented of going to Egypt would escape judgment. One of the great principles of the Christian life is the further we drift from God, the more confused our thinking becomes and the more likely we are to perpetuate our mistakes. Whatever degree of spiritual life the group who went down to Egypt once had now seemed to be lost. They had been fully immersed into local customs of idolatry, debauchery and pagan worship – the things that caused all the trouble in the first place. They stubbornly refused to recognise the source of their problems which was their departure from God's way and breaking the covenant.

FURTHER STUDY

Deut. 4:1-9;
1 Cor. 10:1-13

1. What warning is given to Israel?

2. Why were Israel's failures recorded?

When we forget a lesson we are in danger of repeating the mistake that the lesson was meant to counter. The people of Judah forgot their past and thus found it easy to repeat. Our past is a school of experience. We live foolishly, even dangerously, when we fail to let our past choices point us in the direction God wishes us to take now.

Father, I see that not to learn from my choices is to assure future failure. Just as I remember the lessons I once learned in school, help me remember also the lessons I learn in Your school of experience. In Jesus' name. Amen.

A boost to Baruch

FOR READING & MEDITATION - JEREMIAH 45:1-5

'Should you then seek great things for yourself? Seek them not.'
(v5)

This, the shortest chapter in Jeremiah's prophecy, is chronologically out of order. It links with the events recorded in chapter 36:1-18. Baruch, you remember, was the scribe who wrote down Jeremiah's words. Clearly the scribe is upset. *The Living Bible* puts it graphically: 'You have said, Woe is me ... I am weary of my own sighing and I find no rest.' There is little doubt that Baruch is getting his share of opposition for the influence he supposedly has over Jeremiah (v3). It appears that Baruch had great hopes for himself and his own ministry, but now all those hopes were dashed.

FURTHER STUDY

Matt. 6:25-34;
Mark 10:35-45

1. Contrast pagans and believers.

2. How did Jesus correct the disciples?

God speaks to him through Jeremiah and takes him to task for his negative thinking, but to sustain him he is given a promise of personal survival: 'I will protect you wherever you go' (v5). This brief chapter is evidence of the fact that God comes to the aid of His servants and reassures them of the divine love and compassion. The heart of God's message to Jeremiah is one that we need to hear today: take your eyes off yourself, and think more of the purposes of God for your life than of making a name for yourself.

When we concentrate more on our own careers or our own future than on the purpose of God for our lives we become self-centred rather than God-centred. That does not mean it is wrong to think and plan out a career. It means rather that unless God has first claim on our lives then we live superficially no matter how much money we make or how many possessions we own. True greatness in His kingdom is serving Him and others before ourselves (Luke 22:26-27).

O God, forgive me when I focus in a self-centred way on what I have to give up to serve You. Help me to focus on what I have gained because I know You: real life in this world and eternal life to come. Thank You my Father. Amen.

A message to the nations

FOR READING & MEDITATION - JEREMIAH 46:1-10

'This is the word of the LORD that came to Jeremiah the prophet concerning the nations' (v1)

A superficial reading of the Old Testament may easily lead someone to conclude that God is interested in just one group of people – the Jews. But such is not the case. He is the God of the Jews, but He is also the God of the nations. In fact nearly every Old Testament prophet has something to say about the nations that lay outside Israel. Obadiah, for example, focuses on Edom; Jonah and Nahum direct their message to Nineveh. Jeremiah was called by God not to be a chaplain to the Jews but a prophet to the *nations* (1:5).

Here, Jeremiah's missionary heart is made bare. He had little opportunity to visit the surrounding nations so in chapters 46–51 we see him preparing oracles or written talks for ten different nations: Egypt, Philistia, Moab, Ammon, Edom, Damascus (capital of Syria), Kedar and Hazor (two nomadic tribes), Elam and Babylon. His concern for the surrounding nations is a reflection of God's concern. No one has a greater missionary heart than God. His primary intention in calling Israel into covenant with Himself was *evangelistic*. He wanted them to be a shop window through which other nations could look and see life being lived as God originally intended, and blessings that come from serving the true and living God. But as we well know, Israel failed to reflect the divine purposes.

'Biblical religion,' says Eugene Peterson, 'is aggressively internationalistic.' Our churches ought not to be cosy places to which we retreat but centres from which we draw inspiration to make both individual and corporate evangelistic forays into the world. Jesus' last words were not 'come', but 'go' (Matt. 28:19).

FURTHER STUDY

Acts 1:1-8; 13:1-5

1. Where were God's messengers to go?

2. How was the church an evangelistic centre?

Father, help me never to forget that the first two letters of the Gospel are GO. May there be a GO in my faith, and may I share Your heart for Your people I pray. In Jesus' name. Amen.

A tale of two cities

FOR READING & MEDITATION – JEREMIAH 51:58-64
'Babylon's thick wall will be levelled' (v58)

We do not know how Jeremiah got his talks into the surrounding nations, but we do know he got his message into Babylon. In today's passage we see Jeremiah enlisting the services of Seraiah to take the message addressed to Babylon with him as he makes an official diplomatic journey to the city. Jeremiah commissions him not only to read it but then to take a stone, tie it to the scroll, and throw it into the River Euphrates, announcing: 'So will Babylon sink to rise no more' (v64). Did those words come true? Definitely. Babylon, one of the greatest cities the world has ever known, now lies in ruins. I am told by travellers who have visited its remains that an eerie atmosphere pervades the place. In fact the city was devastated about seventy years later.

FURTHER STUDY

John 17:13-23;
2 Tim. 4:9-10

1. How did Jesus' prayer reflect two cities?

2. Why did Demas desert Paul?

Someone has described the Bible as 'a tale of two cities'. It centres on Babylon, the symbol of pride and Jerusalem, the symbol of peace. Babylon, built on the site of the original tower of Babel, represents the kind of pride and arrogance that comes before God and says: 'We can get along without You'. Jerusalem, on the other hand, represents God-centred worship that says, 'We can't get along without You'. Interestingly, only Jerusalem, the city of God, is standing today. Babylon may have gone, but its spirit is still with us. However, as we see in the book of Revelation, one day that spirit of pride will be eradicated from the earth and the new Jerusalem will hold sway. We live today in both cities; our physical life is in Babylon, but our hearts are in Jerusalem. So which one is uppermost in your life?

Father, I see that I can choose my eternal destiny. I choose life. I choose the New Jerusalem, the city of God. All honour and glory be to Your precious name. Amen.

A strange ending

FOR READING & MEDITATION - JEREMIAH 52:1-34

'It was because of the LORD's anger that all this happened to Jerusalem and Judah' (v3)

The book of Jeremiah ends in a slightly unexpected way with the story of the last days of King Zedekiah. If you know the books of Kings and Chronicles then you will be familiar with the events as both contain these details. Jeremiah has himself referred to the event before (39:1-7). Because of this some have suggested that this chapter happily could have been left out of the Bible. It is without doubt an historical appendix or an editorial edition, but there is no doubt too that it is put here by God for a purpose.

The story tells how Zedekiah (who at this point was Nebuchadnezzar's deputy) rebelled against the Babylonian oppression, and how Nebuchadnezzar came to put down the rebellion and lay siege to Jerusalem. The chapter records the removal of the furnishings from the Temple and the execution of some of Jerusalem's leading citizens. It ends with the much later release of Jehoiachin who became a recipient of the king's favour.

FURTHER STUDY

Psa. 119:89-96; 1 Pet. 1:22-25

1. How did God's Word affect the psalmist?

2. What is the nature of God's Word?

I found myself wondering as I came to the end of these meditations: why doesn't the book end as it began with some reference to Jeremiah? I would have liked to have known how and where he died. But then it occurred to me – the book is not so much about Jeremiah as about the word that came to Jeremiah. So this closing chapter' is very appropriate, as it shows how events turned out exactly as predicted in God's Word. We can be sure that whatever God says will happen. The divine Word has always been fulfilled, is always fulfilled and will always be fulfilled. Nations come and nations go but God's Word endures forever. Hold firmly to it!

O God, I am thankful that Your Word is truth. It is my joy, my daily bread. I trust that Word, and build my life on it. Help me to know it better and deeper day by day. In Jesus' name. Amen.

Average or excellent?

FOR READING & MEDITATION - HEBREWS 11:32-40

'Some faced jeers and flogging, while still others were chained and put in prison.' (v36)

Having spent two months reflecting on the prophecy of Jeremiah, what is our conclusion? Surely it must be this – when life seems humdrum, routine and unexciting, or we feel overrun by life's circumstances and situations, there is hope. We must remind ourselves of God's calling and covenants towards us. We can opt for the average or we can pursue excellence. Excellence does not always mean the exciting or the adventurous. It means doing God's work faithfully, industriously, and without cutting corners.

FURTHER STUDY

Acts 21:10-14;
Phil. 3:7-16

1. Describe Paul's attitude.

2. How should we live?

Whenever I think of Jeremiah I think of Sir Winston Churchill's picturesque remarks concerning one of the generals who led the Russian armies against Germany in World War II. 'He reminded me of a frozen peg hammered into the ground, firm, solid, immovable.' That is the picture I hold in my mind of Jeremiah. We can all choose how we will live – cautiously or courageously. Which one will it be for you? The Word of the Lord came to Jeremiah and despite bouts of discouragement and inward struggles he rose through it all to pursue the task God had given him.

Has the Word of the Lord come to you? Has God spoken into your life and given you clear direction concerning the path He wants you to go? Then go for it – and never give up. Doing the work of God faithfully is the excellence He looks for. The Word of the Lord is your strength. Give Him praise and honour and glory. Flannery O'Connor, the writer, once said that he had an aunt who thought nothing happened in a story unless somebody got married or shot. Jeremiah doesn't get married and he doesn't get shot. But a lot happened in his story because he gave it all to God.

Father, thank You for all You have taught me through Jeremiah. Now I go out to live faithfully too. In Your strength, may I pursue excellence in all I do. In Jesus' name. Amen.

ORDER FORM

EDWJ J/A 2014

4 EASY WAYS TO ORDER:

1. Phone in your credit card order: **01252 784700** (Mon-Fri, 9.30am - 5pm)

2. Visit our online store at **www.cwr.org.uk/store**

3. Send this form together with your payment to:
   CWR, Waverley Abbey House, Waverley Lane, Farnham, Surrey GU9 8EP

4. Visit your local Christian bookshop

r a list of our National Distributors, who supply countries outside the UK, visit www.cwr.org.uk/distributors

YOUR DETAILS (REQUIRED FOR ORDERS AND DONATIONS)

Full Name: **CWR ID No.** (if known):

Home Address:

                                                 Postcode:

Telephone No. (for queries):   **Email:**

PUBLICATIONS

TITLE	QTY	PRICE	TOTAL
Total publications			

All CWR adult Bible-reading notes are also available in eBook and email subscription format.
Visit www.cwr.org.uk for further information.

UK p&p: up to £24.99 = **£2.99**; £25.00 and over = **FREE**

Elsewhere p&p: up to £10 = **£4.95**; £10.01 - £50 = **£6.95**; £50.01 - £99.99 = **£10**; £100 and over = **£30**

Please allow 14 days for delivery   **Total publications and p&p A**

SUBSCRIPTIONS* (NON DIRECT DEBIT)

	QTY	PRICE (INCLUDING P&P)			TOTAL
		UK	**Europe**	**Elsewhere**	
Every Day with Jesus (1yr, 6 issues)		£15.95	£19.95	Please contact nearest National Distributor or CWR direct	
Large Print Every Day with Jesus (1yr, 6 issues)		£15.95	£19.95		
Inspiring Women Every Day (1yr, 6 issues)		£15.95	£19.95		
Life Every Day (Jeff Lucas) (1yr, 6 issues)		£15.95	£19.95		
Cover to Cover Every Day (1yr, 6 issues)		£15.95	£19.95		
Mettle: 14-18s (1yr, 3 issues)		£14.50	£16.60		
YP's: 11-15s (1yr, 6 issues)		£15.95	£19.95		
Topz: 7-11s (1yr, 6 issues)		£15.95	£19.95		
Total Subscriptions (Subscription prices already include postage and packing) **B**					

ase circle which bimonthly issue you would like your subscription to commence from:
/Feb Mar/Apr May/Jun Jul/Aug Sep/Oct Nov/Dec

nly use this section for subscriptions paid for by credit/debit card or
heque. For Direct Debit subscriptions see overleaf.

CONTINUED OVERLEAF >>

PAYMENT DETAILS

☐ I enclose a cheque/PO made payable to CWR for the amount of: **£** _____

☐ Please charge my credit/debit card.

Cardholder's Name (in BLOCK CAPITALS) _____

Card No. ☐☐☐☐ ☐☐☐☐ ☐☐☐☐ ☐☐☐☐

Expires End ☐☐☐☐   Security Code ☐☐☐

GIFT TO CWR ☐ Please send me an acknowledgement of my gift   **C** _____

GIFT AID (YOUR HOME ADDRESS REQUIRED, SEE OVERLEAF)

giftaid it

I am a UK taxpayer and want CWR to reclaim the tax on all my donations for the four years prior to this year **and on** all donations I make from the date of this Gift Aid declaration until further notice.*

Taxpayer's Full Name (in BLOCK CAPITALS) _____

Signature _____ **Date** _____

*I understand I must pay an amount of Income/Capital Gains Tax at least equal to the tax the charity reclaims in the tax year.

GRAND TOTAL (Total of A, B, & C) ☐

SUBSCRIPTIONS BY DIRECT DEBIT (UK BANK ACCOUNT HOLDERS ONLY)

Subscriptions cost £15.95 (except *Mettle*: £14.50) for one year for delivery within the UK. Please tick relevant boxes and fill in the form

☐ *Every Day with Jesus* (1yr, 6 issues)
☐ Large Print *Every Day with Jesus* (1yr, 6 issues)
☐ *Inspiring Women Every Day* (1yr, 6 issues)
☐ *Life Every Day* (Jeff Lucas) (1yr, 6 issues)

☐ *Cover to Cover Every Day* (1yr, 6 issues)
☐ *Mettle*: 14-18s (1yr, 3 issues)
☐ *YP's*: 11-15s (1yr, 6 issues)
☐ *Topz*: 7-11s (1yr, 6 issues)

Issue to commence f
☐ Jan/Feb ☐ Jul/Aug
☐ Mar/Apr ☐ Sep/Oct
☐ May/Jun ☐ Nov/Dec

CWR

Instruction to your Bank or Building Society to pay by Direct Debit

DIREC Debi

Please fill in the form and send to: CWR, Waverley Abbey House, Waverley Lane, Farnham, Surrey GU9 8EP

Name and full postal address of your Bank or Building Society

To: The Manager _____ **Bank/Building Society**

Address _____

_____

_____ **Postcode** _____

Name(s) of Account Holder(s)

_____

Branch Sort Code

☐☐ ☐☐ ☐☐

Bank/Building Society Account Number

☐☐☐☐☐☐☐☐

Originator's Identification Number

4	2	0	4	8	7

Reference

☐☐☐☐☐☐☐☐☐☐☐☐☐☐☐☐☐☐

Instruction to your Bank or Building Society

Please pay CWR Direct Debits from the account detailed in this Instruction s to the safeguards assured by the Direct Debit Guarantee.
I understand that this Instruction may remain with CWR and, if so, details will passed electronically to my Bank/Building Society.

Signature(s) _____

Date _____

Banks and Building Societies may not accept Direct Debit Instructions for some types of account

DEVIL'S WEB

THE DEVIL'S WEB

Who Is Stalking Your Children For Satan?

Pat Pulling
with Kathy Cawthon

WORD PUBLISHING

Word (UK) Ltd
Milton Keynes, England

WORD AUSTRALIA
Kilsyth, Victoria, Australia

STRUIK CHRISTIAN BOOKS (PTY) LTD
Maitland, South Africa

ALBY COMMERCIAL ENTERPRISES PTE LTD
Balmoral Road, Singapore

CHRISTIAN MARKETING NEW ZEALAND LTD
Havelock North, New Zealand

JENSCO LTD
Hong Kong

SALVATION BOOK CENTRE
Malaysia

THE DEVIL'S WEB

Dedication

For "Bink":
My sweet brother why did you die?
Whenever I think of you, I often cry.
My eyes fill up and begin to flow,
I let my tears and my feelings go.
A permanent solution, for a temporary problem.
Why did you leave me? I trusted you.
We didn't know. We didn't have a clue.
You kept it a secret inside your heart.
Now, because of that, we are apart.
That last morning when you said goodbye,
You gave your farewell kiss and final sigh.
Everyone else is hurting, too.
But why did you leave me
      I trusted you.

****

With love, your sister
    Melissa Pulling, 1987

"SON, IN LIFE AND DEATH
YOU CHANGED OUR WORLD"
This book is dedicated to all of
the children and adults who lost their lives
unnecessarily.......

CONTENTS

ACKNOWLEDGEMENTS

My gratitude extends to my friends and family whose emotional support has sustained me over these difficult years.

I am also grateful to the many professionals who have assisted me in my research and investigations. Much would have been impossible without their efforts. Some of those professionals must remain unnamed due to their sensitive positions.

We extend special thanks to the following:

Curtis and Dorothy Adams; Roy and Martha Adams; Lisa Antonelli-Bacon; Paul Banner (S.C. Criminal Justice Academy); Mike Barrett; Jim and Sally Bostad; Billy Bowles; Bob and Jane Brame; Ed Briggs; Father Brennin; Shirley Cawthon; Greg Corrie; Cheryl Cox; Josephine Crafton; Bill Dear; Carl Deavers (Va. State Police); Patrick and Mary Dempsey; Janet Deihl; Grace Diekhaus; Larry Fleece; Lt. Jim Gaertner (Sedalia Police Dpt.); Officer Sandi Gallant; Dr. Dale Griffis; Tipper Gore; Lt. Larry Haake (Richmond Police Dpt.); Dr. Neil Hutcher, M.D., and staff; Jan's Restaurant and the staff; Mr. and Mrs. Robert Kane; Ernest Lowery; Rosemary Loyacono; Teresa Luce; Steve McPheeters; Winston Mathews; Det. Ed Maxwell (New Castle Police Dpt.); Sgt. Elizabeth Merrill (Austin Police Dpt.); Darren Molitor; Nancy Meyer; Jennifer Norwood; Dr. Kenneth Olshansky; Frank Parham; Proctor's Restaurant and the staff; Elexia Pulling; Dr. Thomas Radecki, M.D.; Sean Sellers; Inv. Al Sheppard (New York City Police Dpt.); Det. Jerry Simandl; Sharon Sipos; Officer Jim Skorcz; Stevie Smith; Kathy Snowden, M.S.W.; Inv. Roy Stout (Petersburg Police Dpt.); John Stuart; Bruce Sullivan; Mary Ann Talley; Civia Tamarken; Bill Teed; Maury Terry; Maury Trelford; and Eddie Vaughan.

I also would like to thank the many concerned citizens who have worked so hard over the years to help all children grow up safely.

We extend very special thanks to our families for their patience and for the sacrifices they made in support of this book: to our husbands, Irving Lee Pulling and Roger E. Cawthon, and to our children, Melissa and Rachel Pulling and Ryan and Reid Cawthon.

INTRODUCTION

In the late 1970s, when I began an independent investigation of New York's sensational Son of Sam murders following the arrest of David Berkowitz, the supposed lone gunman in those slayings, my knowledge of cult crimes and the occult in general was minimal. But I quickly discovered that I wasn't alone: as the Son of Sam inquiry progressed and ultimately led to the discovery that the killings were orchestrated by a satanic cult to which Berkowitz belonged, the reaction of most in law enforcement was one of disbelief. The general feeling was simply that there was no such thing as occult-related crime in the United States.

But time and, most importantly, accumulated evidence laid that skepticism to rest, and it is now widely recognized that the Son of Sam case marked the first time that a major, nationally prominent series of murders was definitively linked to satanic cult activity.

Since those "early days," my familiarity with the occult underground has increased dramatically as a result of my involvement with the Berkowitz investigation and others that I've been asked to consult on throughout the 1980s. At the same time, law enforcement awareness of the situation has grown, most notably over the course of the last few years. Ten years ago, it would have been difficult to interest two detectives in the subject. Today, seminars throughout the nation that are devoted to the various aspects of cult crime routinely attract two hundred or more.

The facts and the headlines reveal the reasons for this new concern on the part of law enforcement, clergy, educators, parents and mental health professionals. Occult crime is both on the rise and receiving justifiably increased coverage in the media. David Berkowitz's immersion in devil worship is now well-documented, as is that of other infamous killers such as Charles Manson, California "Night Stalker" Richard Ramirez and more, including those behind the 1989 ritualistic slayings of at least fifteen people in Matamoros, Mexico, just across the U.S. border from Brownsville, Texas. Those cases are familiar to everyone, but just as important are the many isolated occurrences that transpire on an almost-daily basis throughout the country.

From virtually every corner of the United States incidents of murder, rape, animal mutilations and graveyard desecrations are being reported with disturbing regularity by the press. Concurrently, "adult survivors"—victims of generational satanic worship—are coming forward to relate their stories of horror, abuse and degradation suffered at the hands of parents, grandparents, and other relatives who were members of witchcraft or satanic groups that have been in existence for upwards of fifty years, in some instances. Clearly, the various facets of occult crime and the dangers it represents to mainstream America—particularly its young and impressionable—are challenges that must be recognized and faced head on.

America's youth is both its foundation and its future, and it is there that the greatest threat exists. Young people, still struggling through their formative years, are prime targets of sophisticated cult recruiters and are also vulnerable to the superficial lures of satanism. Whether they experiment individually or ultimately become part of an organized group where they are subject to the whims and manipulations of power-crazed leaders, the bottom line is all too often the same: tragedy, death, incarceration, severe mental illness and ruin.

These are not the observations of an alarmist. Rather, they are a cut and dried recital of the everyday facts of life for those who descend into the netherworld of satanic worship and other deviant occult practices.

The key to dealing with the problem is understanding it, becoming aware of the indicators, and knowing how to distinguish between fact and fiction when confronted with the possibility that a family member or friend has become engulfed in harmful occult activities or that a potentially dangerous situation is manifest in a community. Patricia Pulling and Kathy Cawthon have compiled a valuable guide in *The Devil's Web*. The story they have to tell is not pleasant, but it is both informative and important. For centuries, satanism has thrived in the shadows, and it is gratifying to see some of its insidious mysteries exposed to the light of day.

I hope you find the book to be as helpful and interesting as I did. It should serve as a valuable tool for both parents and professionals alike as they seek to take the steps necessary to encounter and conquer what has grown to become a force that must be reckoned with in America as we move into the last decade of the Twentieth Century.

Maury Terry
Author, *The Ultimate Evil*
June 1989

A PERSONAL TRAGEDY

During the last seven years I have investigated the subject of teenage "devil worship." During those years—while doing research and speaking on this subject—I learned much about the evil that stalks our land, about those whose sole purpose is to lead our children away from home, family, church and the moral values which they have learned. Because of the sinister nature of these individuals and the lives that they are destroying daily—it has become necessary to tell this story.

This book is for parents, school officials, law enforcement officers, mental health professionals, the clergy and anyone else concerned.

In it you will discover the ever-growing web being spun by those who desire to lead your children into satanism.

You will also explore and come to understand the historical aspects of the occult and the reasons why this "devil's web" chooses young people as its prey and works so diligently to entrap them.

I entered this work because our family was victimized by the deadly menace of the occult, and because I felt compelled to search for answers to my own cries of "why?"

As a lecturer and consultant on the subject of teen devil worship, it is easy to present the academic side, the facts and statistics, the warning signs.

To talk and write about my own grief and pain and that of others with whom I have come in contact is quite another story.

For that reason, this prologue is very difficult to write. I will share the details now, not because it doesn't still hurt, but because so many others have asked about my family's experience. As you read, know that these pages are filled with much heartache and much love.

The Story of "Bink"

On a warm morning, June 9, 1982, I had a living, breathing, really neat son, 16-year old Irving, who kissed me good-bye before taking his last school bus ride.

My husband Lee and I went shopping after work to buy a "boom box" for Irving, whose nickname was "Bink." He was finishing his junior year in high school with excellent grades, and we wanted to give him a reward. We also stopped by the train station to buy tickets for the whole family to take a trip to Walt Disney World as soon as school was out. Then we went to my brother's house to pick up our nine-year old daughter, Melissa.

Our Montpelier, Virginia, home sits in the middle of an open field on approximately 36 acres of land. The two-story colonial home is elevated somewhat so that the front door is visible from the road.

When we pulled into the driveway, I could see that the house was dark and the front door was open. Chills raced up and down my spine. I knew immediately that something was wrong. Call it a mother's intuition or whatever you like, but panic began to build inside me.

"Hurry up, hurry up!" I told Lee.

He said, "What's wrong with you?"

All I could say was, "Something is wrong! Something is wrong! Where is Bink?"

Lee told me to calm down, that Bink probably had gone out with friends and forgotten to shut the door.

"No, no, hurry!" I said. My sick, gut-wrenching feeling would prove not only to be right, but was the beginning of the most horrible time of our lives.

As the car crested the last rise and the headlights shown on the sidewalk, I could see my son lying on the ground.

I jumped out of the car and ran toward Bink yelling, "Get up! Please get up!"

Simultaneously, I was thinking, "This is a joke, he's just playing around," yet another part of me knew that it was real. He certainly never had played like this before. No, my mind knew that he was dead, but my heart was not ready to accept it.

I could see that his feet were extremely white, the kind of white you expect to see where circulation has ceased.

As I drew closer, I could hear Melissa screaming. I do not remember that she said anything, only that she was screaming in terror.

2

I almost got close enough to bend over, to reach down and touch my son. Then Lee grabbed me around the waist and began tugging me, pulling me back to the car.

I shouted, "No! We can't leave him. We have to get help." I can remember looking down at Bink's face. He seemed to be staring at me in fear and shock.

Lee managed to get Melissa and me back into the car, and he drove us back down that long driveway and then to a neighbor's house. We saw lights on, and we ran to the door. We banged on the door and screamed for help, but no one came.

We got back into the car and drove to Ernest Lowery's house a little further down the road. I heard Lee ask Ernest if we could use his telephone.

Ernest greeted us warmly and invited us in, not realizing our terrorized state just yet. I heard Lee say into the phone, "There is no need to send a rescue squad. He's dead."

Then I started screaming, "No, no, no! He can't be dead! He is my baby, my only son! No!"

Lee left then to go back to our house. Melissa and I just sat crying in the Lowery's kitchen.

My daughter looked at me and said, "Mom, am I going to die like Bink?"

I panicked and ran, out of the Lowery's home and down that long country road back to our home.

As I approached our house, I saw lights flashing in our front yard. It seemed it took me hours to run the length of the driveway. I felt weak, sick, scared, like I was running in a nightmare. I wanted so desperately to wake up, but of course I couldn't because this was real.

As I drew closer to the mob of people in the yard and ran to my son's body, someone tried to stop me, grabbing me and pulling me away, but I kept moving closer and closer to Bink. I fell down inches from his face and reached out to touch his hair. I lay there on the ground and would not move. I did not want to leave my son. People kept trying to pull me away, and I kept telling them to please get my son up off the ground and help him.

Finally, one of the rescue workers pulled me up and led me to the rescue van. He looked at me and asked, "Mrs. Pulling, do you know who I am?"

I said, "Of course I know who you are. Do you think I am out of my mind? I know exactly who you are. I know who I am, I know what has happened. My son is dead, and I want him back!"

I started to cry. No, I started to sob—deep, aching sobs that came up from the pit of my stomach. I had never known that a person could hurt that bad and not die from it.

I remember looking up at the sky, shaking my fist and saying, "God, why did You do this to me, to my son, to us? We don't deserve this! Why? Why?" Then I began begging, "God, if You will please let him live, I will lie down and take his place. Please let him live. Make him get up! I know that You can do anything!"

The police photographer began taking pictures of Bink. The flashes were blinding.

A man approached me and said, "Mrs. Pulling, will you please come with me?"

I said, "Who are you?" and he answered that he was an investigator from the Hanover County Sheriff's Department. He was gentle and softspoken. He took me by the arm and led me in a very wide circle around my son's body and up the steps leading into the house.

We went into the den. Lee was there, and I remember thinking that I had not seen him in awhile. I had lost track of time.

The investigator took Lee out of the room and returned. He said that he needed to ask me a few questions. I just stood there with several other people who were in the room. I must have been in shock at this point because I recall thinking absolutely nothing, staring at the other people, the fireplace, the walls. After a few minutes, I looked at the investigator and nodded that I would answer his questions.

He asked me where I had been that evening. I explained that Lee had picked me up after work and that we had gone out to dinner at a favorite restaurant. I told him about our shopping for a present for Bink, about the train tickets we had bought, about picking Melissa up at my brother's home.

Then he asked me how much insurance we had on our son.

I said, "Oh, not much. Only a small policy through my company. I think it is about $2500. Why?"

Then it occurred to me that I still did not know how my son had died.

I said, "What happened to him? Did someone murder him?"

The investigator replied, "We are looking at all of the possibilities right now, Mrs. Pulling. He appears to have been shot with a .38-caliber revolver, and your husband has told me that the revolver found next to your son's body is your gun."

Then I said, "My God, you don't think we killed him, do you?"

He said that he did not, and that he had found some letters apparently written by Bink. He asked me if I would look at them and identify the handwriting.

"But before you do that," he continued, "I have one other question." He paused, then asked, "Mrs. Pulling, are you or your husband devil worshipers?"

I was speechless, but finally managed to say, "What kind of question is that to ask me at a time like this? Are you crazy?"

I told him to look through my house, to do anything he wanted; he would not find anything connecting our family to something as insane as devil worship.

I thought to myself, "Maybe this is a nightmare. Is this guy really a policeman? Is everybody crazy? Devil worship! That stuff doesn't even exist except in the movies!"

I turned on the investigator and asked, "What is going on here? Are you all crazy? This has got to be a bad dream. I can't even believe you just asked me that. I am Jewish. My son is Jewish. He even went to Hebrew school for awhile. Is that why you think we are devil worshipers?"

He said no and showed me the letters.

There were six letters in all, some addressed to Bink's friends and one to a teacher.

One was written to us. It began, "Dear Mom and Dad ..." and went on to describe how evil he thought he had become. He equated himself with Adolph Hitler and the Antichrist, and said that he had been summoned to commit murder, couldn't bring himself to hurt anyone else, and so must end his own life to rid the world of this evil.

He hoped we would understand and told us not to worry about him. He even said that I would have another child within a year, and that the child would be a boy. He asked that we cremate his body and scatter the ashes. It was signed, "Love, Bink."

I felt my stomach turn inside out. I started heaving, but could not throw up. I couldn't speak.

The investigator took all of the letters back and asked me to sit down and relax. Of course I couldn't relax. My head was pounding and I felt so sick. I wanted to know what had happened.

A doctor approached me and said that he thought I should take some medicine to calm me down.

I shouted, "I don't want any medicine. For God's sake, I should be upset. My son is dead! He is still lying on the ground. I don't think that I should be calm, and I don't want anything that is going to impair my ability to think right now."

Then I asked him why he was even there. He told me he had been called to pronounce my son dead. I asked him to tell me if my son had suffered.

He said, "With the kind of wound he had, a .38-caliber bullet through his heart, the force and the shock to his system would have been so great that he probably felt very little pain, more like being kicked in the stomach or having the wind knocked out of you."

I said, "But did he suffer?"

5

The next words he said chilled me to the bone and I will never forget them as long as I live.

"He probably lived long enough to regret what he had done, but even if you had been here, you couldn't have saved him. We couldn't have saved him if he had done this while lying on an operating table," he replied.

I felt very weak then and sat on the sofa, thoughts rushing through my head. I wondered what my son had thought during those last few moments that he lived, lying there all alone, knowing that he was going to die. This question continues to torment me to this day in those rare moments when I allow myself to dwell on it, but of course I will never know the answer.

Lee came into the den and said to me very gently and quietly, "The hearse is here to take Bink."

I got up slowly, walked out of the house, down the steps and across the yard to the hearse. I looked through the window and saw the body bag on a stretcher. I leaned against the window and kissed the glass as though I might somehow kiss my son good-bye.

When we, in the course of our work, see violent "slasher" movies and a character in the film gets shot, I hear kids in the audience yell and scream with excitement. Some laugh when they see a body put into a body bag and say, "Another one bites the dust." How flip, how insensitive, how unreal the movies are. They never show the anguish, emptiness or feelings of the survivors for the loved one who is dead.

But no horror film that I have ever seen was this bad; nothing else in my life has ever come close to making me feel as sick and empty as the reality of that night.

The days that would follow would be filled with seemingly endless hours of despair and helplessness. Bink died on a Wednesday evening, and we buried him five days later. I kept him out for viewing at the funeral home the maximum time they would allow.

There is no right or wrong way to handle a tragedy, and it varies from individual to individual, from family to family. I guess I just did not want to say that last good-bye. Somehow, even though I knew Bink was dead, I wanted to be with him, to look at him, to remember the good times and the bad, and most of all to touch him. I needed to touch him, touch his hair, in order to try and come to some kind of terms with what had happened to my son and to our family.

The day after Bink's death, I remember going into the kitchen and looking at the table where he had left his school books. I sat down and began to go through his things. He had cleaned out his locker at school as requested since this was three days before the end of the school year.

As I looked through his papers and composition books, I saw many things with which I was unfamiliar. One was the *Advanced Dungeon Master's Guide* which had a picture on the cover of a large, red, monster-like creature. It looked similar to Hollywood renditions of "the devil" with horns on its head. The book beneath was another advanced book called the *Monster Manual*.

I called Lee into the kitchen and said, "What is all this stuff?"

We began thumbing through the books, and none of what we saw made any sense to us at the time. Among the papers was a pre-printed form with the words "Dungeons & Dragons Character Record Sheet" printed at the top.

We found violent, sadistic poems among the papers, poems that appeared to have been written by a demented person. We were shocked to see that some of them had the letter "A" printed in red at the top. Yes, some of these were papers graded by a teacher, and many had notes written by the teacher about style.

"For this he got an A! This is the sickest stuff I have ever seen!" I said.

Lee told me that we had to put all of this aside for awhile because we had to go upstairs and find a suit in which to bury Bink.

I began to cry when we entered his room. Everything that had been his life, his short 16 years, was in that room.

I picked up a shirt that he had worn recently and smelled it. I could smell Bink on the shirt, the smell of life. I hurt so badly and wanted him back so much.

My husband got the suit, a shirt and some underwear. I was pretty useless at this point. My grief ate up all my energy.

We drove into Richmond and took the clothes to the funeral home. The funeral director told us to come back about five o'clock that evening at which time Bink's body would be ready for viewing.

That day went so slowly. People called and came by, trying to talk to me, but I couldn't talk. I could only cry. I was so tired, but I couldn't sleep. With the exception of choosing a casket, everything had been handled by Lee. He made the necessary telephone calls to family and friends who lived out-of-state. Relatives who lived near us took Melissa to be with them. All I did was sit, think and cry.

When we arrived at the funeral home that evening, the attendants were so kind and gentle. They led us to the room where Bink lay. We spent a long time alone with him before the doors were opened to family and friends who had gathered in the hallway.

Watching them come in and show their great love for our son was terribly sad, but somehow comforting, too.

I did not feel shame as I have heard that so many families do when there has been a suicide, but I did feel extreme pain and, to some degree, anger. Yes, anger. Anger that I had not known what was going on in my son's mind, anger and guilt that I must have lacked something that would have allowed me to know that I had a child in trouble. I did not feel that Lee and I were to blame in any way for what had happened, but I wondered why we hadn't seen that something was very wrong. What could have caused our son to become so disturbed, and how did it happen so subtly? Had I not been paying attention?

I talked with those who came to the funeral home. I spoke with his friends and teachers, trying to recapture the last day of his life to see if there was something that I had missed that had triggered Bink's desperate act.

One of his teachers introduced herself as his "talented and gifted" program instructor, and I told her that I needed to speak with her.

I asked her what she knew about a game called "Dungeons & Dragons." She replied that she did not know what I was talking about.

At that time, I did not know that she had introduced this game to the TAG (talented and gifted) students and that they had played it in the classroom during class time, so I did not challenge her denial.

I asked her about a male teacher whose name had appeared on my son's game sheets as the "Dungeon Master."

She said that she only knew that he was an English teacher in the school. Again, she was not being completely truthful with me. I would discover later that she had invited him into the TAG class to act as Dungeon Master for the game.

Several of my son's closest friends came to the funeral home, too. When I tried to talk with them about the game, they either turned and walked away or simply did not respond to my questions.

This certainly was not the time or place to press the issue or make a scene, but it was becoming increasingly obvious to me that, whatever this game was, no one wanted to talk about it or would even admit to knowing anything about it.

The night before we buried Bink, the director of the funeral home handed me a small plastic bag of the belongings found on him. The bag contained some oddly shaped plastic pieces with numbers on them which I learned later were "Dungeons & Dragons" dice. The only other thing which had been in his pockets was a key in a leather case. It was a house key, but to this day we do not know to whom it belongs.

When the funeral was over, I determined to learn all I could about this game called "Dungeons & Dragons." First I went to a local game store and asked the clerk to tell me about "Dungeons & Dragons" and how it is played. She explained to me that it is a game of role-playing, not a board game.

I still did not understand, so she gave me a promotional brochure entitled "Your Personal Invitation to Adventure," published by TSR, and explained that TSR was the company that created the game.

I guess I still looked puzzled and confused because she said, "Look, the best thing for you to do is find yourself a Dungeon Master who can take you on a campaign. This will make things clear for you."

I asked her where I could find such a person, and she showed me a bulletin board filled with personal ads posted by people who wanted to act as Dungeon Masters and others who wanted to join gaming groups.

It all sounded pretty complicated to me and, as an adult, I had better sense than to call up someone I didn't know and ask him to get together with me to play a game I didn't know anything about. Instead, I went to a local college and hung around until I spotted some young men carrying "Dungeons & Dragons" books under their arms.

I introduced myself and asked them if they would show me how to play this game. They said they would, but openly wondered why a woman in her mid-30s was hanging around a college campus looking for someone to teach her to play "Dungeons & Dragons." I told them I had a 16-year old son who had been interested, but that I wanted to learn something about the game before buying it. I did not tell them that my son was dead or any of the circumstances surrounding his death.

Neither did I tell anyone that Bink had received a death curse the day he died. The curse, written by another player in his "Dungeons & Dragons" gaming group, read, "Your soul is mine. I choose the time. At my command, you will reave the land. A follower of evil, a Killer of man."

I did not tell these young men anything that might have made them uncomfortable or would distract them from giving me candid lessons in "Dungeons & Dragons." We played for several hours a day every day for a month.

I also read a great deal about the game to further my understanding of its complexities. At the end of the month, I felt I had had enough.

When my son died and I saw the death curse that had been given to him, I thought that surely no one would take such a curse seriously; **surely** no one would follow a "command" to commit suicide.

Then I began to think about the 900-plus people of Jonestown who committed suicide at the command of a deranged leader named Jim Jones.

Whenever I mention the Jonestown incident and draw a parallel between that incident and fantasy role-playing situations, people will say, "Yes, but those people were brainwashed, completely cut off from society, living in a communal setting. This can't be the same because game players go home to family when the game is over. They are not alienated."

One does not have to live in a commune under the control of an individual or group to be alienated. In role-playing games, players often become so obsessed with the adventure that they mentally withdraw from others to study and prepare.

The Dungeon Master (DM) exerts enormous control over the players in a game of "Dungeons & Dragons." He has the final say in the game, and he creates the world in which the adventure takes place. He has total authority in the world he creates.

The DM is referred to in the *Dungeon Master's Guide* as a "deity."

The book states on page 39, "The deity (you, the DM) will point out all the transgressions, state a course of action which must be followed to regain good graces, grant the spells which the deity deems are necessary to complete the course. ..."

Some may accuse me of taking this out of context; those individuals should read it for themselves. They will see that the context makes no difference in the meaning of this excerpt.

The point I am making is that the DM has such an omnipotent role in this game, a role I believe can lead to tragedy—as with our own son.

We also know that peer pressure plays a major role in the lives of most adolescents. Read what the *Dungeon Master's Guide* has to say about "Handling Troublesome Players" (page 110).

"Some players will find more enjoyment in spoiling a game than in playing it, and this ruins the fun for the rest of the participants, so it must be prevented. Those who enjoy being loud and argumentative, those who pout or act in a childish manner when things go against them, those who use the books as a defense when you rule them out of line should be excluded from the campaign. Simply put, ask them to leave, or do not invite them to participate again. ... Peer pressure is another means which can be used to control players who are not totally obnoxious and who you deem worth saving. ..." the **Guide** points out.

Imagine yourself as a young person not wanting to be excluded or ostracized by your friends. You might begin to lose control of your own ability to reject situations which are wrong for fear of reprisal from the group leader or the group. This type of thinking can be dangerous. It is so subtle that your behavior and attitudes can be modified without your being aware that a change is taking place. As you might expect, right or wrong and good or bad can become relative depending upon the person directing the game, in this case the Dungeon Master.

Admittedly, I did play the game for only a short time. However, I was at a stage in my life where maturity enabled me to see some of the problems inherent in the "Dungeons & Dragons" game which easily could obsess an unsuspecting, immature teenager.

The game is obsessive by design. A participant must spend many, many hours in study and preparation to become a successful player.

Again quoting from the *Dungeon Master's Guide* (page 2), "Esoteric questions aside, one thing is for certain—Dungeon Mastering is, above all, a labor of love. It is demanding, time consuming, and certainly not a task to be undertaken lightly. ..."

When I played, I also became quite concerned about the degree of loyalty players are expected to feel toward the DM. I began to feel that I was participating in some kind of cult.

When reading the *Advanced Dungeons & Dragons Player's Handbook*, I came across the following on page 2: "As diverse as the mélange of enthusiasm is, they all seem to share one commonality: a real love for Dungeons & Dragons and a devotion that few other games can claim. This remarkable loyalty is a great factor in the game's explosion of popularity, and Dungeons & Dragons has become a gaming cult, as avid D & D'ers have ceaselessly 'spread the gospel,' enrolling new players in expanding groups which just seem to grow and grow."

After founding B.A.D.D., Inc. (Bothered About Dungeons & Dragons and Other Harmful Influences on Children) in 1983 and beginning to speak publicly about my concerns, I often was verbally attacked by avid "Dungeons & Dragons" players. They spoke with the kind of vigor that many people exhibit when they talk about their religion. I received some obnoxious and nasty letters and phone calls, some of which included death threats.

One caller was even stupid enough to leave a threat on my telephone answering machine which I later turned over to the police who filed an incident report. I did not take this action for protection (you cannot protect yourself against this type of thing), but for documentation. I have never heard of such an incident or controversy with any other "game."

I continued my Dungeons & Dragons research because some people insisted it was occultic. I read many books on the occult so that I would be prepared to refute or confirm such allegations. The game does, indeed, have a tremendous amount of occult material. Much of what is called "fantasy" in this game is, in reality, drawn from a number of occult philosophies, and it is so specific that it would be ludicrous to suggest that the similarities are mere coincidence.

In January 1983, some concerned friends and Lee and I decided to form an organization to educate the public about potential problems that can occur when impressionable adolescents play. Lee came up with the acronym B.A.D.D. Since I had become pregnant in October, 1982, and had developed some complications which resulted in my being confined to bed, I had a lot of time to think about and work on this new project.

On one occasion, I was hospitalized for several months so that I would not lose the baby. I used my confinement to read in bed. My family rented a typewriter for me, and the nurses helped with the large volume of mail coming in and going out when people began to learn about B.A.D.D. I began receiving phone calls from other parents who had experienced problems similar to ours, and we began to correspond.

My physical condition worsened considerably at one point, but I recovered quickly, and the lengthy stay in bed was invaluable in getting B.A.D.D. started.

The organization grew quickly. We were joined in our efforts by Rosemary Loyacono and Patrick Dempsey, two other parents whose sons had committed suicide following lengthy periods of involvement with Dungeons & Dragons.

Those of us who have lived through the experience of the death of a child have a common bond. We share our grief, of course, but we also share the burden of prejudice and cruelty to which we sometimes are subjected by those who point the finger of blame at the families of the victims. Because of this prejudice, many B.A.D.D. members choose to keep their stories and their pain private. We respect and support their decisions.

However, some of us have chosen to accept the challenge to go public with our cases in the hope that we can help others whose tragedies have followed ours and by preventing other tragedies from occurring. Many of our members have appeared on network television shows to participate in panel discussions about Dungeons & Dragons and other forms of entertainment violence. Some speak at churches and school meetings in their hometowns, warning audiences about the dangers of adolescent occult activity, and some volunteer their time to handle clerical details. Every individual in our organization participates in whatever way he or she feels comfortable.

The decision to write this book was made following a tremendous increase in the number of requests and inquiries pouring into the B.A.D.D. office. This increase is evidence that occult activity is on the rise in every state in the United States. Experts predict that, within the next two years, adolescent occult involvement will rival drug and alcohol-related problems and promiscuous sexual activity in numbers of resultant tragedies. We sincerely hope that this book will provide the answers to questions being asked by parents, law enforcement officers, members of the clergy, school officials and mental health professionals. We hope, too, that the information provided here will help to dismantle the ever-growing web of occultism that threatens to entrap America's children.

ONE

THE DEVIL IN
MATAMOROS

It was on April 2, 1989, that I was home packing and going over my notes in preparation for a trip to Indianapolis to participate in a seminar on ritualistic crime. Though I rarely watch television, I turned on the set to watch Fox's "America's Most Wanted."

The featured case that night involved Mark Kilroy, a University of Texas pre-med student who had disappeared during a "spring break" trip to Matamoros, Mexico with several friends.

According to the television program, the boys had been enjoying themselves in Matamoros like many young people who go there during spring break. They had visited several bars in the tourist section of the city.

As they were leaving in the early hours of the morning on March 14, the three other boys noticed that Mark was behind them talking to a young Hispanic man. Mark's friends walked on, assuming he would catch up to them later. They never saw him alive again.

"America's Most Wanted" aired this program in hopes of receiving some leads in the case or any information related to Mark's disappearance.

The boy's parents had posters printed with a photograph of Mark and offering a $15,000 reward for information which would help them find him. They even went to Matamoros with the posters and searched for Mark themselves.

Since the nature of my work is ritualistic crime, certain details about this case caused me to be more than just a little interested. I had heard rumors and uncorroborated statements from inmates (including Henry Lee Lucas, the reputed serial killer) concerning ritualistic killings that allegedly had occurred in that area just across the United States border into Mexico.

I remembered, Lucas, had tried to convince state and federal authorities, three to four years ago, that if they would investigate, they would find bodies buried near Matamoros. The authorities were understandably skeptical. However, Lucas had pinpointed on a map several locations in Mexico where ritual sacrifices were taking place and desperately tried to convince them to investigate.

In Lucas' biography, *The Hand of Death*, Max Call recites how the authorities asked Lucas to keep silent about this. They felt that if Lucas told the press how the devil worshipers were recruiting and kidnapping for sacrificial purposes, people would be afraid to walk the streets.

After watching the television program, I said to my husband, "Do you think that this boy might have been abducted for a sacrifice?"

He looked at me with his usual skepticism and said, "Pat, get real."

Mark Kilroy was last seen speaking with a young man who appeared to be of Hispanic origin. Being familiar with (but not an expert on) some Hispanic cults such as *Santeria* and *Brujeria*, I knew that March 21 is an important ritual holiday, a religious day in the *Brujeria* calendar, a date for paying homage to the vigil and feast of Santa Teresa la Florecia. It also coincides with the Vernal Equinox. Since this date was so close to the date of Mark's disappearance, I strongly considered the possibility that he had been abducted for purposes of sacrifice.

The details of the disappearance explained in the television program had given me a very strange feeling, what some people might call a "gut response." I seriously considered calling the authorities in Texas to ask if they would consider my theory, but decided they would think I was just another "crazy."

On April 12, I received a call from a well-known investigative reporter who is on the staff of a respected national magazine.

She said, "Pat, are you sitting down?"

When I said I was, she said, "Let me read you what has just come across the wire service."

She read the report to me which said that 12 bodies had been discovered in Matamoros, Mexico, and that the killings were believed to be ritualistic sacrifices. One of the bodies found was that of Mark Kilroy.

Interestingly, the bodies were found on or near the ranch that Lucas had pinpointed for authorities several years before.

While I was saddened to hear of such a tragedy, I was relieved that the case of Mark's disappearance had been solved. I knew that his family would be devastated by the discovery of his body and the circumstances surrounding his death, but I also believe that, in cases such as this one, knowing something for certain is preferable to never having an answer at all to the question of what has happened to a loved one.

I then called some of my police officer friends who specialize in ritualistic crime (called "cult cops" by some). Not one of these officers was surprised by the news out of Matamoros. The typical comment was, "It was just a matter of time before something like this surfaced."

The wire services were flooded with information out of Matamoros during the next few days. The individuals who allegedly participated in the ritual sacrifice of Mark Kilroy and the other victims were practicing a belief system known as *Palo Mayombe* which originated in Africa. Those who adhere to this "black magic" belief system use a *nganga* (a pot filled with body parts, blood, coins and other items deemed sacred) as the focal point of their rituals. A photograph of the *nganga* used by the cult in Matamoros appeared in newspapers across the country and on television news shows in the days following the grisly discovery.

On April 13, I received a call from a producer at Cable News Network who asked if I would come to Washington, D.C. to discuss ritual murder (of the type that had occurred in Matamoros) on the "Larry King Live" show. I agreed to be in Washington that evening.

I appeared on the show that night along with Jim Maddox, the Attorney General of Texas. King asked Maddox to bring the viewers up-to-date on the Matamoros incident.

"Right now we are attempting to apprehend six fugitives," said Maddox, "and we are starting a hunt for two additional bodies. There have been 12 located, including Mark Kilroy. [His] family is now on the scene. They just appeared at a press conference. In fact, they thanked everyone for helping. Of course they are very disappointed to find their son in this situation. At the same time, they are glad that there is some finality to this process. They are very deeply concerned about this kind of worship and concerned also about the use of drugs in our society." (Law enforcement officials already had determined that the ritual activity in Matamoros was drug-related.)

King then asked, "Jim, we now have how many known dead?"

Maddox responded, "Right now, the confessions we have at this location indicate that there are probably two more. The confessions given have been relatively accurate. I would say the leader of this cult has been in this particular area for about nine months. He has lived in other areas, and it is entirely possible that he could be involved in other activities in other places ..."

Later in the program, Attorney General Maddox said that the alleged killers were "not at all remorseful about their activity."

When King expressed surprise, Maddox explained, "They ... were practicing a black magic or a voodoo or some would say a satanic type worship, but they felt that by engaging in both human sacrifice and other kinds of animal sacrifice that they could cast a spell around themselves ... that would protect them from potential danger of arrest and ... danger from bullets."

King asked, "Do you believe that they believed that?"

"I actually believe that they believed that at that time," said Maddox, "and one of the reasons that I think that's the case is that when they were apprehended, one of the reasons they so freely confessed ... was that they were very surprised when their whole cult powers failed them and when they recognized that they were not protected from the police and from bullets. They had been misled, and I should tell you that these are not demented peasants. These are individuals from good families, by and large. One was a student in Texas, and at least one other one was a citizen who was apprehended, and at least two of them speak relatively good English ... These individuals were simply misled, led astray, and they freely admit to following a leader that took them in that direction."

King asked, "Jim, is there some concern that the people loose are doing this kind of thing elsewhere?"

"There is a possibility," said Maddox. "We do not have any evidence about whether or not they might be conducting these crimes elsewhere, but the thing that of course we are concerned about is that we must catch the leader of the cult because, if we don't, he may use that on an even greater basis to show future followers that they can do this with impunity and show that he is protected and that he can get away ... These individuals do not have remorse, and we believe just as the parents have said that they have been taken over by a devil, a devil that they are worshipping and a devil that they believe is protecting them in one form or another."

King: "So drugs were related, but not necessarily causative, right?"

Maddox: "We do not find, based on the confessions, any indication that drugs were being used in any heavy fashion to stimulate hallucinogenic effects or anything else on the individuals [who were] their victims. Every victim was a male. They were all Hispanic males with the exception of Mark. They took them individually. They mutilated and dismembered them, engaging in their worship services in a small chapel or temple as they called it, but it was nothing more than a wooden hut. They were burning candles and drinking liquor. Then they were smoking these fancy cigars, some way or another thinking this stuff would bring them good luck. [They also were] burning their victims in a cauldron with other animal [parts] such as a goat's head, a turtle, chicken feet. They would take the brains out of their victims and boil them, and I must tell you that this was one of the [worst] sights that anybody can ever see."

Larry King asked, "Was Mark in the wrong place at the wrong time?"

Maddox replied, "Not exactly. The leader of this cult picked [the victims] and said that he wanted ... a spring breaker, a college kid, Anglo. [They had] had a particularly good day selling drugs ... and Mark Kilroy was picked at random ..."

At this point a caller telephoned the show and asked what "we" can do to stop the spread of this kind of activity. The caller indicated that he was familiar with a case in Albuquerque in which a middle-class youngster had killed his parents.

Maddox responded by saying, "Parents and others who have loved ones that become involved in any type of ritualistic cult must take it very seriously. They cannot just think that it is a phase through which a child will pass. They must counsel with them, figure out a way to help them through the process or get them professional help. We see this kind of thing growing in Texas. We have seen cases of animal mutilation and other kinds of sacrifices. In our Rio Grande [area] and in northern Mexico, it has been estimated that there could be as many as 10, 000 people that worship Satan in some way ..."

Larry King then asked me if I agreed with Mr. Maddox. I replied, "I definitely agree ... we don't need to be panicked over an epidemic, but I think as a society we are going to have to open our eyes and our minds and stop all this disbelief. The greatest weapon the people who are doing this have is our disbelief."

Larry asked, "Maybe we dismissed that Geraldo Rivera special too quickly, huh, Pat?" (He was referring to a two-hour television special which had aired about a month before. The special had attempted to convince the viewing public that ritual cult activity, including serious criminal activity, is real. It had been dismissed by many as "sensationalistic" and "exploitative.")

"Yes," I answered. "... I think people have wanted to dismiss this too easily simply because it is so offensive and so repulsive that it is difficult to believe."

On to Matamoros

A few days after the show, I was contacted by a friend of mine who is a police officer in Austin, Texas. Sgt. Liz Merrill told me that she and several other officers were going to go to Brownsville, Texas, in order to get a better understanding of what had happened. They were hoping to gather information which could be used to intervene in other cases before more such tragedies occurred. She invited me to go with them. I already was scheduled to go to Dallas to conduct a seminar, so it worked out well. She told me that the Cameron County Sheriff's Office had already been notified, and we were expected and welcome.

Arriving in Texas, I was met by Sgt. Merrill, two of her fellow officers and a detective from Brownsville who would be acting as our guide. We journeyed together to Matamoros, Mexico to view the crime scene.

The day was very warm. Vendors lined the streets, selling all manner of vegetables, goods and wares. The main street of the town was very attractive and provided all of the "flavor" of Mexico.

There were few tourists, however. The locals told us that the tourists had been frightened away by the uncovering of the cult activity.

We drove past the lounge that Mark Kilroy and his friends had visited, then down the road along which Mark had been driven by his alleged abductors.

The detective then said, "We will go out to the ranch."

The ranch was about 20 miles outside the town of Matamoros. The scenery was flat and dotted with the rural dwellings of the very poor.

We turned onto a long driveway that led to the ranch. Nothing appeared unusual as we looked out over miles of open farmland.

We drove past a little shed where the detective told us Mark had been held for 12 hours prior to his death.

A few minutes later, we arrived at the boarded-up shed where the alleged sacrifices took place. We were told that some of the participants in the rituals had referred to this small outbuilding as "the temple."

With cameras in hand, we got out of the car and walked toward the shed. Candles were strewn on the ground, and I saw the *nganga* that I had seen pictures of in the newspaper and on television the week before. It had been filled with blood, animal and human body parts. Feathers, a horseshoe, gold beads and a pot full of pennies (all items used in *Palo Mayombe* rituals) also were found at the scene.

The Shed of Death

As soon as I entered the shed, I was sickened by the strong stench of death and the odor of stale blood. The wooden planks of the walls seemed to have absorbed the smells. I commented on the odor to the detective, and he replied that it was not as bad as it had been the week before. I was amazed that the authorities had managed to recover the bodies and to work in such heat and stench.

Wire hangers hung from the rafters of the shed, apparently used by the alleged killers to hang their victims in order to drain their blood. The walls were heavily stained with splattered blood.

I stood there for a long while trying to imagine what it must have been like for the victims who lived their last moments in this den of horror and death. Nothing in my past experience had prepared me for the overwhelming sensation of evil that was present here.

We left the shed and walked out to the corral and surrounding area where the mass graves had been dug. The detective pointed out the site where Mark Kilroy's body had been found. He showed us where the other bodies had been recovered, telling us what he knew about each of the victims. Some of the graves still contained remnants of scalps with hair attached.

I was curious about how the cult members had chosen their victims. I was told that Adolpho de Jesus Costanzo, the alleged cult leader, instructed his followers to bring individuals to him who met certain criteria. For example, if he wanted a 16-year-old boy, cult members would go into the streets and ask the ages of young boys until they found one who met the requirement.

Standing in the middle of the corral and turning around in a circle, I could view the sites of all the graves. I felt sickened and empty. Many investigators make conscious decisions not to let themselves become emotional in situations such as this one, but I have learned that it is helpful to try to imagine what the victims must have felt. While this is difficult and depressing at times, it helps me never to forget that these were living, breathing human beings whose lives were taken away from them through extremely violent means and with the sole purpose of paying homage to and serving evil.

The detective who accompanied us to the ranch was considerate of our reactions to the horrible events that had occurred there. He described for us the great care and gentleness with which the bodies were handled by the authorities who recovered them.

I went back into the shed for one last look around and to take a few more photographs. This time I became very nauseated. The devastating reality of what had happened there overwhelmed me all at once. It was a relief to leave the area and return home.

The "religious" rituals of the alleged cult members did not succeed in protecting them from being arrested or killed. On May 6, Costanzo ordered his own followers to kill him and his right-hand man Martin Quintana Rodriguez as police officers closed in on the group which had holed up in a Mexico City apartment building. His accomplice, Sarah Aldrete, and four other cult members were arrested following the bloody shootout.

No culture is without its "black magic," its occult practitioners and deviant criminals who will seize upon any belief system to achieve their ends.

In May, 1988, police in Cosenza, Italy, arrested 35 people following an investigation into a bizarre cult which combined satanic rituals with Mafia-style executions. At about the same time, six men in Monrovia, Liberia were found guilty of the ritualistic murder of two boys, ages six and seven. The children had been abducted, killed and mutilated to obtain parts for a *juju* (a West African system of magic) spell intended to increase the chances of one of the participants in his campaign for the office of mayor. The files in the B.A.D.D. office are filled with news clippings detailing such ritualistic crimes that have occurred in other countries.

What happened in Matamoros, Mexico is only the most recent example of the dangers of ritualistic activities and destructive cults. It serves as a reminder to those of us who work in this field that the web extends around the world, that the work we are doing is important, and that evil never sleeps.

TWO

TEENAGERS—A TARGET FOR DEVIL WORSHIPERS

There is an intense effort by many devil-worshiping cult groups to recruit our teenagers.

Sadly, as one well-meaning, conscientious parent said to me, "I have raised my child properly. She goes to church every Sunday, and she knows right from wrong. My daughter could never become involved in devil worship at any level."

This statement is very comforting to the parents, but it is dangerous in that such blind confidence can foster a false sense of security. No child is out of harm's way simply by virtue of his or her "good upbringing." Children and teenagers are curious and imaginative, and adolescents often are rebellious; these traits are normal. These traits also are the very ones that can lead them into danger.

Let's examine a case in point. "Jill" (not her real name) was brought into my office by her mother who said that they needed help. Jill, an attractive 15-year-old, was getting into trouble at school. Her grades had fallen drastically, and she had become obsessed with black metal music.

She was writing fatalistic poetry about death and Satan and drawing pictures of a demonic young girl. These drawings were embellished with occult graffiti in the margins. The family belonged to a mainstream denominational church. Jill's parents were very fearful for their daughter and wanted me to determine her level of occult involvement, whether she was using drugs and whether she needed professional therapy.

By the time I met Jill for the first time, I already had spoken with the principal at her school and several of her teachers. They, too, were very concerned for this young girl.

Jill was reluctant to discuss anything with me during our first session. She was pleasant at first, but became belligerent when I began to question her about her poems and drawings.

After a few more meetings, she began to trust me somewhat. I asked her if she had used any drugs, and she told me that she occasionally used marijuana and alcohol. She did not want to tell me about her friends, and it appeared that she had very little self-esteem; she believed that she was ugly and stupid.

When I asked her why she felt that way, she began to cry. She told me that she had had an abortion when she was 13 because her boyfriend had not wanted her or the baby. Her parents knew nothing about it, and I told her that it was extremely important that she tell them. I offered to be present and to have a therapist present when she was ready to reveal this information to them. She insisted that she could not tell her parents under any circumstances "because they might find out more."

After much coaxing, she explained to me that a family member (not her mother or father) had had sex with her when she was 12-years-old. He threatened her into keeping this secret. She also feared that, if she told anyone, she would not be believed and that serious family problems would ensue.

Seeding Process

From that first sexual encounter, Jill progressed to promiscuous behavior followed by drug use. She fell in with "the wrong crowd" and began going to heavy metal rock concerts. That was where her occult involvement began. The rock concerts were the beginning of a "seeding process" for what was to follow. It began with the friends with whom she attended the concerts and the acceptance of black metal music, destructive violent music and occult imagery promoted at these concerts.

After explaining this progression, Jill stated that she had gone "too far to turn back."

When I asked her what she meant, she said that she didn't want to talk about it anymore.

Jill's mother was extremely cooperative, and I told her that Jill needed professional counseling and should be watched closely. I was convinced that this was a desperate young girl.

A therapist then was brought into our sessions. Jill did not want to talk to the counselor without me present.

During the first meeting of our little group, Jill asked the counselor to leave the room. She wanted to try to explain how she had become involved with what she called "devil worship."

Recruitment

She said that she and some friends had attended a rock concert and that they were approached by some adults who invited them to a party where they could have "all the beer, pot and head-banging music" they wanted. They went and were invited back for many more parties over a period of several months. Jill stated that she and her friends never knew the last names of these adults but didn't care because "we were having fun, and everything was free."

Of course these young people never told their parents about the parties because alcohol and drugs were involved. They attended the parties by sneaking out of their houses in the middle of the night and meeting the adults several blocks away. They got into the adults' car and were blindfolded so that they would not know where they were going.

I asked Jill if she hadn't found this very strange and frightening. She said that she hadn't because the adults always had been "nice" and told the teenagers that it was necessary for everyone's protection —the adults from being harassed by the kids' parents because of the drugs and alcohol, and the teens from being in a bad position if any of them got caught. They couldn't "snitch" if they honestly did not know where they had been, and no teenager wants to be a snitch.

As the teenagers got to know these people better, the parties became sexually oriented. The teens first had sex with the adults and with each other; later, small children were brought into the activities.

I wondered aloud if having sex with little children hadn't bothered her, and she said that it had at first, but didn't after she learned that the adults present were the parents of the children.

Jill began to cry, however, when she talked about a little girl of 4 or 5 years of age who had been present several times and for whom she had "felt sorry." The little girl suddenly had stopped appearing at the parties, but Jill did not know what had happened to her and to speculate on the possibilities caused her a great deal of pain.

Addiction and Blackmail

I asked her if she could describe the little girl and why she had not told anyone about this. She gave a detailed description of the child and explained that she had not told anyone because of the threat of blackmail. The teenagers had been shown photographs of themselves engaged in bizarre sexual acts (some of which included animals) and told that the pictures would be sent to their parents if they ever told anyone about the parties.

Jill went on to explain that, by that time, she had become addicted to the drugs which were distributed so freely and that there was no way she would ever let her parents see those photographs.

After hearing all of this, I told Jill that this sounded to me like a clear-cut case of child molestation, but that I didn't see where any occultism had come into play.

She said, "Oh, no, there's more."

After the teens were heavily involved with the drugs and sexual activities, and with the threat of blackmail hanging over their heads, they were exposed to the religious beliefs of the group of adults. (Note: In spite of what follows, the only criminal charges that could have been brought against these adults, had they been apprehended at that time, would have been child molestation charges and others such as "contributing to the delinquency of minors.")

Introduction to "Devil Worship"

During one party, the teenagers were taken into a room where a man who called himself a priest began to read to them from a large, hand-written book which was referred to as "Satan's Bible." This was not Anton LaVey's *Satanic Bible*, according to Jill's account; it was not even commercially printed.

She said that the room was decked out with red and black candles on what was called an altar and that chairs were arranged in aisles much like chairs or pews in any church.

Jill said that the adults in the room began chanting as the "priest" read from the book.

The teenagers then were given a "promise" that, after a few more meetings, they would be ready for their initiation ceremonies after which there would be "no turning back." They must denounce the God of their own faiths and accept Satan as their master.

As Jill's story began to pour out, I stopped asking questions. I just allowed her to talk. She alleged rituals which had included murder and described in great detail how these took place.

This went on for several grueling hours. Jill cried, withdrew at several points, and then began again.

I then told her that we had no choice at this time but to tell her parents and the police. She was terrified, but finally allowed her parents to be told. Then the police were told. At last report, this case still was open and under active investigation.

Some will say that Jill made up the entire story, but solid police work provided verification of the places and people she described, and the details of the rest of her statements were substantial enough to convince seasoned interrogators that her story was not born in her imagination.

Additionally, the specifics regarding the rituals are not known by most persons unless they have a thoroughly grounded occult education. Simply put, Jill could not have made them up. Nothing existed in her background that could have provided her with the kind of information she revealed.

As much as we would like not to, those of us involved in Jill's case believe her story to be true. To offer here the corroborating details would be a conflict of interest and a breach of confidentiality, not to mention the fact that it certainly would hamper the ongoing investigation.

I have related most of Jill's story as a means of leading up to a very important fact: I now am consulting on a number of cases in several other states that involve an identical method of operation. The question which remains to be answered is whether the adults engaged in this type of "recruitment" are child molesters using the bizarre cover of satanic intimidation, or actual practitioners of a form of satanism.

A number of other teenagers have described similar practices, but only up to the stage of the drug and sex parties. My response to them is, "There are no free rides in our society. There always is a price to pay. If you are not yet at a stage where criminal and/or satanic activity is going on, get out before it is too late."

I also speak with the parents of such teens and advise them of the necessity of getting professional help for their children.

Further evidence of this kind of recruitment practice appeared in *The Pottsville Republican* (Pennsylvania) April 8, 1988. The headline read, "Sex, drug cult alleged in Coaldale; 6 nabbed."

A police officer on patrol had found a teenage boy lying drunk on the pavement a few blocks from a house where he said he had attended a party. The information he furnished to the police resulted in a three-day investigation leading to the arrests of six adults, including the apparent cult leader Diane Prentice Leon (age 31) whom cult members called "Princess."

"Virgin Party"

According to statements from one of the suspects who turned state's evidence and seven youngsters ranging in ages from 11 to 17, Leon used sexual rituals to "christen" youngsters who had been lured to her home with drugs and alcohol. Leon recorded the names of her initiates and wrote detailed descriptions of the rituals in a black diary which police confiscated as evidence.

Police also found a calendar with a date marked as a "virgin party" for an 11-year-old boy.

According to Police Chief John Tonkin (who called this "the most bizarre case" he had ever investigated), the youngsters had been bound in chains which were hooked to walls in Leon's house. Leon and the other adults then engaged in sex with the children. According to reports, Leon was a practitioner of witchcraft, and a number of books on the subject where found at her home.

She gave new members cult names following their initiations; some of them were "Cosmic Star," "Krash Tec," "Arroff," "Arf," "Ace," and "Saylor."

When asked to comment on the occult aspects of this case, Tonkin said, "It's not a satanic cult. It's more witchcraft and definitely sex-oriented."

What is the final outcome of all of this? According to a report I received, the defendants were charged with contributing to the delinquency of minors, and one defendant was sentenced to community service work.

In a Lawton, Oklahoma case, 17-year-old Steven Kemp pled guilty in the shooting death of 41-year-old Joseph Ferrante. Kemp claimed that he had been recruited into a satanic cult by Ferrante through the lures of drugs and alcohol. He alleged that he was forced to participate in ritualistic animal killings and homosexual activities.

The boy testified that he became frightened and wanted out, but that Ferrante continued to follow and threaten him. Kemp began to carry a gun.

As Kemp was on his way home one day in March 1988, Ferrante pulled his car up to the curb and convinced the youth to go home with him.

According to the teenager, Ferrante told him that he could pull out if he wanted, "but let's talk about it first." Kemp went along.

According to court records, Ferrante then attacked Kemp, chasing him around the house with a knife. Kemp pulled his .32-calibre pistol, shot Ferrante in the head and chest and then set him on fire. The killing was ruled self defense, and Kemp was acquitted. Terrified of death threats, the teenager left the area at last report.

The investigation into this case revealed that Ferrante had not held a job for two years. He lived with his 16-year-old daughter and a niece in his home (the house had only one bed). Evidence surfaced which linked him to a cult in Oklahoma City in 1975.

During military duty at Fort Sill, he had told a number of people that he was a practicing satanist.

Kemp himself had been a believer in occult philosophies, making him an easy target for Ferrante and his partners in crime. He is a frightened and confused young man today, and probably will spend the rest of his life trying to come to terms with what happened, in spite of the fact that he was acquitted.

Fantasy Games Used As Seduction Tool

Fantasy role-playing games such as "Dungeons & Dragons" also have been used by some adults to seduce and entrap adolescents into sexual activity. The games themselves did not cause the molestation, but they were the vehicle by which the molestation was carried out.

In May 1985, *The Houston Chronicle* reported that "a former prison psychologist and his wife used the fantasy game Dungeons & Dragons to entice a 15-year-old girl into a sex act. ..."

The teenager testified that she had played the game a number of times at the residence of Armando Simon, a Texas Department of Corrections psychologist, and his wife Angela.

Simon allegedly acted as a character who was obsessed by women, and his wife played the part of a lesbian. The two adults took turns being the Dungeon Master (the leader of the fantasy game). Armando Simon was found guilty of the charges against him (which included rape) and sentenced to nine years in prison.

In a 1988 Delaware case, a 24-year-old vagrant whose nickname was "Hatchet" also relied on "Dungeons & Dragons" as a means of enticing teenagers into sexual activity. Jackson Franklin Morgan was charged with four counts of unlawful sexual intercourse, two counts of attempted unlawful sexual intercourse and six counts of unlawful sexual contact.

Residents of two Claymont apartment complexes had complained to local authorities about Morgan for two years. The 300-pound man lived in the dark basements and laundry rooms of the complexes, vandalizing, smoking dope and playing "Dungeons & Dragons" with neighborhood children and young adolescents.

He was arrested after a maintenance man found a bag on apartment property which contained game pieces, satanic and wiccan materials and handbooks, letters from Morgan which indicated possible sexual activity with some of the area children, photos of two of the children, and items of intimate female clothing.

The apartment manager of one of the complexes compared Morgan to the Pied Piper, saying that the neighborhood children "followed him around. It was not unusual for him to have four or five kids with him."

According to Lt. Stanley Yackoski of the New Castle County Police, Morgan and his friends also were believed to be responsible for satanic graffiti found on nearby railroad bridges: "Pentagrams, triple sixes, that kind of thing."

Several days after the bag was found, an adolescent girl telephoned Detective Ed Maxwell of the New Castle County Police Department and informed him that the bag belonged to her. She and her mother went to Detective Maxwell's office to claim the bag.

Well-versed in ritualistic crime and interrogation procedures, Maxwell questioned the girl about her relationship with the suspect.

Visibly shaken, the teenager confessed that she had been forced into sexual relations with and by Morgan in order to stay in the game; she also believed Morgan had cast a satanic spell on her. She indicated that Morgan had lured other young people into similar activity by promising to bestow magical powers on them. She told Maxwell that her first sexual encounter with Morgan had taken place in a local cemetery, a wooded area that was verified later as a regular meeting place for groups of teenagers who were suspected of acts of satanic vandalism.

Other reported victims were interviewed during the course of the investigation, and one revealed that Morgan had lured her into sexual activity by telling her that it was the only way to regain her depleted magical powers.

Reports from additional witnesses revealed that Morgan had tried to recruit other adult satanists to create a coven and to help him lure more teenagers; that Morgan had made area children sign ritualistic documents in their own blood which he then used to blackmail the children; and that he threatened at least one victim with death if she told of their activities.

Another informant, an avowed satanist who played "Dungeons & Dragons" with Morgan, stated that the defendant "really believes that he can do this stuff," referring to Morgan's belief in the power of ritual magic.

I have known and worked with Detective Maxwell for several years and spoke with him recently regarding this case. He told me that the police were able to uncover the serious case of child molestation due to the training he has received in the area of ritualistic crime, particularly the training he has received through B.A.D.D. (Bothered About Dungeons & Dragons and Other Harmful Influences on Children) seminars. He also stated that this training was the result of the support he has been given by his department in allowing him to attend conferences and seminars and to train his fellow police officers in the investigative procedures unique to ritualistic crime.

Teenage runaways and adolescents who spend a lot of time just "hanging out" on the streets are especially vulnerable to recruitment by satanists and other occultists.

Detective Don Rimer of the Juveniles Division of the Virginia Beach Police Department in Virginia stated recently, "When kids are on the street, they'll take a handout from anybody."

Detective Rimer has observed an increase in the number of Virginia Beach teenagers claiming to have been approached by adults with "satanic" motives.

He tells of one area teen who, after having been missing for several days, showed up at home with burns all over her body and inverted crosses cut into her chest.

The girl's mother had reported nothing unusual about her daughter's behavior to Detective Rimer; he had to point out to her that the girl's room was painted black and decorated with pentagrams (from an article in *The Beacon*, May 8, 1987).

Disbelief Among Authorities

Detective Jerry Simandl, a veteran Chicago police officer, calls ritualistic crime "a very complex subject that makes street gang activity look like a nursery rhyme."

Detective Al Sheppard of the Intelligence Division of the New York City Police Department, a highly regarded ritual crime investigator, states, "Police, prosecutors and others in the law enforcement field need more training." He states that the biggest problem in this area is that of disbelieving investigators; their disbelief leads to inattention.

Many law enforcement officials have told me that, prior to attending a B.A.D.D. seminar or other training sessions on ritualistic crime, they didn't believe that this type of criminal activity was enough of an issue to warrant attention; some have admitted they didn't believe it existed at all. They feel differently after the sessions are over.

One officer commented, "When we first started [investigating ritualistic crime], people were saying, 'You're crazy. This stuff isn't going on.' Police are the biggest skeptics in the world. But when you're done with the presentation, the biggest question is, 'Why didn't we learn this before?' They think back to cases they've had in the past, and it starts to make sense to them."

A friend and colleague with whom I have had the pleasure of teaching law enforcement seminars is Detective Jim Skorcz of the Milwaukee Gang Crimes Unit.

In a recent conversation, he said, "I can see now that there is a lot more awareness [of ritual crime], but we still need to work on drawing the attention of parents to what their kids are reading and listening to."

There are many other incidents which support the theory that satanists are networking and actively recruiting our young people.

Dallas police officers were puzzled and shocked recently when a number of young girls (ages 11 to 14) reported that they had been involved in ritualistic activities during which men gave them alcohol and other drugs, read from "a satanic bible," and forced them to engage in perverted sexual acts.

Physical examinations showed that 11 girls had been sexually assaulted.

In Fort Worth, a teen club was opened by a group of adults who lured area teenagers with free alcohol and drugs and then instructed them to learn about Aleister Crowley, the satanist considered by many to be the father of modern occultism. Within the next two years, police departments in other Texas cities uncovered other teen clubs with identical recruitment methods.

Many people work very hard to discredit the theory of a conspiracy of adults luring young people into devil worship. At this point, the existence of a ritualistic criminal conspiracy on a worldwide or even national level cannot be proven. This is irrelevant.

What is much more important is for us to realize and admit that a number of cases which are surfacing and going to court involve very similar elements. Whether or not this indicates a conspiracy, it is, at the very least, indicative of a relatively new and extremely dangerous trend.

We can, however, look at the conspiracy theory on a smaller scale. My dictionary defines conspiracy as "an evil, unlawful, treacherous or surreptitious plan formulated in secret by two or more persons." The vast majority of the crimes we have examined have involved two or more persons, making them conspiracies in the technical sense.

In the Coaldale case, one of the charges brought against Diane Leon was that of criminal conspiracy.

Whether or not a large-scale conspiracy exists, it is apparent that many small conspiracies of deviant criminal adults do exist. This is an issue we must face.

Trust, but Verify

No, we do not hold totally blameless the older children and teenagers who should "know better" than to be enticed by alcohol, drugs and sexual activity. Most of us have labored diligently to teach our children right from wrong; we have warned them of the dangers of drugs, begged them not to drink, and taught them that sexual relations are for adults who love one another within the secure confines of marriage. But the days are past when children only come into contact with other children under the supervision of parents and other relatives in safe quarters or in small, closely-supervised church, school and community activities in which all of the parents took part.

Today's parents have much less control over the influences that affect their children's attitudes and belief systems. What we teach them at home and at church on Sunday may be openly argued and denied at school on Monday morning or at a party on Friday night. It is more imperative than ever that parents be watchful, supportive and, sometimes, suspicious. It doesn't hurt to take to heart the currently popular political axiom, "Trust, but verify."

THREE

WIDESPREAD TEEN OCCULT ACTIVITY

Until the last few years, it has been difficult to profile the type of teenager that is most likely to be attracted to satanism and other kinds of occult ritual activity. It was also difficult to answer some of the questions that many parents, law enforcement officers, mental health professionals and members of the clergy asked me when they learned of my work. The reason I found these questions difficult was that I was still searching for the answers myself.

As the phone calls and letters requesting assistance poured into my office, and as more and more concerned citizens around the country sent me newspaper clippings about occult activity in their own hometowns, it became increasingly evident that our organization had to quicken its pace toward addressing certain critical questions such as: "Who" are the children that are most vulnerable to teen devil worship? Exactly "what" should we look for when trying to determine whether a child is involved in occult activity? "When" and "where" are these activities most likely to occur? And, perhaps the most important question, "why" do children and teenagers turn to the black arts in the first place?

Another reason that these questions have been difficult to answer until recently is that there has been little scientific research into this highly specialized investigative area. There is no national or central agency that is compiling factual information on the subject of occult activity involving young people.

We do have, however, a large number of caring and concerned individuals around the country and the world who continue to provide the B.A.D.D. office with detailed reports of activity in their localities. We have heard from professional personnel and private citizens in every one of the 50 states as well as Canada, England, Germany and Australia.

Our office now has accumulated sufficient documents and case histories to enable our staff of volunteers to work alongside social workers and mental health professionals in developing guidelines for everyone concerned with the physical safety and emotional stability of children and teenagers.

We expect that these guidelines will become even more fine-tuned as we continue to grow in our knowledge and understanding of this complex and frightening subject. We add new information to our files almost daily, and we continue to welcome reports and inquiries from the public.

When presenting seminars or participating in panel discussions on teen occult involvement, I prefer to use the terms "teen satanism" and "teen devil worship" simply to clarify several issues.

First, my concern is with children and teenagers whose interest in the occult either presents a threat to their emotional and/or physical safety or indicates criminal activity. I do not investigate adult ritual practitioners or adult criminals except where their offenses include the recruitment, abduction, molestation, murder or ritualistic abuse of children and teenagers or the likelihood that such offenses will occur.

Second, the terms "devil worship" and "satanism" clearly define my areas of concern, serving to differentiate them from the areas of pagan and neo-pagan ritualistic activity, or so-called "white witchcraft." I see many more teenagers actively identifying with "the devil" based on the Judeo-Christian concept of that figure as a dark, powerful and very evil being who will reward those who follow him.

Satanic Rituals—Three Categories

Until recently, investigators used three categories to delineate those individuals who practiced satanic rituals: (1) religious satanists such as Anton LaVey and Michael Aquino who have established tax-exempt churches and who "generally" are not associated with criminal activity; (2) "dabblers" who are primarily teenagers interested in the black arts; and (3) self-styled satanists, individuals with psychotic personality disorders who become obsessed with satanic themes (men like Charles Manson, the California cult leader who killed actress Sharon Tate and others, and Richard Ramirez, the so-called "Night Stalker" killer) who may practice their gruesome rituals alone or in small groups.

A Fourth Category—Generational Satanists

In the last few years, we have added a fourth category: **generational satanists**. The existence of generational satanists had been hotly debated among investigators for many years due to a lack of substantial evidence.

Widespread rumors persisted, however, and very recent investigations as well as careful and professional interviewing of victims have led to the general acceptance of this category by the law enforcement and mental health communities.

Generational satanists are believed to constitute networks of individuals whose families have been involved with criminal ritual activity for many generations. They count among their numbers members of every professional field (including the clergy) and people who appear to be upstanding citizens professing to belong to mainstream religious denominations by day and practicing deviant rituals by night.

Teenage "Dabbler"

At B.A.D.D., our concern is the teenaged "dabbler," the young person who develops an interest in the black arts and whose interest grows into an obsession.

This is not to say that we do not have an interest in cases where children and teenagers have been victimized by satanic practitioners who would fall under one of the other three categories; our office works closely with investigators in those areas, too.

However, we feel that the category of the dabbler is where we can work the greatest preventive good if we can intervene and mediate as soon as a young person's curiosity with the black arts begins to take on obsessive characteristics. We can work to get him back "on track" before he becomes involved in criminal activity and before he becomes a victim himself.

To be more specific, a dabbler is someone who experiments with the occult. He may try to cast spells and perform certain rituals based on instructions he has found in books and magazines on the occult or by imitating the actions of characters in occultic movies and television shows.

Characteristically, the dabbler takes his information from a variety of sources and mixes them together to arrive at his own unique philosophy.

Until recently, many investigators and mental health professionals have discounted dabblers as being non-threatening, little more than bored teenagers looking for something different to play around with for awhile; instead, they have argued, the highly organized adult occultists were the ones on whom the greatest attention should be focused.

It is true that the vast majority of teenage dabblers will experiment with the occult for a short while and then lose interest, but we are finding more and more often that certain segments of the teenage population are likely to progress from curious dabbling to violent occult-related criminal behavior.

Those who once ignored the category of dabblers now agree that this group is not only vulnerable to great danger but capable of causing untold emotional and physical harm to others. In fact, the greatest amount of documentation now on file and the greatest number of criminal cases that have gone to court and been adjudicated have involved teenage occult dabblers in devil worship.

Many parents as well as professionals mistakenly think that dabblers are those adolescents who have been rejected by society, are habitual criminal offenders and juvenile delinquents, have low intelligence, and are unpopular with their peers. Some even believe that those most likely to become dabblers are black and Hispanic youths from indigent families.

On the contrary, and almost without exception, the teenagers most likely to become involved in satanic activity are white males from middle- and upper-income families.

While some cities have reported an increase in the involvement of females as well as black and Hispanic youths, white males still constitute the greatest proportion of teenage dabblers.

Creative and Curious— Most Likely To Be Seduced

A white male who is intelligent, creative and curious is the most likely to be seduced by the occult. He may be either an underachiever or an overachiever, and he may be going through a stage of rebellion against family, school, church and society in general.

Conversion to satanism or devil worship is the ultimate form of rebellion for a child raised in a family with a strong religious faith. Some dabblers have low self-esteem and are loners by nature, but many have healthy egos and are gregarious and friendly. It is inaccurate to say, as many have, that the teenager who is rebellious and lonely and who has a low level of self-esteem is the one who is most vulnerable. It is true that some of these children fall victim, but they are far from the majority.

It is particularly inaccurate to say that a child became involved in satanic worship because "he was a loner." Satanic worship is a form of religious philosophy, and children do not suddenly convert to satanism on their own. More often than not, they do so after coming in contact with others who lead the way. These children may have appeared to be loners in that they did not socialize to any great degree with their peers at school, but they almost always have their own small group of friends with whom they regularly spend time.

Some teenaged dabblers have been abused, either sexually, emotionally or physically. This is a possibility that we always have to expect and examine. When I began my investigative work, this area was the most difficult for me to deal with personally, and it still is.

When parents bring their children to my office, I always want to think that these are good parents who want to do the very best for their children and that they have brought their children to me because they love them and want to get to the bottom of whatever is troubling them. I have been severely disappointed in some cases to learn that the parents themselves have abused the children. In these cases, the children have become involved in occultic rituals and satanic worship because the pain of the abuse is so great that they do not want to identify with anything their parents represent.

Story of Sam

The case of "Sam" clearly illustrates how confusing and painful this area of investigative work can be for all concerned.

Very early in my career, I was asked through a police department contact to consult with Sam and his family.

This 15-year-old young man repeatedly had run away from home, and his parents had discovered that he was spending time with a girlfriend. The two were actively involved in devil worship. Sam's family had a mainstream denominational background, and the parents were both well-educated and had good jobs.

The police and Sam's parents wanted me to explain to the family the principles of teen devil worship and to help them examine some ways in which we might be able to help this troubled youngster.

I met only with the parents during the first session. They were very pleasant people and deeply concerned about their son. I shared some of our organization's materials with them, explained what teen devil worship is and some of the ways in which children get involved. I felt confident that we were intervening in Sam's case at an early stage and that we would be able to turn him around fairly easily. Far more serious, I told them, were the cases where children had been molested or ritually abused.

During our second session, I again met only with the parents. This time we discussed the problems they had experienced with Sam, problems which were pretty typical of most families with adolescent children. Nothing seemed extraordinary.

The third session was for Sam and me to get acquainted. His parents waited in the outer office.

Sam was mistrustful at first. He questioned me extensively to see if I had any respect for and understanding of his belief system. He went through quite a lengthy procedure of interviewing me in order to decide whether he even wanted to talk about his troubles.

He then began to talk about a friend with whom he identified closely, a friend who had been severely and repeatedly sexually abused. I tried to make Sam understand that he could not know how his friend felt and neither could I. No one, I told him, could understand that kind of anguish unless he had experienced it himself. Sam kept insisting that he did understand.

Then it hit me. You see, I hadn't really been listening. I had naively overlooked the one critical question that this child needed to be asked. So I asked it, not wanting to hear the answer, but knowing that I had to. There was so much pain on his young face, and both of us were acutely aware of his parents waiting in the next room. He told me quietly that he, too, had been sexually abused.

I asked him if he had been abused by his mother, and he shook his head.

I said, "Was it your father?"

Sam nodded.

I asked him if it had only happened a few times, and he told me that the abuse had begun when he was 6-years-old and had continued until about a year prior to our meeting.

Sam also had an older brother who had some serious emotional problems, and Sam explained that his brother also had been sexually abused by their father.

Then I understood why he had been attracted to devil worship and other black arts. I believed it was because he felt powerless to get away from his abusive father.

He said, "I thought that maybe I could find some spells and rituals that would stop the pain."

At that point, I was completely disgusted and filled with contempt for Sam's parents. I met with them at the end of our session, and it was extremely difficult for me to look Sam's father in the face. I recommended professional counseling for the entire family. They took my advice, and I understand that they are doing quite well today in overcoming their tragic and painful past. The abuse certainly has stopped.

Sam and I continued to meet together to discuss and explore Judeo-Christian belief systems as well as occult belief systems. I am happy to say that Sam later re-converted of his own accord to his family's religion. He finally understood that what had happened to him was not the fault of God or the Holy Bible or his church. What had happened to Sam was the result of his father's actions.

I learned a great deal from this experience with Sam and his family, knowledge which has seen me through countless similar cases. Abuse of any type is cyclical, that is it can be passed down from one generation to the next. In these cases, the entire family is in dire need of intensive rehabilitative therapy. Intervention and mediation often can break the cycle and thus prevent the youngest generation in an abusive family from turning to occult practices, drug use and other dangerous activities.

Any Child Can Fall Victim

It is important to emphasize at this point that, while white males who are intelligent, curious and creative and who are from middle- to upper-income families appear to be the most likely to be seduced by the occult, *any* child can fall victim. If other evidence indicates occult involvement, do not discount such involvement as a possibility simply because the child is female, non-white, of low intelligence or from a low-income family.

Law enforcement officers in large urban areas are seeing an increase in teen devil worship by young people from all segments of society. Still, the largest number of teenagers who practice occultic rituals continue to match the white male profile.

The most vulnerable ages appear to be from age 11 to 17. This, of course, does not include children born into families of generational satanists who are raised with occultic rituals from the first day of life. We have seen children as young as nine years of age and up into the 18-to-20 age bracket becoming obsessed with the occult. Again, every child is vulnerable if other circumstances occur to draw him in, but we find that *most* of the children we work with are between the ages of 11 and 17.

The answer to the "where" question also requires the disclaimer that a child can be victimized anywhere, but several places, events and activities appear to be favorites with those who try to recruit youngsters into teen devil worship and satanism.

Rock concerts are especially popular with recruiters, particularly those concerts where "heavy metal" or "black metal" rock groups perform.

Children also may be recruited through "gaming clubs" formed either privately or through school and community sponsorship and in which members are taught to play fantasy role-playing games such as "Dungeons & Dragons."

Teenagers also may be recruited at popular neighborhood hang-outs such as video arcades, teen clubs and other social spots where children gather with little or no adult supervision.

Private parties at homes are also favorites with recruiters; in fact, some parties are organized and planned by occult practitioners for the specific purpose of recruiting new members into their organizations. Plentiful drugs and promiscuous sex are usually the drawing cards at such parties where participants are carefully observed to determine the best candidates for initiation into the cult.

Behavior Patterns To Look For

To answer the "what" question, the following list serves as a general guide to the types of behaviors that can be expected when a child begins to engage in occult practices:

1. Obsession with occult entertainment.
2. Minor and major behavior disorders.
3. Committing crimes and status offenses such as:
   a. running away from home
   b. grave robbing for the purpose of removing bones and body parts rather than jewelry and other valuables
   c. breaking and entering to steal religious artifacts or small, worthless items to prove loyalty to the group
   d. defacing public or private property with occult graffiti such as "Satan Rules," "Satan is my master," "666," and inverted pentagrams
   e. self-mutilation (cutting and inking-in tattoos and otherwise injuring self) and threatening to kill self or others; suicide attempts
   f. aggression toward family, teachers and authority figures
   g. contempt for organized traditional religions
   h. supremacist attitudes, i.e. that they are members of an elite group better and more powerful than most Americans
   i. kidnapping or assisting in kidnapping
   j. animal killing and mutilation for purposes of ritual sacrifices and the drinking of blood
   k. murder for purpose of ritual sacrifice
   l. suicide pacts among members of group

The obsession with occult entertainment is one of the most subtle and often overlooked stages. I don't want to imply that the youngster who watches one or two occult movies, reads an occult book, attends a few heavy metal or black metal concerts and buys those groups' albums, or plays one fantasy role-playing game is in serious danger of becoming a teen satanist. I emphasize the word obsession. Many parents do not notice the gradual transition from a child's curiosity about occult entertainment to true obsession. An obsessed child is one who only enjoys movies, television shows, music and other forms of entertainment that contain occult themes.

Our office assisted in the case of a young man who was obsessed with occult entertainment, and this case serves well to illustrate the dangers of such a preoccupation.

"Mike" was 14-years-old when he became an occult dabbler through the encouragement of a friend. Like the vast majority of dabblers, he did not wake up one day to discover that he liked occult entertainment or wanted to become involved with devil worship. Mike became belligerent and had a serious behavior problem at home and school. He was suspended on several occasions. Then he ran away from home.

When his mother telephoned me to ask if I could help, she had no idea that he was dabbling in the occult, but she did acknowledge that he was a fan of heavy metal music. She was frantic and only wanted to know if I could find her son. Together we went to Mike's school to begin laying the groundwork, inquiring of teachers, counselors and administrators regarding recent changes in Mike's behavior.

The principal of the school showed us a letter that Mike had written which he had disregarded because, as the principal said, "It is unintelligible, doesn't make any sense, isn't even written in English."

The letter is reprinted here in its entirety with the permission of Mike's family:

"I saw nekowa eno thgin yb siht live tirips. I t'nod wonk yhw tub i tog tuo fo ym deb dna tnew nwod ot eht dne fo ym yawevird. Reiht i saw gnidnats thgir ta ym xobliam, meht tuoba evif setunim retal a kcalb rac htiw siht nam desserd ni kcalb, a draeb, dna gnol der slianregnif eh dlot em ot teg ni eht rac os i deklaw dnuora ot eht edisrehto fo sih rac.

"Nehw i tog ni eh dlot em eh saw na tirips. I deksa mih saw eh a tirips from **NATAS**, esuaceb fi uoy t'nera m'i annog og thgir kcab. Neht eh dehgual dna dias "sey" i ma morf drol **NATAS**. I deksa him tahw did drol **NATAS** tnaw fo em. Eh dlot em taht eh detnaw em ot krow rof mih dna ot trats ffo yb gnivahebsim ta loohcs, dna osla ot trats pu gnikoms niga. I dias enif htiw em os i ma. Neht eh dias ot teem mih ta eht dne fo ym yawevird dna t'nod llet enoyna tuoba mih, tpecxe [name of friend]. Eh osla dias ot etirw lla fo siht nwod drawkcab os ydobon lliw erugif ti tuo dna os i lliw, dna ot

39

kool ta it yreve thgin os i lliw rebmemer tahw ot od. Neht eh
dlot em ot evael dna og kcab ot deb. Eh dias sih eman saw "ILAC
ni ATTUCLAC," dna REVEN llet ydobyna. Ro ESLE!!!"

The words are printed backwards which is typical of many occultic writings. Neither the principal nor Mike's mother recognized
the manner of writing until I pointed it out to them. The letter trans-
lates as follows (with spellings as they appeared in the original letter):

"I was awoken one night by this evil spirit. I don't know
why but i got out of my bed and went down to the end of my
driveway. Thier i was standing right at my mailbox, then
about five minutes later a black car with this man dressed in
black, beard, and long red fingernails he told me to get in the
car so I walked around to the otherside of his car.
"When I got in he told me he was an spirit. I asked him
was he a spirit from **SATAN**, because if you aren't i'm gonna
go right back. Then he laughed and said "yes" I am from lord
SATAN. I asked him what did lord **SATAN** want of me. He
told me that he wanted me to work for him and to start off by
misbehaving at school, and also to start up smoking again. I
said fine with me so i am. Then he said to meet him at the end
of my driveway and don't tell anyone about him, except
[name of friend]. He also said to write all of this down backward so nobody will figure it out and so i will, and to look at it
every night so i will remember what to do. Then he told me to
leave and go back to bed. He said his name was "Cali in
Calcutta," and NEVER tell anybody. Or ELSE!!!

This letter written by Mike was the first indication to his family
and the school that he was dabbling in the occult.
The local and state police were able to find Mike and bring him
home, but the greater problem remained of what to do once he had
returned.
Was this man he claimed to have met real or was the incident a
dream or hallucination of some kind?
We had extensive interviews with Mike in which he maintained
that the man was real. His descriptions of the man were quite detailed
and realistic, but we have never been able to determine whether Mike
ever met such a man.
We discovered later that Mike was using drugs, but it is important
to note that he was dabbling in the occult *before* he began using drugs.
He said (as do many young people who are dabblers) that drugs en-
hanced his occult experiences. The drug use certainly suggests that

the incident described in the letter may have been imagined but, again, this has never been determined.

Mike is currently under treatment in a psychiatric and drug treatment facility, and there is every indication that his recovery is progressing well.

The fascinating points regarding his letter are that he did write completely backwards and that he wrote about things (Cali of Calcutta) that he could not have known about had he not read occult books other than *The Satanic Bible*, the only book on the occult he admitted to having read.

Mike also admitted to having tried some ritual spells. He was convinced that these spells worked, particularly one in which he had asked for money. Whether or not these spells worked is irrelevant; the fact that he *believed* they worked supported his belief system and encouraged him to delve deeper and deeper into the occult.

Frequent Activities of Teen Satanists

Grave robbing and the desecration of churches are other frequent activities among teen satanists and, as mentioned earlier, the grave robbing does not include the opening of graves for the purpose of stealing things like jewelry and other valuables. Occultic grave robbing is easily recognized by the absence of skulls, bones and body parts from the grave. Hair and fingernails from deceased persons are required in many occult rituals, and their absence is easily overlooked by investigators. Individual gravesites often are desecrated as are entire cemeteries. This desecration may take the form of spray-painting satanic graffiti on tombstones and the walls of mausoleums, the turning upside-down of crosses and other religious symbols, the beheading of angels and other religious figures, and the general destruction of the surface of graves. There has been an increase in police incident reports of cemetery and grave vandalism since 1983.

Similarly, there has been an increase in reports of church desecrations (again, the spray-painting of satanic graffiti is typical as is the turning upside-down of religious symbols and figures) and the theft of religious artifacts from churches. Most occult rituals require the use of chalices and robes, and those taken from Catholic churches are the most highly prized in devil worshiping.

Law enforcement officials and mental health professionals now recognize the fact that adolescent occult involvement is *progressive*. The child who is obsessed with occult entertainment may stop there, but he often moves on to satanic graffiti and cemetery vandalism. From that point, he easily moves into grave robbing for items needed for occult rituals, and he is just a step away from blood-letting.

Blood-letting begins with animal killings and mutilations and progresses to murder if intervention does not take place.

I often am asked by seminar participants if I think that drugs are the "real problem." I have interviewed hundreds of adolescents who are in drug treatment facilities, some of whom have committed murder. Most of these youngsters' crimes were drug-related robberies and homicides. They did not commit murder in the name of the devil and they did not worship the devil. Drugs may enhance the occult experience and push some children over the edge, but they are not the cause.

Self-mutilation and blood sacrifices are considered ultimate tributes to Satan. Evidence of this may appear early in a teenager's occult dabblings with "tattoos" he creates for himself. This is usually done by scratching an occult symbol (such as an upside-down cross, an inverted pentagram, the number 666 or the word "Satan") into the skin, usually of the arm. Ink is then rubbed into the scratched symbol, thus creating a very primitive but recognizable tattoo. Such a tattoo is an example of self-mutilation and should serve as a warning to family and friends that something very serious is beginning to take place in the teenager's life.

Mutilation Killings of Animals

The next step in this dangerous progression is the mutilation killings of animals, a step which sometimes leads to homicide and suicide. We in traditional, mainstream America may not see the logic behind this practice but, for occultists, the practice is very logical indeed.

Richard Cavendish, noted author on the occult, writes in his book *The Black Arts*:

"In the altar **grimoires** [a **grimoire** is a magical ritual ceremony], the sacrifice tends to be more closely associated with the ceremony itself, and in modern rituals, the victim is sometimes slaughtered at the height of the ceremony. This is done to increase the supply of force in the circle [meaning a magic circle which is literally drawn on the ground or floor for the protection of those holding the ritual and for the purpose of containing energy].

"In occult theory, a living creature is a storehouse of energy, and when it is killed, most of this energy is suddenly liberated. The killing is done inside the circle to keep the animal energy in and concentrated. The animal should be young, healthy and virgin so that its supply of force has been dissipated as little as possible. The amount of energy let loose when the victim is killed is very great, out of all proportion to the animal's size or strength, and the magician must not allow it to get out of hand. If he is unsure of himself or lets his concentration slacken, he may be overwhelmed by the force he has unleashed. ... It is an ancient magical principle that blood is the vehicle in which an animal's life energy is carried. The spirit or force which is summoned in the ceremony is normally invisible. It can appear visibly to the magician by fastening on a source of energy on a physical plane of existence. It may do this by taking possession of one of the human beings involved in the ritual. The most important reason for the sacrifice, however, is the psychological charge which the magician obtains from it, the frenzy which he induces in himself by concentration, by incantations, by burning fumes and heightened by the savage act of slaughter and the pumping gush of red blood.

"It would obviously be more effective to sacrifice a human being because of the far greater psychological 'kick' involved. Although this is highly unlikely, there is a tradition that the most effective sacrifice to demons is the murder of a human being.

"Aleister Crowley could not pass over such an opportunity to scandalize his readers. 'For the highest spiritual working, one must choose that victim which contains the greatest and purest force. A male child of perfect innocence and high intelligence is the most satisfactory and suitable victim.' In practice, human beings normally being in short supply, the magician's bloody sacrifice is the killing of an animal or the wounding of the magician himself or one of his assistants whose skin is gashed until the blood runs. If this is combined with the release of sexual energy in orgasm, the effect is to heighten the magician's frenzy and the supply of force in the circle still further.

"In many satanic cults, a member may achieve the status of high priest or priestess only after having performed a blood sacrifice ritual. For some, the ultimate homage to Satan is the sacrifice of a human being either through the killing of someone else or the taking of one's own life."

Teenagers and other children who engage in satanic rituals may practice those rituals at any time and, while some may practice such rituals alone, the majority prefer to do so with one or more other individuals. They may form groups of 13 members and call themselves a "coven," although it is seldom that a teenage dabbler can find 12 like-minded friends.

Unholy Days

There are certain dates which occultists consider "high holy days" in satanism and witchcraft. These dates are important ones on which certain rituals are expected to be performed in order to pay the highest possible tribute to the demons and deities being worshiped or summoned.

These dates are January 1 (traditionally a Druid feast day), January 20 (St. Agnes' Eve), February 2 (Candlemas, a witches' sabbat), April 24 (St. Mark's Eve), April 30 (Walpurgis Night), May 1 (Beltane or May Day), June 23 (Midsummer's Eve), July 25 (St. James' Day), August 1 (Lammas, considered the Great Sabbat), August 24 (St. Bartholomew's Day), October 31 (Halloween, traditionally the night the dead were thought to return to this earth), and December 21 (St. Thomas' Day).

Other significant dates in the occult calendar are a member's birthday, any date on which there is a full moon, and Easter and Christmas for the purpose of mocking Christianity's holiest days. Midnight is the time of choice for many rituals, but most may be practiced at any time of day.

The Attraction of Evil

Without question, the most difficult aspect to understand regarding teen satanism and devil worship is the "why." Why on earth would basically good, decent children from loving families, children who have been raised with strong values and religious backgrounds, be seduced into the dark, evil practices of the occult?

The occult *is* interesting, and many intelligent, creative children are drawn to read and study the subject. Also, as mentioned earlier, most will do just that and then leave it alone, going on to explore other (and healthier) areas of interest. The ones who don't leave it alone and who are drawn deeper into the occult may be rebelling against authority or experiencing severe psychological and emotional disorders as a result of abuse.

The sociological implications can vary infinitely. By far the most compelling reason, however, appears to be the desire for personal power, power over self and others, power to control events that are ordinarily beyond human control.

Whether this power is truly obtainable through the casting of spells and the practicing of rituals is for others to debate. The critical issue for us is that the children so involved *believe* that their spells and rituals work, and this appears to give them something that they are lacking, to fill some kind of void in their lives, no matter how that void was created.

44

Is Teen Devil Worship Widespread?

Some readers may doubt that the problem of teen satanism and devil worship is widespread enough to warrant any great concern. Others simply may wish to know upon what grounds I have based an entire career devoted to the investigation of teen occultism and the counseling of youngsters who have fallen victim to its subtle seduction. My office is filled with files on hundreds of cases, many of which had tragic results.

Consider the following excerpts from newspapers and wire services around the country:

USA Today, 4/26/84: (Northport, N.Y.) A 17-year-old Long Island youth was charged with opening a 19th century grave. Richard Kasso, Jr., a self-proclaimed devil worshipper, planned to use the remains in satanic rituals, police say ...

New York Times, 7/8/84: A teenage youth charged with slaying and mutilating a 17-year-old Long Island boy in what authorities said was a ritual carried out before followers of a satanic cult was found hanged early yesterday in his cell at the Suffolk County Jail. The Suffolk County Sheriff, John Finnerty, listed the death of the suspect, Richard Kasso, 17-years-old, of Northport, L.I., as an apparent suicide. Deputies had found him hanging from a bedsheet ...

USA Today, 5/31/84: (Sanford, Me.) The suspected strangler of Gycelle Cote, 12, was depicted in police documents as a devil worshipper. The documents, released by a judge Wednesday, say police found satanic writings and art work in the school locker of Scott Waterhouse, 18 ...

Centralia Sentinel, 8/23/84: (Salem, Ill.) Nine persons were apprehended by Marion County authorities last night in connection with what has been described as "cult" or "devil-worship" activities on Texaco Oil Co. lease property southwest of Salem ... Deputies at the scene reported that the group had placed "a couple of dead dog carcasses" on a bale of straw and were preparing to light the bale as a sort of "burnt offering." ... [Symbols found at the sight included] pentagrams within circles, two red crosses within circles, and the number "666." ... [Six of those arrested in this case were teenagers.]

Prattville Progress, 10/2/84: (Gadsden, Ala.) Two teen-agers who face charges of vandalizing a cemetery and 30 tombstones have taken credit for rigging up what police say appears to be a devil worship site in western Etowah County. Walnut Grove Police Chief Terry Greer and another officer last Saturday found a site in a wooded area with two crosses — one with blood on it — an altar with bones of a small animal, remains of bonfires and signs with pictures of Satan and a goat's head warning trespassers of death ...

Houston Chronicle, 9/11/85 (Houston, Tex.) Five teens allegedly lured a 19-year-old laborer to a field behind a ceme-tery where they tortured him for the thrill of it and then killed him because "they wanted to watch somebody die. They sat around and talked about it for a week and then lured him out to the field and killed him for kicks," Harris County Sheriff's Detective Max Cox said Tuesday ... All of the suspects claim to believe in Satanism ...

Associated Press, 9/29/85: (Santa Maria, Cal.) Under the guise of worshiping Satan, teenagers are reveling in sado-masochistic sex orgies, police said, terming the practice a "fad." An investigation revealed that 15 teenagers from local schools have engaged in the sexual rituals, and a smaller group of them have added devil worship to the activities ...

The Montgomery Journal, 1/3/86 (Rockville, Md.) A wooded thicket just blocks from expensive homes in Chevy Chase hides a satanic worship site with cages, nooses, sacrifi-cial pits, satanic symbols and inverted crosses made of nails, Maryland-National Capital Park Police say. ... [A] priest ad-vised officers not to return to the site at night alone ... A per-son familiar with satanic worship said the site is probably the work of teenagers who have researched the black arts. ...

El Paso Times, 2/16/86 (El Paso, Tex.) [A teenaged girl] thought she was at a regular party with classmates and some of their friends. Then a boy told the 14-year-old student that some of the 25 people at the party were angry with her be-cause she would not become one of them. Suddenly, a group of girls converged on [her] and started beating her up. She cried out to one of the adults for help, but the man encour-aged the fight to continue. "I didn't know they were *all* satan-ists," said [the girl], who spent eight hours in the hospital. She was beaten, she said, because she had refused to become a satanist. ...

The Albuquerque Journal, 4/22/86 (Albuquerque, N.M.) A 15-year-old boy who is sought in connection with the fatal shooting of his father with a bow and arrow had threatened to get revenge on the victim for tearing up the youth's Satan bible, according to an arrest warrant filed Monday. ... The affidavit filed in Children's Court by police detective Barbara Cantwell also says Satanic symbols were found in the youth's bedroom. ...

San Jose Mercury News, 9/5/86 (Denair, Cal.) The evidence: one open grave, 4 feet deep; a shattered coffin, once sealed by concrete; an elderly man's bones, removed sloppily with the head severed; ceremonial burn marks around a gravesite; 14 headstones tilted; and nearby, occult symbols painted on the walls of a high school. The questions: Who were the people responsible? And did the devil make them do it? And why did it happen in this pastoral central California town, known to the 2,000 or so who live here as the "Oasis of the San Joaquin Valley"?

The Florida Times-Union, 11/13/86 (Fernandina Beach, Fla.) Law enforcement officials in Nassau County say there is little they can do about a satanic cult that has panicked local residents. City and county officials say they are powerless to prevent the bizarre worship ceremonies of the cult unless those services involve some violation of the law. Although evidence indicates the ceremonies involve sacrifices of domestic animals, the use of drugs and alcohol and trespassing onto private property, neither Nassau County sheriff's deputies nor Fernandina Beach police officers have been able to link that evidence to individual cult members ...

Casper State Tribune, 2/12/87 (Powell, Wyo.) Police are closing in on a Satan-worshiping cult called the "Warlocks of the Crimson Circle" that they say is behind several burglaries that have occurred in Powell over the last few months, officials say ... 12 high school-age boys are involved in the cult. ... The group's activities have included the ritualistic mutilation of several cats and may be drug-related. ...

The Cincinnati Enquirer, 2/19/87 (Fairfield, Ohio) Evidence of devil worship was discovered Wednesday by police searching the trailer home of an acquaintance of the Price Hill woman whose severed legs were found in an Indiana churchyard. Smeared red stains, which may be blood, were found on the floor of a bedroom converted into a satanic worship area, investigators said ...

Chicago Tribune, 8/27/87 (Machesney Park, Ill.) The 19-year-old son of Illinois wildlife artist Walter P. Oswald, Sr., was arraigned Wednesday on charges that he shot his father to death in the family home near Rockford and also killed a friend with a knife, authorities said. [The] bodies were found Monday night in the rustic Oswald home, amid books and writings on the subject of satanic worship, police said. ...

Executive News Service, 8/29/87 (Jacksonville, N.C.) Two teenagers were taken to hospitals after claiming they were possessed by a demon, leading Onslow County Sheriff's Department deputies to investigate claims that a "satanic cult" was meeting. [A woman] said that she and her husband ... confronted their 14-year-old son Thursday morning after discovering he had sneaked out of the house four nights in a row ... [The woman said], "My son began drawing satanic symbols and explaining that the seven kids involved in the cult had to go through the 'six gates of hell' to get to the top of the pyramid. Once you got to the top, he said, you must make a human sacrifice to become a high priest. ..."

Scranton Tribune, 10/29/87 (Scranton, Penn.) A Satanic cult holds rituals at midnight in a wooded area a few miles east of Lake Scranton and kills cats and dogs that are offered as "sacrifices to Satan," says a woman who was asked to join the cult. The rituals, she said, consist of cultists standing around a fire, talking in a form of Latin, and honoring Satan as their god. [The woman told police that she had dated a man who was a member of the cult. She said that] one night he took off his shirt and showed her a tattoo of a Satanic pig-faced beast that was on his back. She said as she watched in horror, the man took out a knife, slit his chest, let his blood pour into a cup, and asked her to drink it. ... With the help of some neighbors, this bizarre ritual ended. ...

Scranton Tribune, 11/12/87 (Scranton, Penn.) "We're concerned that someone might get killed and we're concerned about the moral fiber of the youth of today." These are the words of Lt. William Gowden of the Borough of Dunmore Police Department, who with Officer Joseph Carra of the department's juvenile division, has been investigating Satanic cults for 22 months and identified four ritual sites. The officers say the cults are real and dangerous, and that a number of teenagers have admitted to participating in Satanic rites. ...

Tallahassee Democrat, 12/19/87 (Tallahassee, Fla.) Satan worship and a mission to sacrifice four Christian souls were among the bizarre details of the devil-made-me-do-it discussions murder defendant Tommy Malone had with a psychologist ... Malone admitted shooting to death his girlfriend's parents, Jesse and Doris Foster, while the couple slept in their Runnymede subdivision home on May 13, according to court documents filed by his lawyer. ...

AP Wire Service, 1/11/88 (Jefferson Township, N.J.) A youth obsessed with Satanism committed suicide after stabbing his mother to death with his Boy Scout knife and trying to kill the rest of his family by setting a fire as they slept, officials said. Thomas Sullivan, Jr., a 14-year-old eighth-grader and Boy Scout, began reading books on the occult and Satan worship about a month ago, Morris County Prosecutor Lee S. Trumbull said yesterday. His "mind was taken control of by his interest in the Satanism," Trumbull said ...

The Florida Times-Union, 6/10/88 (Douglasville, Ga.) A teenager, convicted of murder last month, testified in the trial of another teen charged in the same death that he joined a satanic cult when he was 13 and later formed his own group that ultimately performed a human sacrifice. Terry Belcher, 16, testified that after he participated in the strangulation death of Theresa Simmons, he and 16-year-old murder defendant Robert McIntyre performed a crude ritual over her body, chanting to the devil. Belcher said he and McIntyre were "calling upon Satan to bring him ... to be with us, to give him the sacrifice ..."

Parkersburg News, 8/18/88 (Coal City, West Va.) Rumors of animal sacrifices and devil worship are running rampant in a small Raleigh County community where cultists allegedly threatened to blow up a church, desecrated graves and terrorized a teenage girl. [A local minister] said Wednesday that most of the tales floating around are just that. But he added that some stories are true, and strange things are going on in the community of 750 residents. "There have been a lot of rumors, and there have been some things that happened, like one girl who [cultists] tried to pull out of a window in her bedroom and an older woman who was taken out of her house," [the minister] said. ... "we are convinced there are things happening and young people are being threatened to join the satanic worship group ..."

Sunday News, 9/11/88 (Lancaster, Penn.) A Strasburg Pike church is vandalized, with a fire set in the basement; mirrors and a spot of blood left on the altar; hymnals carefully arranged on the floor, and debris scattered in the aisles. Strange symbols are carefully painted on buildings in Lancaster County's Central Park in West Lampeter Township, and a goat's head is later found in the same park. Tombstones are upset, broken and scattered in a handful of area cemeteries ... Some police officers, clergy and school officials around the county believe these and other pieces of evidence indicate that satanic activity—behavior and rites designed to glorify Satan—is increasing in Lancaster County and on the East Coast in general. ...

The Richmond News Leader, 10/28/88 (Richmond, Va.) Behind an automobile dealership on bustling Midlothian Turnpike in Chesterfield County sits a run-down, abandoned dwelling that some area residents believe is being used by teenagers who indulge in Satan worship or other rituals. The interior walls of the house are covered with graffiti that glorifies Satan and sacrificial killing, and some residents are convinced the messages are the work of devil- or demon-worshiping youths, Chesterfield police say ...

The Ledger Star, 1/2/89 (Norfolk, Va.) It was the most gruesome thing Robert Kirby had seen in his 12 years as Norfolk's superintendent of cemeteries. On the night of November 25, someone broke open a padlock on the gate of an Elmwood Cemetery mausoleum ... The casket of a woman, entombed in 1961, was dragged halfway out and the casket's lid was opened, revealing her skeletal hands folded atop her black dress. [A Norfolk investigator and a Virginia Beach in-

vestigator] said more animal mutilations and graveyard van-
dalisms occurred in 1988 than in any year they can remember.
[The investigators] said they believe most of the acts might
have been committed by "experimenters" or "dabblers" in the
occult. ...

If these incidents aren't enough to convince the most skeptical
reader, know that there are hundreds more like them on file in the
B.A.D.D. office and the offices of the Cult Awareness Network,
Parents' Music Resource Center, National Coalition on Television
Violence, Advisory Board on Ritualistic Crime for the American
Federation of Police and Advisory Board of the Cult Crime Impact
Network.

All of these organizations are working together to gather and dis-
tribute information and to alert parents and others concerned with
the welfare of America's children to the dangers of occult involvement and the methods used by recruiters.

It is the responsibility of every person who cares about the welfare of children to inform himself regarding the who, where, what,
when and why of teen occult involvement. Additionally, it is the responsibility of every such person to recognize the evidence when he
sees it, to address the problem instead of ignoring it, to befriend a
child in trouble.

THE SATANIC
NETWORK

The subjects of satanic worship in particular and the occult in general have become hot topics within the last few years. As new cases surface and evidence comes to light through the court system and the media, these subjects will receive more attention than ever before.

Along with all of this new information, there also will be a corresponding increase in the number of people who call themselves "experts," "occult researchers" and "investigators," and many of these will join the ranks of those who currently are trying to convince the public that none of this is real.

Sadly for all of us and especially our children, these individuals are determined to downplay every criminal incident that has occult overtones. Many of them are sincere skeptics; some have questionable motives. The vast majority simply are uninformed.

The Richmond News Leader recently carried the headline "Experts say tales are bunk; Rumors abound but nothing proves that cults exist."

The reporter had gone to a great deal of trouble to find a number of "authorities" who would support the angle of his article.

Additionally, a member of the Intelligence Division of the Richmond Police Department and I were interviewed.

The two-part series quoted a number of people who have set themselves up as experts on the subject of occult activity and used these quotes to argue the statements made by the police officer and me.

The reporter failed to mention, however, that one of his naysaying sources is a former member of the Church of Satan whose current level of involvement is unknown.

Another source has been "investigating" this subject for less than a year, and his "research" consists of little more than reading a smattering of articles and books.

The reporter, of course, failed to mention these important facts, leaving the unwary reader to assume these sources were qualified. A number of the sources in this and other similar articles have referred to the idea of satanic cults involved in criminal activity as an "urban legend." It is time to put this argument to rest once and for all.

Most of the individuals who minimize the significance of occult crime have never dealt with the documented cases which involve adolescents and children. When confronted with such cases, they dismiss them as "isolated incidents" and say that they are simply examples of "deviant behavior." Certainly murder is deviant behavior, but we must not ignore the motives in cases where there is evidence of occult involvement.

In the Scott Waterhouse case (which concerned the strangulation killing of a 12-year-old girl; the presence of semen on the victim's clothing indicated that the perpetrator had masturbated over the victim's body), the court clearly stated, "We conclude that the evidence of satanism and the defendant's belief therein is relevant for the permissible purposes of proving the identity of the perpetrator as well as his intent. In the tape-recorded conversation introduced at trial, the defendant described sex and destruction rituals as part of the system of satanic beliefs. The defendant stated that satanism represents that darker side of humanity and urges indulgence of man's carnal needs rather than abstinence. He characterized the 'seven cardinal sins' of the Christian faith as representing abstinence."

Scott Waterhouse was convicted, evidence that these facts were relevant even through the appellate court.

The David Berkowitz case provides further proof that the so-called urban legend is, in fact, quite real. Berkowitz, the .44-caliber killer who came to be known as the "Son of Sam," terrorized the city of New York in 1977. He was arrested and charged with shooting 13 young people.

Berkowitz claimed that his neighbor's dog was possessed by evil spirits and that this dog had instructed him to carry out the shootings. The obviously deranged young man was convicted of the crimes and sentenced to prison.

Ten years later, however, noted occult investigator Maury Terry turned up new evidence which indicated that Berkowitz did not act alone, but was instead a member of a nationwide satanic network which is still operating today and to which the Charles Manson "family" was tied. This evidence, revealed in Terry's book *The Ultimate Evil*, was so convincing and well-documented that it resulted in the reopening of the "Son of Sam" case.

Hand of Death

Another interesting case which lends credence to the theory of a large satanic network is that out of Texas of convicted killer Henry Lee Lucas. Lucas claimed to have killed 360 people between 1975 and 1983, and said in interviews that many of the murders had been ordered by a cult to which he belonged called "The Hand of Death." He explained that the cult made sacrifices to summon the devil, and the sacrifices often involved ritual crucifixions of both animals and human beings.

Ottis Edward Toole, a one-time companion of Lucas now imprisoned in Florida, also spoke of satanic cult activities in which he had participated, some of which activities included the eating of human flesh.

I first learned of the Lucas case in 1984 and, while I thought it bizarre, was not surprised by the mention of "The Hand of Death" cult. I had heard of this cult several years before from law enforcement officers in two other states who had, in turn, received their information from two prisoners who had no knowledge of Lucas.

I became intrigued with Lucas's case and with "The Hand of Death" cult and later read a book about Lucas by Max Call entitled *The Hand of Death*. I was amazed at the accuracy with which Henry Lee Lucas (who is almost illiterate and who has little more than a fifth-grade education) related his alleged involvement with this cult. He described rituals and methodology that only could be known by someone who has participated in cult activities.

Many detractors have called this entire story a hoax and insist that we must not believe anything said by someone who is deranged enough to commit even one murder, much less 360. However, investigators claim that information provided by Lucas helped them close the books on over 100 murder cases by giving detailed descriptions of how and where the victims were killed.

Why do we choose to believe Lucas regarding the details of these murders and simultaneously disregard everything he says which pertains to satanic cult activity? Others have suggested that Lucas read about occult rituals in a book and concocted his entire story. I reject this notion based on the fact that there was very little written and published about this subject in 1984 when he began making these allegations about "The Hand of Death."

I wanted to get a "feel" for this case, so I made arrangements to see Henry Lee Lucas on death row. We limited our conversation to the events and details in Call's book. After meeting with him, I was convinced his allegations are true regarding this lethal cult which reportedly has several hundred members nationwide. To the best of my knowledge, no one is at this time actively trying to prove or disprove the existence of "The Hand of Death" cult, a mistake I consider to be deadly and, with Lucas' accuracy in pinpointing the ranch near Matamoros where the bodies of Kilroy and others were found, it is obvious more should be done. When critics of our investigations challenge us with demands for proof in the form of dead bodies, I often respond that perhaps we need to find more suspects who are as cooperative as Henry Lee Lucas, and at the very least, pay more attention to the confessions of people like Lucas.

Many other cases have proven beyond a shadow of a doubt that satanic cults exist and that, whether large or small, they can be extremely dangerous.

In 1987, Clifford St. Joseph was charged with the murder of a man who had been bled to death. The victim's body showed signs of a satanic ritual: a pentagram had been carved into his flesh and he had a stab wound in his neck, whip marks on his buttocks, and wax in his hair and right eye. Other evidence suggested cannibalism.

A number of witnesses were called to testify in this case which resulted in startling allegations of a homosexual satanic cult. Some of the witnesses had participated in other rituals with St. Joseph. One claimed he had been drugged and chained to a fireplace while cult members gang-raped him and forced him to participate in sex acts with a dog. This witness said that St. Joseph had intended him as his next human sacrifice. The suspect was convicted and sentenced to 25-years-to-life on the murder charge and a total of 12 years on other charges.

Human Sacrifice

The Cincinnati Enquirer, in 1987, followed closely the case of 21-year-old Monica Lemen who disappeared after leaving work one February evening.

One article began as follows: "Evidence of devil worship was discovered ... by police searching the trailer home of an acquaintance of the Price Hill woman whose severed legs were found in an Indiana churchyard. Smeared red stains, which may be blood, were found on the floor of a bedroom converted into a satanic worship area, investigators said. 'In one of the bedrooms, the walls, the ceilings, the floor, everything is painted black,' Fairfield Police Detective Eddie Roberts said ... of the trailer home of John Fryman, 24. 'He's got a table made like a podium, and on top of the podium is a granite headstone. There are all kinds of black candles. There's a name on the headstone, and it's a legitimate headstone.' Roberts said satanic literature was found in the trailer."

Other occult evidence found in the trailer included an inverted cross, a black notebook, a chalice, a black bell, a black ceramic ram's head, and a satanic prayer and swastika painted on a closet door.

The resulting murder trial revealed that Lemen had been fascinated with the occult and had been involved with Fryman and his girlfriend, Beverly Cox, as well as with other occult practitioners, including Harry Powell, an occultist from Tennessee. Subsequent testimony revealed that Cox's own father was a practicing satanist.

This case is but one example of what we often find to be true, that is, if enough witnesses are interviewed for long enough periods of time, sometimes a real (though somewhat disorganized) conspiracy will reveal itself, a conspiracy which occasionally involves more than one generation.

In each of these cases, the occult activity progressed to the point of human sacrifice.

FBI Agent Ken Lanning defines sacrifice as "a murder, committed by two or more people, which is logically and rationally planned, and the primary purpose of which is to fulfill a religious or satanic ritual."

I agree with this definition, but I like to take it one step further by saying "one or more people." In many cases, one person has performed the sacrifice.

This practice is mentioned in Old Testament accounts of human sacrifices made to pagan gods, and individuals acting alone have made sacrifices throughout the ages. It is no different today.

The Evidence Mounts

Other occult-related crimes are on the record books which do not include the sacrificing of animals or humans.

In 1987, a large New York-based company hired a private agency to investigate a senior executive officer whose "business trips" to Europe were highly questionable. He often drew large cash advances prior to these trips and used the company's credit card at a strange bookstore. The investigators found that the bookstore specialized in occult and pornographic materials. Further detective work revealed that this elderly corporate executive was also a priest in a satanic organization and that he financed many of his group's ritual activities with funds from his company.

William P. Callahan, president of United Intelligence, Inc., the agency hired to track the executive, said in an interview with the *Daily Herald*, "We've had cases in which four or five executives were involved in satanic cults. These are men in their 60's and 70's. Nothing surprises us anymore."

The question concerning "organized satanic networks" comes up at seminars and conferences where I speak. To date, there may not be sufficient information or evidence gathered to say without a doubt that such networks exist. However, there is quite a bit of information to suggest that the non-criminal occultists do network with one another through newsletters and computer bulletin board systems. If these hard-line occultists are actively networking, it would be quite naive of us to assume that the destructive criminal cults do not do the same.

Another example of possible networking unfolded several years ago. I received a document in a plain brown envelope that I have not shared with anyone prior to the writing of this book. The lengthy report was on official government investigative report forms; it is frightening in the information it contains.

That report, dated and signed on April 10, 1975, is summarized here. Passages within quotation marks are quoted verbatim from the document, with the exception of the deletion of names and some minor details which would identify the persons involved.

According to the document, the investigation was requested by a U.S. Attorney's office as a result of reports of an occult group operating throughout the Midwest and southern sections of the United States. These reports concerned numerous cattle mutilations which had occurred in the Midwest and in Minnesota, and indicated that these mutilations might be the result of occult ritual activity.

The investigator who wrote the report had investigated these cattle mutilations (prior to this investigation) at the request of others who were looking into the possibility that the mutilations had something to do with UFO phenomenon. He had determined that they did not. Due to his already extensive knowledge of the cattle mutilations, his services were requested once more, this time to investigate the possibility that practitioners of occult rituals might be involved.

The investigator had determined that a certain pattern existed in the cattle mutilation cases (which numbered over a hundred in an eight-state area). In most of these cases, the animal had been found in the middle of an open field. Body parts (which included eyes, ears, lips, tongue, teats and sex organs) had been removed surgically. In many of the cases, the animals had been drained of all blood; in several of the cases, veterinarians had been unable to determine the cause of death. In nearly every case, no tracks were visible on the ground near the animals' bodies, and no blood spills or stains were found. In the cases where the carcasses were found in a field of snow, the snow had been melted in a circle around the body.

Several letters written by an inmate in a federal prison were brought to the investigator's attention. The letters had been written to authorities and alleged that the inmate had extensive knowledge about the cattle mutilations. The investigator had the inmate transferred to a county jail for an interview.

The inmate (whom we will call "Bill") reported a lengthy acquaintance with two other inmates ("Eddie" and "Joe") who had told him of their participation in the animal mutilations. Eddie and Joe had talked quite freely about their involvement with an occult group which they said had killed and dismembered the animals for ritual purposes.

The investigator decided to interview Joe.

"[Joe] stated that around 1965 while he was residing in (city, state), he became a heavy user of drugs," the investigator wrote in his report. "Through his contacts in the drug world, he learned of a group of people involved in 'Satanism' or 'Devil Worship' who wanted members. The occult group had unlimited access to drugs, so [Joe] got into it initially as a means of more freely obtaining drugs. He said at that time the group would regularly conduct rituals and ceremonies and would use parts of small animals in the rites. He described the killing of dogs, cats and rabbits in various areas which would be bled, the sex organs would be cut off, and all of these parts would be used in the rites. He was told by the leaders of the occult group that most of their beliefs, etc. were based on passages from the Bible, namely Revelations, and that astrology also played a major role in their activities. It was believed by all the members of the group that their 'religion' called for sacrifices of human life later on. [Joe] didn't particularly believe they meant that part of their religion until an event occurred in 1969 near (city, state) which jolted him to the realization that human sacrifices would become very real.

"[Joe] stated that during the late summer of 1969, he and several members of the (city) occult group had traveled to (city, state) where they met several members of the occult from nearby universities. They were camped on a lake near (city) and planned to conduct one of their ceremonies. Four young people, two boys and two girls, were camped nearby who had no connection with the occult and appeared to [Joe] to be transients traveling through the area. About this time, a tranquilizer drug, PCP, was being used to tranquilize some of the animals before the mutilations took place. The leaders of the occult this night were interested in the effects of PCP on humans, as they felt they might use this drug later when they began sacrificing humans on a large scale, so it was agreed that they would try it out on the four youngsters camped nearby. [Joe] stated that he accompanied four members of the cult who had tranquilizer rifles and watched as they shot each of the four youngsters. [Joe] said it appeared that the dosage of PCP was too great as about two hours later the teenagers were dead, apparently from the drug. It was decided that being as they were dead, they would use their bodies in the planned ceremonies. [Joe] then described how the sex organs were removed from the bodies, syringes were used to withdraw the blood, nipples were cut from their breasts, ears were sliced off and all these parts were used in the ceremony. [Joe] described the ceremony that took place as being the same type ceremony held anywhere in the country. He said one of the female members of the group would act as 'the sacrifice' for that particular ceremony. Everyone present would get extremely high on a variety of drugs, would begin 'chants' to the Devil and offer prayers to him. The female 'sacrificial lamb' would begin by drinking blood from the victims and then would pass the blood around for all the members to drink. The sex organs would be used in sexual activities performed by the members, among other atrocities too horrible to mention at this point. [Joe] stated that after this ceremony was over, he watched the bodies of the four young people being cut up and placed in burlap bags. He did not see what became of the bodies, but felt they were probably buried in a nearby gravel pit.

"[Joe] went on to state that he had participated in the killing and mutilation of a number of small animals and cattle throughout [three states], but this was the first and only time he had ever participated in human sacrifice. He described the killing of the cattle in a similar way. The animals would be shot with tranquilizer pellets. He and others would then lay down pieces of cardboard which they would step on, working their way up to the animal, thereby leaving no tracks. A stimulant, amial nitrate, would then be used by holding it against the [animal's] nostrils to speed up the body functions. Then large veterinarian syringes would be used to withdraw the blood. After the animal was dead, the sex organs, etc. would be removed. In some cases if snow were on the ground, either [Joe] or one of the others would melt it in a circular area around the body by ... use of a blowtorch. He said they all got a particular 'thrill' over not leaving any tracks and often talked about how the authorities would sooner or later begin blaming the whole thing on UFO's, which is what came to pass."

Joe told the investigator that he withdrew from the occult group when members began to talk about sacrificing more humans. He was arrested in 1973 on charges stemming from his involvement in a car theft ring and had been in prison from that time until the time this interview was conducted.

What follows in the report is a list of 13 individuals (six males and seven females) with their current (at the time this report was filed) addresses and information from law enforcement officials regarding their activities at that time.

One female whose name appears on the list is a former assistant district attorney whom local authorities stated associated with "disreputable people."

Others on the list (including one female who was once one of the F.B.I.'s top 10 fugitives) were reported by local authorities to be suspected of occult activities; some were under surveillance at the time this report was filed, and several were suspected of drug trafficking.

The investigator who filed the report indicated that his interviews with authorities in the areas where the listed individuals lived revealed that other investigations were ongoing which concerned the cattle mutilations as well as several murders which were thought to be occult-related.

In two murder cases, the young female victims had been battered to death. They were found nude and had "satanic messages" clipped to their bodies. Coroners' reports indicated that the bodies showed signs of ritual activities as there were indications the victims had been kneeling for a length of time prior to their deaths.

Joe had told the investigator of a certain ritual during which "symbolic sacrifices were made of females who were required to be in a kneeling position for an extended period while various acts of 'fertility' were committed on her body."

According to the investigator's report, authorities near the city where the four teenagers allegedly were killed verified the existence of the gravel pit described by Joe and indicated that they intended to dig there "as soon as weather permits" to "attempt to locate any body parts that might be buried there. They also verified that location has been the gathering spot for a number of years for occult groups, hippies, etc., mainly during the summer months, and that occult 'ceremonies' had been held there."

Reports from other authorities contacted during the course of this investigation indicated that murders had taken place in their localities which had details similar to those described by Joe. In one such case, officials described the killing of a local male "who had his sex organs removed, ears cut off, drained of blood and has been trussed up in a 'fetal' position held by wire and used at the scene of several rituals in (city). Members of the occult transported the body to (city, state) where (city) authorities were able to make two arrests and recover the body."

The investigator also told in his report of several incidents that occurred during the course of his investigation and interviews with Bill and Joe.

Several nights in a row, a car pulled up outside the jail where Bill and Joe were being held. The occupants of the car called out the names of the two inmates while turning the car's headlights on and off.

The evening after this activity ceased, Bill and Joe said they received a package in their cellblock which they alleged was delivered to them by a jailer-deputy. They said the package contained a .25-caliber semi-automatic pistol, a hunting knife and a note which read "We hope this will help you. We need you both. Try to use these before March 30. Peace."

According to the report, the inmates contacted the investigator and turned the pistol and knife over to him. He wrote that they "were obviously shaken over this experience."

Following this incident, the two subjects were moved (under fictitious names) to another jail in a neighboring county. Shortly after this move, the investigator received a call from a man who said that he had been an inmate with Bill at the jail from which the inmates had been moved. The caller said that he needed to get in touch with Bill, but hung up when asked to come to the investigator's office to discuss the matter.

The investigator checked with officials at the first jail and learned that the name the caller had given him did not appear on the jail's log of previous and current inmates. The investigator stated in the report, "It became obvious to me that someone was making an effort to locate the two prisoners for some purpose that did not appear to be legitimate."

The report goes into detail at this point regarding the reliability of the inmates interviewed. Federal prison officials who had knowledge of the two "assured me that both were considered to be sane and very reliable. Both were considered model prisoners. [Bill] had provided the warden at [a federal prison] with reliable information in the past pertaining to activities inside the prison. [Joe] cooperated with the F.B.I. in its investigation of his case and testified against co-defendants as well as providing the information necessary for the F.B.I. to make the case against several others. [One F.B.I. agent] remarked to me that he considered [Joe] to be 100% reliable."

And the report concludes:

"[Bill and Joe] have repeatedly stressed to me the fact that the occult believes its '10-year cycle' is coming to an end around

August or September of 1975, and from that point on, human sacrifices will occur throughout the United States. They insist that [the leader of the group whose names appeared on the list of thirteen] and others in the occult have detailed lists of intended victims to be included in the human sacrifices ...

"In my opinion, the alleged activities of such a group and the activities referred to by [Bill and Joe] should be looked into more closely. Each name given to me by them turned out to be someone who was suspected of either this type of activity or other unlawful activities in their respective areas. The cattle mutilations have been very real indeed, occurring in [eight states]. Events such as the pistol and knife given to them and the ensuing phone call to my office have appeared to be symptoms of some type of effort to either get them away from authorities or quiet them once and for all. In several states ... doctors of veterinary medicine have agreed that some type of tranquilizing agent was used in bringing down several animals. Murders have taken place in other states that at least appear at this point to be occult-related.

"It should be pointed out that none of the names described by [Bill and Joe] as being part of the occult, or activities and events described by them can be either proven or disproved at this point. It is possible that [Bill and Joe] have concocted a fantastic, bizarre and grisly story which is so complicated that they could never be proven as liars, yet I cannot see what they could hope to gain from concocting such a story. They would probably gain a great deal if it all proved to be true.

"Investigators from (state) have interviewed both [subjects] and stated they feel both men are telling the truth. Both ... have given information to [the chief jailer] for [the county jail] ... about certain activities of other inmates in that jail which have proven to be absolutely true. Such an organization is not as fantastic as it may first appear if compared to the famous 'Manson family' as described in the recent book *Helter Skelter* written by the district attorney from California who prosecuted Manson.

"Throughout the initial interviews of [Bill and Joe] I was assisted by (another investigator) ... [He] is a skilled investigator, and both he and I inserted certain false allegations about the cattle mutilations during our questions in an attempt to trip up [the two subjects], but both passed the 'test' with flying colors. I felt if they were concocting the story, they would have seized upon those allegations or at least some of them and incorporated them into their story.

"The information from the various states concerning the names given by [the subjects] and information contained in those states' investigative files appear to corroborate most of what [the subjects] have said. An example of this would be the information supplied to [an investigator for a cattlemen's association] wherein four totally independent sources have described the occult movement in detail which coincides with [the subjects'] story. The name [a 'satanic church' mentioned by both subjects] ... has never been publicized until recently, so it would be unlikely [the subjects] could have picked up the name by reading about it in some newspaper. Likewise, (city, state) authorities advise that the grave-robbing antics of [a female whose name appeared on the list of thirteen] in 1969 were not publicized, so it would appear [the subjects] could only have gained that information through an association with [her] or someone close to her.

"A proper investigation into this whole matter would naturally require considerable manpower and coordination. I must admit to having mixed emotions about such a horror story being true, but at the same time cannot help but feel such an investigation would be justified. If it were established that such a thing does exist, then the persons involved should most certainly be brought to justice."

In summary, this document which was given to me was an official report done by an investigator and prepared for an elected official. This report is highly significant in that it was signed in the spring of 1975; the allegations regarding the cattle mutilations are believable in their detail and accuracy, and the information regarding the occult groups and their human sacrifice rituals are too close to what we are experiencing in the 1980s to be considered mere coincidence. In other words, the information provided by this investigation and the written report was (and is) extremely valuable.

It is also significant that this report was written long before occult activity was a recognized subject with widespread media attention. Also, we know that the government has spent large amounts of tax-payers' money studying the "UFO connection" and that they have found nothing.

The subjects interviewed for this report went into great detail explaining how the cattle mutilations were made to look as if they were related somehow to UFO activity, and that this was a source of great pride to the perpetrators in that they were able to get the best of the government investigators.

The discussion of PCP in this report is significant, too, in that this was not a subject of great issue in the mid-70s. It is unlikely that the subjects could have invented the part of the story concerning the sophisticated method of using amial nitrate to efficiently bleed the cattle.

While it is possible that these subjects made up this entire story, the accuracy of the story is significant in that the methods described are identical to those reported by victims of satanic cults whom we have interviewed in recent years. Furthermore, there has been extensive evidence of many animals and some humans killed whose body parts were removed and used in the methods described by the two subjects interviewed for this report.

In this report, a total of 16 different people from eight states were mentioned who allegedly had participated *together* in ritual activities. Additionally, four other individuals who were not named in the report corroborated (according to an investigator) similar events and indicated knowledge of an occult meeting that would be held in a midwestern state; they also named the city mentioned by the two subjects. These unnamed individuals even referred to the '10-year cycle' when discussing human sacrifices.

Far too much information in this report has been verified by reliable sources (including law enforcement officials) to be considered mere coincidence or fictitious. Our office has attempted to contact people close to this investigation, but we have been given precious little information.

One of the key figures in the report is dead. Another has been promoted to a much higher position and has stated simply that the entire matter was "a hoax."

Another individual was reported to have stated that the jailer-deputy who allegedly gave the gun and knife to the two subjects took a polygraph test. He failed the polygraph, but it was reported that that was probably due to the fact that he was "nervous," and that, therefore, he was not guilty of the allegations against him.

It is not known if the two subjects ever took a polygraph test or, if they did, what the results were; we do know, however, that they agreed to take the test. None of the other details of this report have been explained regarding the information provided by the subjects including how they could have had such detailed knowledge regarding verified murders and other crimes as well as a large number of people spread out over eight states.

As time-consuming and frustrating as our investigations have been regarding this and other reports on file, our office continues to move forward. We are convinced that occult practitioners in this and other countries do communicate with one another and that they share information. It is likely that (as many victims have reported) these individuals come together at specific times and places to conduct rituals.

We also believe that, from time to time, innocent bystanders become victims by being in the wrong place at the wrong time.

FIVE

CHILD ABUSE
AND THE OCCULT

Probably nothing stirs our emotions more than the subject of child abuse, and the investigation of such abuse is the most controversial aspect of occult research. The subject has polarized families as well as entire communities.

When I began my research in 1982, a friend gave me a book entitled *Michelle Remembers*. This is a nonfiction book written by Dr. Larry Pazder with and about a patient of his, Michelle Smith. As an adult, Michelle had begun to experience a number of problems for which her doctors could find no physical basis.

Psychiatrists were consulted and, after several years of intensive therapy, Dr. Pazder was able to help Michelle recall her early childhood. Michelle had been molested, and the details of the incidents of molestation were quite bizarre. She recalled having been taken to "satanic rituals" by her mother. In one particular ceremony, after lengthy incantations she was "married" to the beast "Satan."

When I read the book, I was certain that the story was the result of someone's very vivid imagination. I simply could not believe that the incidents recounted really had happened or that a mother would do such things to her own child.

Of course, in 1982, I did not believe that there were really people called "witches" and "satanists," nor did I know that there were tax-exempt satanic religious organizations. It was only after a great deal of research that in 1983 I became aware of the reality of their existence.

By becoming involved at the adolescent level, I was "getting my feet wet" by investigating the bizarre occult activities of teenagers, but dealing with or accepting such practices as "ritual abuse" was, in my opinion, making the quantum leap.

I had the pleasure of meeting Dr. Pazder at a seminar in 1985. He gave the participants a definition of ritual abuse which is the most complete I have found to this day: "Repeated physical, emotional, mental and spiritual assaults combined with a systematic use of symbols, ceremonies and machinations designed and orchestrated to attain malevolent effect [to turn the victim against self, society and God]."

One of the most interesting ritual child abuse cases which I have been involved is that of Casandra Hoyer. "Sam" (as she is called by her friends) is a tall, nice-looking woman in her early 40's who used to work as a model. Today she lives in fear that members of a "destructive satanic cult" will come to get her.

Sam had kept her story to herself until 1988 and, with the exception of her therapist and a handful of trusted friends, no one knew who she was or that she even existed.

After several years of intense therapy, she was diagnosed as having a "multiple personality disorder." This is a very complex psychiatric disorder but, simply stated, it means that the patient, who, in most cases, has suffered tremendous abuse (often sexual), develops a number of alter-personalities as a way to "escape" the abuse psychologically while continuing to endure it physically. Once the abuse has ended for whatever reason, the individual may lead a relatively normal life for years before symptoms resurface, causing him or her to seek counseling. Intense therapy often reveals the existence of these alter-personalities, and the goal of the therapy then becomes the "integration" of the various personalities into a whole, healthy human being once more. What is significant is that most patients diagnosed by psychiatrists as victims of generational satanic abuse have multiple personality disorders.

Sam relates her story publicly to church groups, on television shows and with members of the media. She talks about ritual abuse and the abuse of children. She first told her story at the New Covenant Baptist Church in Richmond, Virginia. She explained to the audience that she had been "satanically abused" since she was 3-years-old. At that tender age, Sam stated, her own mother turned her over to a "satanic cult." She was a twin, a perfectly formed child, but her identical sister had been born with a deformed foot. According to Sam, her twin sister was murdered in a ritual because she was not perfect.

Sam also explained processes of brainwashing to the audience, the use of clinical drugs (as opposed to street drugs) and hypnosis to deeply embed suggestions in her mind that she would not act upon for many years. At the age of 17, Sam was "released" into what she calls "the normal world" with little memory of what she had experienced as a child. Only through therapy was she able to recall vivid details of those horrible years.

Today she recounts specific events such as ceremonies of sacrifice with adults and adolescents clad in black or brown robes, moving in procession around a fire, holding black or white candles. She remembers naked women draped across an altar, symbols of human free will, according to Sam. She states that there were goblets and bottles filled with the blood of animals such as cats and cows, and some which contained human blood.

She also recalls bottles of preservatives such as formaldehyde which were used by the cultists for preserving flesh, and that there were small animals hung on the sides of the altar.

The rituals also included all manner of sexual perversions which involved children and animals.

A parody of a Christian hymn was sung: "Open the gate, haste, haste, for Satan waits."

Ritual ceremonies were held in barns and in open fields on private property. The most important ceremonies, Sam says, were held on Christmas and Easter in order to blaspheme the most holy Christian days.

In *Insight* magazine (January 11, 1988) Jeffrey Burton Russell, professor of history at the University of California at Santa Barbara and an authority on the idea of the devil in Western civilization, traced the current religious satanism to the rise of an interest in the occult that began in the 1960s as part of the New Age counterculture.

"The rash of appallingly degenerate crime, including the violation of children and the mutilation of animals, can be tolerated only by a society determined to deny at any cost the radical existence of evil," says Russell.

A Burnet, Texas, case, tried in February of 1986, involved allegations of sexual abuse of a pre-teenage girl, abuse which appears to have been ritual. This case was distinguished from other sexual abuse cases by two factors: testimony was given regarding bizarre occurrences with reference to the abuse, and the district attorney questioned prospective jurors with regard to witchcraft and satanism. However, the most important distinguishing element of this case (as opposed to other cases where "ritual abuse" has been alleged) is that there was a conviction.

Trial testimony included graphic details of sexual orgies which involved children and animals. The young victim testified in lengthy periods over two days, describing the events and stating that the ritual ceremonies had been filmed.

On trial was Gerry Herring, the young girl's uncle. Herring and five other persons had been indicted in 1983 on charges of sexually abusing five children.

His niece was 8-years-old at the time of the alleged sexual abuse by her uncle. Her parents had been away for the weekend with relatives, and Herring (the brother of the girl's mother) had volunteered to baby-sit. The child testified that Herring had threatened her with a knife during the sexual attacks, and that he had cut her leg on one occasion when she tried to run out of the bedroom. She showed the jury a scar on her leg which she said resulted from the knife cut. She told the jury that a group of adults and several children had come to her home on Saturday, a few days after she had been raped by Herring. She said that she and the other children had been given injections that made her "feel sick, dizzy and numb."

The young victim also testified that she had watched while her older brother was whipped and sexually abused, that the adults had injected themselves and a horse that was kept on the premises, that several of the adults used "bright lights and a camera on legs" to photograph the activities, and that she was made to take off her clothes and get into bed with three male adults and a female adult. Several of the adults, she said, were naked at various times.

A psychiatrist hired by the defense testified that, in his opinion, "the accusations of the two children stemmed from fantasy and not reality."

At another point in the questioning, he stated in response to a question from the prosecutor, "My research is incomplete, but it seems your case is preposterous."

An interesting note here is that this psychiatrist, a Dr. Gilbert Klinman, had never interviewed the children and had never testified for the prosecution in an abuse case. He had only interviewed the defendants in this case.

Dr. David Poole, a psychiatrist hired by the prosecution and who had testified in a number of sexual abuse cases, stated that he had administered tests to the children to determine various aspects of their developmental stages and whether they knew the difference between fantasy and reality. He said, "In my opinion, the children have certainly been traumatized. They fit the profile of children who have been sexually abused." Several of the children interviewed by Dr. Poole reported witnessing what they thought were staged murders.

Gerry Herring was convicted of the charges against him and sentenced to seven years in prison. The charges against the other defendants eventually were dropped.

It is crucial to understand why these charges were dropped because, when charges such as these are dismissed, the public often has the impression that this means the alleged activities never occurred. In this particular case, the district attorney explained that the charges against the other adults were dropped for a number of reasons, some of which stemmed from the fact that the defendants were indicted separately.

D.A. Sam Oatman told reporters that the defendants had been indicted separately because sexual abuse was not covered under the state's organized crime statutes. Separate indictments meant separate trials; the children would have to testify again and again. He stated that the case already had "traumatized the children to the extent that the State is of the opinion that the further prosecution of this case would result in victimizing the children far more than justice should allow."

Shirley King, the sister of Gerry Herring, stated in response to the dismissal of charges against the other adults, "I just felt like my children couldn't take anymore, and I didn't want to have them go through another trial," adding that the trial was the worst part of the entire experience for her children.

In addition, a $3 million slander suit had been brought against the family with what she called "devastating" results. She stated that existing laws regarding the sexual abuse of children were inadequate. "People have to believe these children if we are going to do anything about this problem," she added. "I believe my children."

Additional reasons for the dismissal of charges were cited by D.A. Oatman. He stated that his office's caseload was such that further trials would be delayed indefinitely, thus weakening the prosecution's case and making convictions unlikely. Further, he stated that he had been denied a request for additional time to investigate leads which had resulted from Herring's trial. He also stated that motions granted by the court had the potential of causing great expense to the county. Because the expense "may well exceed that of the Gerry Herring case," it "does not warrant the further prosecution of this case."

In this particular case, the children discussed sex with animals, being injected and "feeling dizzy," orgiastic involvement with alleged multiple offenders, the staging of "murders," the taking of photographs, all with an occult thread weaving them together.

These allegations are virtually identical to those made in a number of cases in which I have been involved. I have interviewed children, their parents, other family members, therapists and law enforcement officials in each of these cases, and the consistencies go far beyond the possibility of coincidence.

The consistent descriptions of ceremonies include participants dressed in black robes, chanting, burning candles, references to the devil and Satan, being forced to drink liquids which taste like human excrement, blood and (in a few cases) cannibalism.

Ritually abused children often describe being placed in open graves and having dirt thrown on them and being thrown into ponds, swimming pools or lakes and then being rescued (which experts believe may be a means of simulating near-death experiences).

Difficulty in the Courts

Clearly, it is very difficult to prosecute cases of ritual child abuse, and even harder to gain convictions. It concerns me that a great many people believe that it is so difficult because the children's allegations are basically untrue. If the children are telling the truth, they ask, then why isn't there a conviction? And why, in some cases, isn't there even an indictment?

One of the most obvious reasons that these cases never go to trial is to spare the children any further emotional trauma. In a case where there are multiple allegations of sexual abuse, the children must testify in individual trials. This becomes a very lengthy process and each case can drag on for several years. With these kinds of delays, the children begin to forget certain critical details, and, too, the children begin to sound rehearsed after having been interviewed and having testified over and over again. Defense attorneys often pick up on this and state that the children have been coached.

Another problem in prosecuting these cases is that, in most states, the children must testify in an open court and face the accused. This is very traumatic for young children, especially when their allegations are true. Facing someone who truly has abused them is emotionally devastating to most children. Too, quite a few cases involve children under the age of seven, and most states will not allow a child under seven to testify unless their psychological maturity can be firmly established. This is extremely difficult to do.

Next comes the problem of physical evidence. In most cases, children are so traumatized by the abuse and so terrified by threats of what will happen to them or their families if they "tell" that they do not tell anyone what has happened to them for months or even years. By this time, of course, there is no physical evidence present such as semen or saliva. Vaginal or anal tears most likely have healed as well.

During the Herring trial, Dr. Beth Nauert, a pediatrician who specializes in cases of physically and sexually abused children, stated, "We do not necessarily have findings when an adult has intercourse with a child. If the findings are not present, that does not mean they were not abused. Most things like small tears will go away in about six weeks. Also lubricants and muscle relaxant drugs make intercourse easier ... Finding no physical evidence today does not mean these children were not abused."

Another reason why some children who have been sexually abused do not show signs of physical injury is that they were made to engage in sexual activities with small animals, usually dogs, and/or they were raped with small items or mechanical devices.

If vaginal or anal scarring is found, the defense often will allege that the abuse could have been committed by anyone, even the children's parents, and was not necessarily committed by the individuals identified by the children. A defense attorney does not have to prove this, but the use of such a tactic will plant small seeds of doubt in the minds of jurors, seeds that will play havoc with the prosecution's case. The defense even may bring in expert witnesses to testify to *the possibility* of this, further creating doubts in the jurors' minds.

A problem with manpower also exists. Caseloads are often overwhelming, especially when a community has many other criminal issues to deal with, and investigators are stretched pretty thin. Money is also a major issue, as unpleasant as this is to admit. It takes money to investigate, prosecute and hire the experts needed in cases such as these in order to obtain convictions. States and cities have budgets with very real limits, budgets that only will allow certain expenses to be incurred in cases they must investigate and prosecute. If a victim's family wants more expert witnesses than the budget will allow, that family is expected to assist the state or city with the costs. Many families simply do not have these funds.

Victims' families must also consider from the outset the possibility of liable suits. If a case does not make it into court, or if it does go to court but charges are dismissed or the defendant is found "not guilty," the family is left wide open to civil actions by the defendant.

Details such as these may seem insignificant, but are critical to our understanding of the reasons some cases are not prosecuted and why, in other cases, charges are dismissed.

Cases involving adult survivors (such as that of Cassandra Hoyer) can be extremely difficult because, in most cases, such survivors either have been patients in mental institutions or under the care of therapists for years. Defense attorneys will destroy their credibility immediately.

Just because something cannot be proven "beyond a reasonable doubt" in a court of law does not mean that it did not happen, but this appears to be the measure of believability for the public. Charges of sexual abuse are probably the easiest to allege, the most difficult to bring to trial, and nearly impossible to prove. Convictions are rare and hard-won.

Am I painting a very bleak picture? Perhaps, but it is important to continue trying to improve the system which is supposed to protect our children. We cannot work toward such improvement if society does not demonstrate greater concern for the safety and welfare of its smallest, most helpless citizens. The irony is that we feel *lucky* when a conviction is obtained and a child molester goes to prison; he may even be given the option of treatment in a psychiatric facility.

In January 1988, the *Commercial Appeal* of Memphis, Tennessee, investigated 36 cases of ritual abuse in more than 30 communities. That newspaper reported the following: Charged-91; dismissed-45; acquitted-11; convicted-23; pending-12.

Charges Dismissed

What are the real numbers? No one really knows. While the figures above appear to be significant, the cases represented do not include several with which I am familiar. There is no central reporting agency or agency which collects information on cases involving allegations of ritual child abuse. However, I feel that the sampling cited here significant enough to warrant more in-depth studies and extensive investigation into this apparent phenomenon.

Often I am asked where the bodies are in cases where children have alleged witnessing one or more murders during ritual ceremonies.

Some investigators have stated that cult members who are involved in this kind of criminal activity are quite good at covering their tracks by disposing of the bodies in creative ways such as burning them to ashes, distributing them in pieces in various locations, to eating them as part of a ritual ceremony.

This always ruffles the feathers of critics who say, "Oh, how convenient. No proof of ritual murder." Some even have referred to the idea of ritual murder as a hoax and (as discussed earlier) have called it an "urban legend."

My concern is not where the bodies are, but how many of the bodies and body parts found every year by law enforcement officials throughout the country may be connected to these types of crimes. Many "John Does" are found every year and never identified. Many bodies are found each year so badly decomposed that the cause of death cannot be determined nor the identity established. No suspects ever are arrested in John Doe cases; if officials cannot identify the deceased or determine the cause of death, they cannot build a case against a suspect or establish a motive. There are plenty of bodies out there connected to plenty of questions about who they are and how they died. These cases are seldom investigated because of the manpower and money problems mentioned earlier.

One of the most widely publicized cases involving allegations of ritual abuse was the McMartin Preschool case. A total of 323 charges were filed against ten defendants after 380 children were interviewed by Children's Institute International, a Los Angeles sex abuse center.

The children alleged that they had been repeatedly sexually molested and that animal mutilations, drugs and threats were frequent elements of the abuse. Some contended that they had been made to drink blood and participate in satanic rituals.

In another case, children at the Rogers Park Jewish Community Center in Chicago alleged that they had been sexually abused. Their reports included detailed descriptions of satanic rituals and animal mutilations.

In the McMartin Preschool case, charges were dropped against all of the defendants except Peggy Buckey and her son, and they may yet be acquitted. In the Rogers Park case, one defendant (a janitor) was tried and acquitted although the children had made allegations against all of the teachers at the school.

Major investigations of alleged preschool ritual abuse cases have taken place in cities all across the nation. Nearly every case faded into obscurity as the children began to forget details and to speak like little robots. Every time that charges against child molesters are dismissed for reasons other than that those charges were determined to be unfounded, not only do the children, families, police officers and prosecutors suffer, but also the young children whom the molester will make his next victims.

It saddens me that, when the general public reads in a newspaper article that "charges were dismissed," they assume this means that the defendants were innocent. Often this is not the case, and those involved in the case continue to be plagued by fear, remorse, guilt and shame. Victimized children and their families often spend many years in therapy trying to come to terms with the trauma they have experienced. This is the other side of these stories which the public never sees.

Green Light to Offenders

Roland Summit, a psychiatrist at the Harbor/UCLA Medical Center, says that there are three ways of looking at such cases. "Either there are a number of people who have discovered a way to entrap preschool children; or this is a case of mass hysteria formed by naive people; or these cases are, at the core, conventional child molestation cases in which the victims have somehow exaggerated the experiences into fantasy ... What is striking about these cases is that the children, unless they are speaking a different language that we can't understand, are telling stories so similar to each other. Their descriptions of ritual cult practices come out of nowhere in their backgrounds, and the stories are told to adults — parents or therapists — with no background or knowledge of ritual cults. And they match perfectly the descriptions of adults who have survived these things."

He went on to say that these allegations are hard to believe because responsible people don't want to believe that such atrocities can happen. "But if there is something to this, those who are doing it now have unchallenged power."

A 1985 case was reported only locally by the *Albany Herald* of Albany, Georgia.

Two men and two women were convicted of child molestation and sentenced to serve three years in prison.

Following his sentencing of the four adults, the judge commented, "... this is one of the strangest cases I have ever sat on. I must admit that there are some things that bother me about this case. I certainly am not going to comment on these things with the news media present, but there are some things that bother me."

The prosecution's key witness was 46-year-old Gloria Bohannon who was confined to a wheelchair due to a physical handicap. She had lived with Robert "Redhawk" Hunt and his wife Mardy "Bluestar" Hunt, two of the defendants, for 18 months. She testified that the Hunts and two other adults had engaged in "wicca" (the religion of witchcraft) ceremonies and rituals and also had inducted her into their cult. She claimed that she had been "skyclad" (naked) for the initiation ceremony and that the other adults had engaged in sexual activities.

The charges were brought because the Hunt's 4-year-old daughter was present during all of the rituals.

Bohannon described twice-monthly ceremonies during which the defendants donned black robes with pentagrams, offered prayers to the "land of the dead," and placed curses upon their enemies. The witness claimed that, following these ceremonial curses, all of the adults and the child removed their clothes. The adults engaged in orgiastic activities and, at the end of the services, the child was sexually molested by her own father who said to her, "Daddy's going to make you feel good."

The witness was able to escape the home and the rituals practiced there by giving a note to a nurse's aid who visited her.

The city of Richmond, Virginia, was shocked in 1984 by allegations of satanic ritual abuse and murder in the case of 12-year-old Jessica Hatch who disappeared on a February evening while walking to her grandmother's house just nine blocks from her home. Jessica's body was found several months later, too decomposed to determine the cause of death. Identification was established through the use of X-rays taken prior to her death and compared to X-rays of the body.

Reporters Frank Greene and Ed Briggs of the *Richmond Times Dispatch*, probed the case further. It was determined later that year, that suspicions of cult activity were confirmed after authorities took two young girls into custody. The girls were 7-and 5-years-old.

They had allegedly been sexually abused by their mother and her boyfriend.

"The mother in that case ... was into satanism," said a Richmond law enforcement official. It was reported that the oldest child said she witnessed the murder of Jessica Hatch. She talked of brutality ... she also claimed her mother and others would make her eat human entrails. The police, however, were not able to verify these allegations due to the emotional condition of both girls. Mental health persons did not feel the girls were capable of testifying.

Police officials were granted search warrants for the mother's Richmond apartment and her new residence outside of the city. Items which were discovered during the search of the rural home included seven ceremonial chalices, three red robes and one black robe, a ceramic witch and a satanic painting.

Additional evidence which corroborated the statements of an informant was found during the search of the apartment in Richmond.

One investigator stated in the search warrant application "that the acts of sodomy against the two girls occurred as a part of devil worship." Currently, the homicide of Jessica Hatch remains an open and unsolved case.

Such cases are not confined to the United States. A Canadian case went to trial last year with charges of ritual abuse; a conviction was obtained.

In July 1988, three High Court appeals judges in Nottingham County, England, reviewed evidence in the cases of 17 children during closed wardship hearings. The Nottingham County Council won adoption orders for all of the children, and the justices turned evidence over to police officials for investigation of 15 adults.

At one party it is claimed by the children that they had been forced by the adults to participate in satanic rituals during which sheep were killed and their blood drunk. During one ritual, a child's blood was drained using a craft knife, and the other children were made to drink the blood from a silver cup. Cases of ritual child abuse have occurred in virtually every country in the world.

A crime is a crime, and every criminal incident should, of course, be investigated thoroughly and prosecuted to the full extent of the law. When a criminal's religious beliefs (be those beliefs wiccan, satanic or whatever) spill over into the commission of a crime, that information should be documented. This is **not** religious persecution; this is criminal prosecution utilizing all information available to determine motive and intent.

Linda Wallace Pete, a Los Angeles attorney who represents child abuse victims, states, "More people believe in UFOs than in ritual abuse. When you talk about black robes and human sacrifice, the case goes out the window."

The evidence surrounding ritual abuse of children is substantial, but no one seems to care enough to compile the documentation. How many children must die or sustain permanent emotional injury before we, as a nation, decide that this horror must end?

SIX

FANTASY ROLE-PLAYING GAMES

As a child, you may have dreamed of flying on a magic carpet or accompanying Alice on one of her delightful adventures in Wonderland. As a little boy, perhaps you imagined that you were a knight riding away from your castle to slay the evil dragon that stood guard over your kingdom's stolen wealth. As a little girl, you pictured yourself a princess held captive in an ivy-covered tower, knowing that the prince would arrive just in time to rescue you from a terrible fate. Such is the stuff of childhood fantasies.

As you grew and matured, the fairy tales of youth paled in comparison to real life adventures like feeling the solid crack of ball-on-bat, camping out in the woods, sleeping over at the home of a friend, taking family trips to faraway places. Still later came the excitement of dating, driving a car and finally, venturing away from the security of your parents' home to face the world as an independent adult.

At each step along the way to maturity, fantasies and make-believe played smaller and smaller roles in your life. Reality, while not as easily manipulated, was preferable to daydreams simply because it was real. You discovered that real life, for all its hardships, brings real joy and real accomplishment, better by far than any that exist only in the mind. As an adult, you have been able to enjoy adventure films and mystery novels, and have returned easily to the real world once the last credit has rolled or the last page has been turned.

Sadly, there are those who, for a variety of reasons, do not have a solid grasp on reality. Some of these individuals find the fantasies of childhood far more rewarding than the day-to-day details of their lives. There also are those who are functioning happily and have a world of endless possibilities ahead of them, but who occasionally look for a little extra "kick," a temporary yet powerful rush of excitement. For all of these people, fantasy role-playing games present a very dangerous and very real threat.

Dungeons and Dragons

While many are familiar with the term "fantasy role-playing games," few are sure of exactly what they are. The first and most critical concept to accept is that these games are *not* board games like "Monopoly" and "Chutes and Ladders." The games with which we are concerned are about role playing; they are mind games acted out in the imagination which sometimes spill over with deadly results into the real world. Many role-playing games are on the market today, but the granddaddy of them all and still the most popular is "Dungeons & Dragons," commonly referred to as D & D.

D & D was created in the mid-70s by Dave Arneson and E. Gary Gygax. It is manufactured by TSR Inc. of Lake Geneva, Wisconsin. The company was opened with an investment of just $1,000 in 1974. The earliest game sets were in the form of paperback booklets which contained concepts along the lines of war games and were marketed primarily to adults.

It soon became popular with junior high and high school students, and a major transformation began to take place toward the end of the decade. The game soon was marketed in three sets: the Basic Set (a box with a booklet and oddly shaped dice), the Expert Set (similarly boxed) and the Advanced D & D set which consisted of hardbound books.

Role-playing, a technique originally used by therapists for behavior modification, is the foundation of the game. Each player is instructed to merge or "become one" with his game character.

As stated in a publication from TSR entitled *Your Personal Invitation to Adventure* (copyright 1980), "... Once past the portal, you will find that Dungeons & Dragons adventure games are unlike any games you have ever played before. There is no playing board, no piece to move from space to consecutive space, and no play money. In Dungeons & Dragons role-playing games, the action takes place in the imagination of the players themselves. Role-playing requires that the players become so familiar with their game personas that they become one with their characters in their imaginations while playing the game. They will react throughout the game as the characters would in each given situation. The player becomes an actor. Through the character, he or she may vicariously 'act out' heroic deeds, fight great battles with courage and brilliance, or perhaps flee to fight yet another day."

Fantasy Role-Playing Games

How the Game Is Played

The game itself is set in the middle ages. Each player is solely responsible for the actions of his character, and all players are under the direction of the Dungeon Master. Play begins with six rolls of the dice by each participant who then uses the six numbers he has rolled to organize the traits of his character (based upon strength, intelligence, wisdom, constitution, dexterity and charisma). If he wishes, he may roll again to determine the physical size of his character after which he assigns his persona a race (such as elf, dwarf, etc.), a class (occupation) and an alignment (attitude or outlook).

The classes include cleric (druid), fighter (paladin, ranger), magic-user (illusionist), thief (assassin), monk and bard. The alignments are lawful-good, lawful-neutral, lawful-evil, neutral, chaotic-good, chaotic-neutral, and chaotic-evil.

After these assignments have been made, each player rolls the dice again to obtain his character's "hit points." Hit points represent the persona's stamina or the amount of damage the character can sustain in an encounter with the enemy. This damage can be minor or severe, ranging from a stab wound to a coma and even death.

The dice are rolled again to give the character money, supplies, weapons and armor. The players whose characters are clerics or magic users roll yet again to obtain the spells he will be able to use. Finally, each player chooses a name for his character.

The Dungeon Master (DM) is usually a far more experienced player; his is a very powerful role in the game. He controls everything that happens with the exception of the characters' actions, although he may restrict them as he chooses. He also controls the lives of the characters in that he may destroy them. The DM is not supposed to destroy a character unless that character has lost control and altered the game.

His major responsibility is to create an adventure or dungeon for the characters. Books are available with prepared dungeons, but most DMs prefer to create the dungeons themselves. He must invent the scenery that the characters may encounter in the course of the adventure, the climate, the smells, the monsters and the treasure. This process can take from 36 to 48 hours of work. One woman has left her career to be a full-time DM; she is supported entirely by her D & D players.

A game of D & D is played with two or more players. The average number of players is five (including the DM). The DM begins by providing the players with a detailed description of the countryside he has created, the action that is taking place there, sounds and smells the players may notice, and other pertinent information. Each player then decides the action his character will take, and the DM informs him of the results.

A character may do *anything* the player controlling him wants him to do. For example, the DM might tell the players that they have come upon the entrance to a cave at midday. It is warm and they can hear what sounds like running water coming from inside the cave. Each player decides whether his character will enter the cave, throw in a rock to locate the water, yell into the cave, ignore it or take some other course of action.

Or perhaps the DM tells the players that they have discovered an underground chamber. In it are a table, some chairs, a desk with a number of jars on top, and a chest. Everything is covered with dust. The characters might first check the chamber for traps and then try to open the chest. While engaged in this activity, they are attacked by armed and angry orcs (human-like monsters resembling pigs).

A character who has spells at his disposal may protect himself and/or disable the enemy with an incantation. Most characters must choose to fight. They choose their weapons and begin a series of rolls of the dice. The DM rolls a six-sided die for the orcs, and each player rolls it as well; these rolls are to determine initiative. Another series of rolls (using four-, six-, eight-, 10-, 12- and 20-sided dice) determines the injuries sustained by the characters and their enemies. The process continues until the character or the enemies are dead.

According to many young friends of mine who have been serious D & D players (and who, by the way, have chosen not to play anymore), all of this play is described so vividly that the participants actually can visualize it in their minds, almost as if they are watching it on a movie screen. Since it is imperative for the players to "become one" with their characters, the players feel extremes of emotion relative to the action of the game. They experience anger, frustration, fear, elation, triumph and despair.

During the course of most D & D games, characters must commit robbery and murder, and may choose to commit rape, mutilation and other atrocities. These activities are expected and condoned. The object of the game is survival, and a character may do anything he deems necessary to survive and have "fun" at the same time. The longer a character survives, the more powerful and wealthy he becomes.

According to Darren Molitor (a former D & D player who was convicted of murder and now is serving a life sentence with no parole in Oxford Federal Prison), "... the game is played or imagined entirely in the mind ... if it is played, let's say three to five times a week, four to eight hours each time, the conscious mind becomes accustomed to [the] violence. Suddenly you are no longer in total control of your mind. The 'fantasy game' becomes a 'reality game.' You begin to live it for real. Everything you do or say involves ... the game itself. You no longer play the game for enjoyment; you play it because you feel you have to. [Your mind] is possessed by the game. It is more dangerous than I can fully explain."

D & D has stimulated a great deal of controversy during the last nine years. Proponents such as Dr. Joyce Brothers have stated that the game stimulates the imagination and encourages group cooperation. In 1982, Dr. Brothers was hired by TSR, Hobbies, Inc., to tour nationally in order to promote the game to high school librarians, principals and teachers, and to encourage them to use D & D in the talented-and-gifted programs.

For men, D & D is the ultimate macho fantasy, a chance to be the heroic adventurers they can't be in the real world. According to the woman who introduced me to the game, it is "women's liberation with a vengeance. Not only does the D & D game allow women to stab people, it's accepted. You even get a bonus for striking from behind."

Hypnotic Control

D & D is limited only by the players' imaginations. For those with particularly vivid imaginations, the game can become a mystical experience, consuming, addictive and potentially dangerous.

Gary Gygax, one of the game's creators, has stated, "When you start playing out a fantasy, it can really eat up time and capture you totally. Most people can handle it, but there probably are exceptions. You can get very emotionally involved. I've got several characters I've nurtured through many tension-filled, terror-fraught D & D games, and I'd really be crushed if I lost one of them. They can become very much a part of you."

As a result of a number of cases that have been made public in the last few years, many parents, educators and mental health professionals have come to agree that this is a violent game and that youngsters who play it can over-identify with their characters to the extent that their safety is in jeopardy.

The game is extremely complex which means that many hours of preparation and study are required. Some children reach a point where they are "gaming" all the time in their minds whether they are at the game table are not. This constant gaming can result in a growing inability to distinguish the fantasy from reality. Many players have described real incidents in their lives during which they determined courses of action based upon what they thought their game characters would do.

Another major concern is that D & D and similar fantasy roleplaying games deal with the supernatural and magical powers. Some youngsters believe that they can gain these powers by playing the game and that, ultimately, they are indestructible and capable of doing anything they want. A few have gone so far as to become convinced that they are deities.

Deities (gods) play an important role in D & D. Serving a deity is a significant part of the game, and all characters are expected to have a patron god. Alignment assumes its full importance when tied to the worship of a deity. The only deities in this game are mythological gods and those of occult "religions."

Dr. Thomas Radecki, M.D., chairman of the National Coalition on Television Violence, has stated, "There is no doubt in my mind that the game 'Dungeons & Dragons' is causing young men to kill themselves and others. This game is one of nonstop combat and violence. Although I am sure that the people at TSR mean no harm, that is exactly what their games are causing. Based on player interviews and game materials, it is clear to me that this game is desensitizing players to violence and also causing an increased tendency to violent behavior."

The Experts Speak Out

"While TSR with its millions of dollars in profits can find some psychologists and psychiatrists to applaud its violence, nine out of 10 expert aggression researchers with whom I have spoken about this game expressed concern. All ten stated that, in their opinions based on entertainment violence research, the playing of violent games does cause an increased tendency toward violent behavior in many participants. While 'Dungeons & Dragons' is a game of cooperation and working together, that cooperation involves cooperating in violence, premeditated murder and war. While it does stimulate creative fantasies, these fantasies are of killing and horror. There is a need to get the honest information out to the American people. The research is overwhelming that violent entertainment is having a harmful effect on its participants. The changes are most often gradual and subtle. Few become murderers, but many become more aggressive. When a children's game is documented to cause many deaths, it should not be promoted through advertising and cartoon programming ..."

Dr. Arnold Goldstein, Ph.D., director of the Center for Research on Aggression at the University of Syracuse, has made the following statement: "Like many psychologists, I feel quite negatively about violent toys and violent play. With desensitization effects that start with childhood games, we help make violence a part of the American lifestyle. I think it's a bad idea to play a violent role-playing game such as 'Dungeons & Dragons.' For many, such play causes subtle changes which increase both a desensitization towards violence and a tendency to commit aggressive behavior. We psychologists use role-playing in therapy ... to bring about good effects. I must assume that the same teaching of destructive behavior will have harmful effects."

According to Dr. Goldstein, there are over 150 studies on the effects of role-playing on attitudes and behavior change in teaching positive behavior. "There is every reason to suspect that the role-playing of antisocial behavior will increase its probability of occurrence, especially when the behavior is practiced and rewarded as in a game-playing situation," Dr. Goldstein said.

Dr. John P. Murray, Ph.D., a psychologist at Boys' Town in Nebraska and an editor of the Surgeon General's original study of the effects of television violence, said, "The effect of being involved with aggressive symbols is an increased tendency to anger and violence in real life. A violent role-playing game would reinforce aggressive behavior. We routinely discharge violent games and violent play and encourage parents not to buy violent toys or games for their children since these increase violent fantasy and the tendencies towards violence."

I have observed the same in the course of my work. The vast majority of the information in the D & D manuals is violence-oriented. It consists of detailed descriptions of killing including occultic human sacrifice, assassination and premeditated murder as well as sadism and curses of insanity which include suicidal and homicidal mania. Much of the material draws upon ancient systems of demonology.

Magic and Demonology

The *Advanced Dungeon Master's Guide* notes for instance: "Suicidal Mania: This form of insanity causes the afflicted character to have overwhelming urges to destroy himself or herself whenever means are presented, a perilous situation, a weapon or anything else. The more dangerous the situation or item, the more likely the individual is to react self-destructively."

Here is one of the many occultic spells (The Summoning of the Cacodemon) from the *Advanced Player's Handbook*: "... This perilous exercise in dweomercraeft summons up a powerful demon of type IV, V, or VI, depending upon the demon's name being known to the magic user. The spell caster must be within a circle of protection [or a thaumaturgic triangle with protection from evil] and the demon confined to a pentagram [circled pentacle] if he or she is to avoid being slain or carried off by the summoned cacodemon. The summoned demon can be treated with as follows: ... by tribute of fresh human blood and the promise of one or more human sacrifices, the summoner can bargain with the demon for willing service ... the components of this spell are five flaming black candles, a brazier of hot coals upon which must be burned sulphur, bat hairs, lard, soot, mercurinitric acid crystals, mandrake root, alcohol, and a piece of parchment with the demon's name inscribed in runes inside a pentacle; and a dish of blood from some mammal [preferably a human, of course] placed inside the area where the cacodemon is to be held."

The information in this spell is authentic occult information including the references to pentagrams (the occult five-pointed star), runes (mystical cryptic writings) and the use of blood, as well as the components of the spell itself. Still, proponents of the game say that this is a game of good overcoming evil.

Writer Ed Greenwood stated in an article titled "Devilish Questions" which appeared in *Dragon* magazine (a monthly publication by TSR), "The perennial question is: Why did I not include Satan/Lucifer/the BIG DEVIL of Christian mythology and religious lore? Simply, I did not because Mr. Gygax has not, and I tried to adhere to official AD&D ["Advanced Dungeons & Dragons"] game rules whenever possible. His reasons for excluding Satan are best given by him; my own objections, from a game designer's point of view, boil down to the simple judgement that there is no room in the AD&D game system for a devil more powerful than Asmodeus. The few [in number] forces of good have enough to worry about without tipping the balance any further on the side of the diabolic [November, 1984]."

In my opinion, this is a complete how-to system, a basic primer on the occult. Even more frightening, while studies have proven a relationship between television violence and aggression/crime, and while the Surgeon General has made strong statements regarding this relationship, D & D is a *participatory* game in which the players actually become *involved* instead of just sitting back and watching as television viewers do. If television violence can result in negative behaviors of viewers, how can anyone question whether a participatory role-playing game might have less than positive effects on behavior?

Other concerns of mine and of Dr. Radecki are the apparent submissiveness of females and the depiction of rape and torture.

On the "Michael Jackson Show" (an ABC national radio talk show) which aired on September 17, 1985, Gary Gygax repeatedly denied that Dungeons & Dragons had ever caused a single incident of real harm of any kind. He denied, during a debate with one panelist, that D & D contains any mention of rape or torture. Dr. Radecki challenged him on this, pointing out that one player's handbook clearly explains that hirelings (mercenary soldiers that D & D players hire to assist them in combat) are prone to rape and pillage at random.

The basic *Player's Handbook* (Advanced D & D) informs the reader as follows: "Non-human Soldiers: The less-intelligent non-human will serve for 10% to 60% less cost, but these evil creatures will certainly expect to loot, pillage and rape freely at every chance, and kill [and probably eat] captives [page 31]."

Women objecting to rape are treated as follows in the *D & D Dungeon Master's Guide*: "Random Monster Encounters: Good-wife: Encounters are with a single woman, any seeming party of assault, rape, theft, murder [page 192]."

Darren Molitor was asked about the concepts of good and evil in D & D during an interview at Oxford Federal Prison. Darren responded, "There is good in the game, but very little, and anyone who has played [it] will tell you that evil will triumph over good in this game."

Accumulated evidence now indicates that fantasy role-playing games have been significant factors in at least 125 deaths. In one case in Great Britain (which was not reported by the American media), a 27-year-old man machine-gunned to death 16 people before killing himself. The action was part of a fantasy role-playing game which was played by mail. The killer/player had been instructed to kill in order to earn certain powers.

In a Utah case, an adolescent killed his brother as part of a D & D game.

In 1985, two active-duty Marines in Arizona were charged with a murder. The crime later was linked to heavy D & D involvement, and the Marines were convicted and sentenced to prison.

TSR continues to discount the growing evidence. When questioned regarding specific incidents, company officials have stated, "We always find there were many different factors [and] haven't yet, out of all the names, seen one shred of evidence to indicate the 'game' was the cause of death. They [B.A.D.D] cannot scientifically prove these deaths were connected."

Our organization has sought to obtain posteriori (from effect to cause) evidence by conducting investigations into D & D-related deaths. Evidence has been collected in the form of police incident reports, coroners' reports, physicians' evaluations, victims' suicide notes, and statements by murderers as well as statements from witnesses and friends of the deceased victims.

On a talk show broadcast from Toledo, Ohio, Patrick Dempsey (board member of B.A.D.D., retired Seattle police officer and family member of a D & D-related suicide victim) asked Dieter Sturm, a TSR representative, how he had investigated the deaths in question. He was asked if he had interviewed the parents or other family members of Mike Dempsey, Steve Loyacono or Irving Pulling, three young men whose deaths have been linked to D & D involvement.

He replied that he had not. Mr. Dempsey then stated that our organization not only had interviewed the parents and other family members, but also had reviewed the evidence in each case and determined that the deaths were D & D-related.

Such denial of responsibility has been an ongoing practice of TSR. In some instances, they also have attempted to discredit the families of the teenaged victims by indicating that the youngsters were already seriously emotionally disturbed prior to their involvement with D & D. No evidence exists to substantiate such claims.

Sturm's statements must be viewed in light of the salary he received as a hired spokesman for the $27 million company he represented. It appears that TSR's denial of responsibility will continue.

The motives of the B.A.D.D. organization are based on a concerted effort to inform the public of the negative effects of fantasy role-playing games and, we hope, to save lives. If our efforts prevent only one tragedy, we have achieved our goal.

Our efforts have involved lengthy and often tedious investigative procedures. In order for evidence to be accepted in a court of law, it must fall under these guidelines:

> Evidence is a statement of a witness, victim or suspect.
> Evidence can be a tangible object which establishes the point in question.
> EVIDENCE IS RELATED TO THE CRIME OR INCIDENT AND HAS A BEARING ON SAME.
> Scientific evidence can be latent prints, fibers, and/or hair and blood samples linking a person to an incident, crime or crime scene.

In a suicide investigation, blood samples are taken to determine whether the system of the deceased contained any evidence of alcohol, drugs or poisons at the time of death, the presence of which substances would direct police to consider a motive of suicide in the absence of a note left by the victim. If no note is found, tangible evidence near the body must be taken into account. At times, such evidence is overlooked. These items might include records or tapes containing suicidal lyrics and fantasy role-playing game manuals. Such manuals often contain suicide phraseology, commands, curses and themes of murder and assassination.

Frequently, a suicide note is found which directs police to a motivating factor connected with games like D & D. These notes normally are placed into evidence by police officers and accepted as evidence in court. If fantasy role-playing manuals are found at the crime scene, they commonly are seized as evidence. Tangible or real evidence (such as D & D items) often are connected later to the incident through statements from the victims' families and friends and/or incident witnesses. Statements are important links in solving crimes as well as establishing cases. Statements by murder suspects often reveal the motivating factors behind the crime.

How, then, can we link an individual's death to a fantasy role-playing game? The answer to this question can be found in the Advanced D & D manuals and in the fantasies of the players.

Once "hooked" on the game, a player's mind may accept the violent events without a second thought. When this begins to occur, negative behavior modification has taken place. Traditional values are pushed aside, and ethics become situational. Mind alteration has begun. The player's character becomes the player's alter-ego. Consider how such a player might respond to the following:

Command Spell: "The individual will obey to the best of his or her ability only as long as the command is absolutely clear and unequivocal—For example: Suicide (From *Advanced Dungeons & Dragons Player's Handbook*, page 43)."

Detection of Magic: "Furthermore, if the creature dominated is forced to do something totally against its nature or self-destructive, the expenditure of strength points is doubled (From *Advanced Dungeons & Dragons Player's Handbook*, page 112)."

Clone Spell: "If one [clone] cannot destroy the other, one will go insane [75% likely to be the clone] and destroy itself, or possibly [5%] both will become mad and commit suicide (From *Advanced Dungeons & Dragons Player's Handbook*, page 90)."

Fanatical-Spies: "These spies will never become double agents. On any dice total over 60, they simply kill themselves (From *Advanced Dungeon Master's Guide*, page 19)."

Death: "The character faces death in many forms. The most common, death due to combat, is no great matter in most cases, for the character can be brought back by means of a clerical spell or alter-reality wish (From *Advanced Dungeon Master's Guide*, page 15)."

Alignment-Chaotic Evil: "Life has no value (From *Advanced Dungeons & Dragons Player's Handbook*, page 33)."

Alignment-Lawful Evil: "Life, beauty, truth, freedom and the like are held as valueless (From *Advanced Dungeons & Dragons Player's Handbook*, page 33)."

In the introduction to the *Dungeon Master's Guide*, Gygax gives prospective players some advice, stating, "Never give a sucker an even break."

Evidence that Demands Action

Darren Molitor, mentioned earlier in this chapter, was one of two young men convicted of the 1985 murder of Mary Towey. When Darren was picked up by the FBI after the murder, he signed his confession with the names of two of his D & D characters. Both of these characters were of an evil "alignment."

Darren works hard today, writing from his prison cell to warn others about the dangers of fantasy role-playing games. In one of his essays on the subject, he wrote, "I and many others have had some bad experiences because of the game, and I am writing on their behalf, too, to warn or make you aware of the game [D & D]. It is dangerous."

TSR representatives have said they have not seen one "shred of evidence" that specifically links any criminal activity to D & D. Here are some of our shreds of evidence:

In 1985, a 15-year-old girl in Angleton, Texas, was raped. The lead sentence in the story printed by the *Houston Chronicle* on 5/8/85 read, "A former prison psychologist and his wife used the fantasy game of Dungeons & Dragons to entice a 15-year-old girl into a sex act, Brazoria County prosecutors stated."

The attorney of 16-year-old Toby Napier said that his client was legally insane when he killed a store clerk in Orlando, Florida. The attorney stated that Toby "had an obsession with guns, violent movies, paramilitary magazines and the game of Dungeons & Dragons."

Jeffrey Jacklovich, age 14, wrote in his 1985 suicide note, "I want to go to the fantasy world of elves and dwarfs instead of the world of reality with conflict."

Juan De Carlos Kimbrough, age 14, was shot and killed by his brother in 1985. According to the investigating police officer, the shooting was part of a D & D game. Others familiar with the boys said that both were avid D & D players, and that the victim believed he was a deity. He asked his brother to shoot him in the head to prove that he was invulnerable.

An Illinois fifth-grader developed a psychosis clearly linked to D & D gaming and had to be admitted to a state psychiatric hospital. His teacher said that the boy (who had good grades and never had been a behavior problem) had been sitting in the back of the room staring at the wall, unwilling to follow directions.

When confronted, he said, "The wizard tells me to do this."

The boy was heavily involved in D & D play and told the principal that voices told him to do things. He admitted to frequent nightmares of being chased by a dragon through a cave and a wizard master telling him to kill his friends and parents. The principal also noted the boy hinted at suicidal "commands."

The boy's father told the principal he wondered if his (the father's) 17-year-old brother, who had booby-trapped his room and jumped out at his own father with a knife, might have been influenced by his heavy D & D involvement.

A third-grader was placed in foster care after becoming too violent for his mother to handle. The mother reported a clear deterioration in the boy's behavior after he began playing D & D. He had put D & D-type curses on his mother and sister and also had physically assaulted them.

One 16-year-old and two 15-year-old boys in a southern state (all bright students and frequent D & D players) were arrested in early 1984 for making poisons and bombs and threatening to murder a fellow student.

A bizarre note to the intended victim read, "You have been marked for termination ... You may choose from the following forms: poison, bomb, stabbing, strangled, shot, hung by the neck until dead, burned alive, heart ripped from the chest, decapitation ... on the day of the Angel of Darkness, during your lunch period. This is not a threat, but a promise."

The list goes on and on. Well over 100 incidents have been widely publicized in newspapers all over the country. A considerably larger number have not been made public. All mere coincidences, or perhaps just "isolated cases" with very similar characteristics? I think not.

Dr. Radecki and I have testified in a number of murder trials. In some cases, we have testified in the same trials. Regarding the trials in which Dr. Radecki has testified, he provides us with the following case capsules:

"As a practicing psychiatrist as well as the research director of the National Coalition on Television Violence, I have now testified in eight trials connected to entertainment violence. Six of these have been murder trials, one reckless manslaughter, and one burglary-assault-bomb making. Six of these have involved Dungeons & Dragons as at least one element. All have involved young men between the ages of 14 and 20 who have become seriously desensitized to violence and intoxicated with violent entertainment. In each case, the entertainment appeared to have played a major role in leading to their criminal behavior.

"[One] trial involves a 19-year-old American youth who became heavily involved in Dungeons & Dragons during his military training. He undoubtedly had been affected by his upbringing, being abused seriously by his father and stepfather, as well as his stepfather's family who were into teaching their boy children to fight. At the time of his brutal rape-murder of a 14-year-old girl, he was heavily into Dungeons & Dragons. It was his almost constant obsession, when not working or sleeping. In his games, female characters would often switch into demons after male players had had fantasy sex with them. The females would 'have to be killed.' In real life, the youth admits to committing unpremeditated choking, rape and murder of the girl saying that it was like 'I was looking over my shoulder watching the whole thing.' While in jail, the young man is writing an extremely violent book with a plot which is a clear outgrowth of his Dungeons & Dragons. It includes killer weapons that come alive and numerous assassins. At the time of the killing, the young man's god was Asmodeus, the most powerful satanic god in the Dungeons & Dragons game. Asmodeus is listed in the *Satanic Bible*.

"Yet another case involved a young member of the National Guard in Hartford, Connecticut, who picked up the game of D & D in his early teenage years. He had been admitted to a psychiatric hospital at age 15 at which time his obsessions with D & D were noted. He was arrested for committing a series of burglaries, both on his own and with his fellow D & D players. At least one (burglary) included an assault and another arson. He and his friends were finally caught as they were going out into a field to test a gasoline bomb they had made.

"There was an enormous amount of evidence to show that the burglaries were committed on nights that the young man had heavily prepared to play the D & D game, but had been unable to because his fellow players couldn't make it. The young man markedly preferred thief roles for his D & D characters. When asked why he committed different actions during the actual burglaries, he repeatedly stated, 'That is how my character would have done it.' Although ... this young man was barely able to differentiate fantasy from reality, his fantasies had a marked effect on his real life behavior.

"In each ... case, although there was a preoccupation with Dungeons & Dragons and the playing of [the game] 15-30 hours per week, there was also a heavy consumption of other forms of violent entertainment, including martial arts training and weaponry, heavy metal music, extremely violent war and horror movies and frequent indulgence in war magazines. The youths who had first learned D & D in the military noted that it has become a popular pastime in the U.S. military."

Of the trials in which I have been involved, three are especially relevant.

The first was Darren Molitor's. My involvement began with a phone call from Darren's attorney, Lee Patton of St. Louis, Missouri. He told me that his client was on trial for first degree murder and that the state was seeking the death penalty (the gas chamber at that time). Patton explained that the case involved Darren and two friends with whom he frequently played D & D. The friends were Ron Adcox and Mary Towey. He said that, while the teenagers were not actively playing a game of D & D at the time of the murder, it appeared that the game had a great deal of influence over Darren's thoughts and possibly his behavior at the time of the murder.

Patton continued by explaining that, while Mary's parents were out of town, the three friends were preparing for a "Friday the 13th" party to which everyone was to come dressed in black. They began "horsing around" during their preparations for the party, and Mary Towey wound up dead.

My role was that of jury education, explaining to the jury members the game of "Dungeons & Dragons" and how it is played. As I began to review the information regarding the case, one news article in particular struck me.

In an article in the *St. Louis Dispatch* dated April 26, 1984, county detectives were quoted as saying that there was "no connection between the strangulation of Miss Towey and a game called Dungeons & Dragons in which players pretend to be various characters acting out roles in fantasy adventures."

A Detective Ventimiglia was quoted in the article: "Socially, they got together for the game, but it has nothing to do with the murder. It's just a game that they play with each other. It's not a physical game. It's a mental game ..."

I was disturbed by these quotations for two reasons. One, it appeared that the investigating officers knew little or nothing about the game they were discussing. Two, most crimes begin with thoughts and later progress to physical violence. I felt certain that the St. Louis police were diligent and competent, but I was concerned that they did not appear to have information regarding other criminal situations involving young people who had played D & D and similar games.

To the best of my knowledge, this was the first case of its kind in which D & D would be discussed as a possible mitigating circumstance in a murder. Educating those involved in the case was to be a gruelling task simply because I was starting from scratch with people who had very little knowledge of fantasy role-playing games.

Convincing the court of the relevance of D & D-related lines of questioning was difficult. Every time the defense attorney asked a D & D-related question, the prosecuting attorney objected. The two attorneys approached the bench, had whispering conversations with the judge and returned to their places.

On several occasions, the jury was removed from the courtroom. This went on for several very frustrating days as the prosecution continued to object to any testimony related to "Dungeons & Dragons."

Finally, I was allowed to testify with my statements strictly confined to an overview of D & D. I could not mention other criminal incidents connected to fantasy role-playing games because they were not relevant to this case, according to legal procedures.

When I stepped down from the witness stand, Darren stood up at the defense table and, with a little bow, said, "Thank you, Mrs. Pulling."

I have corresponded by mail with Darren since that day and have seen him being interviewed on television, but we have not had the opportunity to speak to each other again. In his own defense, Darren never tried to excuse his actions and readily admits his guilt. Prior to his involvement with fantasy role-playing games, he had no criminal record and no obvious behavior problems.

The next case in which I became involved was that of Sean Sellers. I was contacted in 1986 by one of Sean's attorneys, Kindy Jones of the Public Defender's office in Oklahoma City, Oklahoma. Sean, she told me, had been accused of murdering his parents and a convenience store clerk. He was charged with capital murder, and the state was seeking the death penalty.

I interviewed Sean with his attorney present, and we talked about many things. In particular, we discussed his obsession with violent entertainment.

Sean had become involved with D & D when he was around 13-years-old and, while he had used some of the typical game characters, he stated that he preferred the Egyptian gods. This interest had created a desire in Sean to dig deeper into a variety of occult topics.

He told me that, at the age of 15, he had met a female witch who taught him much about the occult and peaked his interest all the more. He said that he then formed his own "coven" based on the D & D level system and that, while most members were teenagers, some were in their 20s.

He said he had tried to commit suicide several times and that he heard voices. He had tried self-hypnosis and stated that he could slow his heartbeat and go into a trance. He had been involved in blood-letting and the drinking of blood because, he said, that is what he had read about in books. He owned a copy of the *Satanic Bible* and at one time had an altar set up in his room. Sean's related interests included Zen meditation, witchcraft, satanism, knives, guns and other weapons.

His mother had taken him to visit a clergyman after she found his *Satanic Bible*. Sean and the clergyman had discussed the validity of the *Holy Bible* as opposed to that of the *Satanic Bible*.

According to Sean, the clergyman stated that some of the events in the *Holy Bible* were probably mythological, such as the story of Adam and Eve, but that the philosophies were good.

Sean told the clergyman that he felt there was more truth in his own book, and asked why he should believe in the *Holy Bible* if the clergyman did not. The clergyman, said Sean, recommended to Sean's mother that she respect her son's rights of privacy.

The rest is basically history. Sean was convicted of murder in October 1986, and is sentenced to die by lethal injection. The following is a document written by Sean which was entered into evidence at his trial:

> I renounce God.
> I renounce Christ.
> I will serve only Satan.
> To my enemies death. To my friends love,
> > Regie Satanas
> > Ave Satanas
> > Hail Satan
> > > Sean

The last three lines are, curiously, the same three phrases with which Anton LaVey ended the prologue of the *Satanic Bible*.

Sean said that this was written in his own blood. He said that he often bled himself for certain rituals and sometimes collected the blood, storing it in the butter compartment of the refrigerator. I asked him if his mother hadn't noticed this.

He replied, "Yes. One time the bottle fell out on the floor and she asked me what it was for. I told her that we were doing a project at school, examining blood on slides under a microscope, and that this was animal blood."

Sounds logical, doesn't it? You see, there are always clues, but sometimes they are subtle and, in many cases, the helping professionals don't take them seriously.

The third case was that of Jeffrey Meyers. Jeff was convicted of murder in November, 1988, and sentenced to death. Several concerned individuals had mailed articles to me about the case. The articles stated that Jeff and a friend (both soldiers) had been charged in the brutal slaying of an elderly couple and that, when arrested, the two men were wearing "Ninja-type outfits" (associated with the martial arts). Confiscated during the investigation were two butterfly knives, three darts, a blowgun and a copy of *Advanced Dungeons & Dragons Oriental Adventures Book*.

I was contacted in November 1987, by Mary Ann Talley of the North Carolina Public Defender's office. She asked me if I would come to North Carolina, interview Jeff and consult with her and her co-counsel, John Britt.

Jeff was a nice-looking young man, cooperative and pleasant. He related in what appeared to be an open and honest manner about himself and his experiences. He discussed his involvement with D & D, weaponry, the martial arts and Eastern mysticism. He had read a variety of books on the occult, but his primary obsession was "Dungeons & Dragons." He had dabbled with drugs in the past. Some of his favorite movies were "Thief of Hearts," "Sword and Sorcerer," "Conan," "Poltergeist," and "The Exorcist." He enjoyed any form of entertainment that dealt with possession, and he believed in ESP. His D & D character's name was Manteiv which is Vietnam spelled backwards.

According to Dr. Radecki's testimony which was based on his psychiatric evaluation of Jeff, "His [Jeff's] explanation to an inmate on the night of the arrest about the game, involving acquiring gold pieces and the killing of opponents for experience points, closely fits much of the material stolen by the patient [Jeff], including eleven gold chains, a gold-colored wristwatch, a gold-colored wedding band, a silver chain and a silver watch. Jeff admits that he was working on developing a character, a Bushido Ninja Warrior with a chaotic-neutral alignment ... Neutral means that the character has no moral alignment or feelings towards good or evil. Chaotic means that his actions are unplanned and do not follow any laws. Hired assassins are a standard part of the Dungeons & Dragons game, and Jeff states that his Ninja character was essentially that, and that he was gaining experience points and developing the character although not officially playing the game. Jeff describes the murder at times as an 'adventure' which is the typical language of Dungeons & Dragons."

After deliberation by the jury, the order was signed. "This the 15th day of November, 1988. We, the jury, unanimously recommend that the defendant Jeffrey Karl Meyers be sentenced to death."

One recent tragedy is the homicide/suicide involving a 14-year-old boy named Tommy Sullivan who lived in New Jersey. Tommy was a good boy who had never been in any kind of legal trouble, but in January 1988, Tommy stabbed his mother to death with his Boy Scout knife and then tried to set the house on fire while his father and younger brother slept. The fire was unsuccessful, but Tommy ran next door and cut his own throat so severely that reports said it appeared he almost decapitated himself with his Boy Scout knife.

Among Tommy's belongings, police investigators found mystical writings, heavy metal music, and a "book of shadows" written by Tommy which included demonic scribblings and an apparent pact that he had entered into with the devil.

This case was covered extensively by the media, and everyone talked about how quickly young Tommy must have gotten involved in the occult. No one talked about the fact that Tommy's first involvement was with "Dungeons & Dragons," followed by heavy metal music and, finally, satanism.

The list of tragedies continues to grow. The last *official* reporting of deaths related to fantasy role-playing games stated that there were 125 such deaths. That was at the end of 1987. More have occurred since that time, but statistics have not been updated yet to reflect the new numbers. Many, many more remain unpublicized; the cases are in files marked "confidential." This is not hype. This is not speculation. The cases are there. However, those of us who track such incidents were convinced that, once the number reached 100, the public would recognize the danger and voice their concerns.

So why do we continue to gather documentation on this subject? Because, more and more frequently, it is becoming necessary to - *prove* to the public that fantasy role-playing games are dangerous. And because the information we have been able to gather provides us with very specific indicators of the types of children who are in danger of serious occult involvement which may endanger their lives.

Not every child who plays fantasy role-playing games is going to commit murder, suicide or other crimes, but we must be aware of these indicators in order to spot the child who is in danger of going over the edge. Not every child who develops a problem with fantasy role-playing games is going to become a practicing satanist either, but these games most assuredly are a starting point for many who later become involved with devil worship.

A reporter asked me recently, "How many human sacrifices are there a year?"

I said, "How would I know?"

He asked, "How many cases have gone to court in Virginia [my home state]?"

I said I didn't know that either.

He appeared to be very perplexed and frustrated, so I explained. For one thing, I told him, there is no central reporting agency for this type of crime. Secondly, there have been cases which have gone to court in which the link to occult activity was not allowed in evidence even when both the defense and the prosecution were aware of the occult involvement.

We are in a "catch-22" situation. If occult involvement of victims and/or perpetrators of crimes is not documented and entered as evidence in court, how can we prove the criminal/occult link to the public? And if no one believes it, how will we convince the courts to admit the evidence?

I did tell the reporter that there have been a number of cases involving adolescents and teen devil worship which have resulted in murder.

He said, "Oh, yeah, I know that, but what about the adults?"

I leaned forward in my chair and asked, "How do you know about them?"

He said he knew about those cases *because* they have been in court.

I said, "Exactly, but five years ago, you would not have thought adults were involved in devil worship because it was not an issue in court!"

Did that mean it wasn't happening then? Of course not. We must become more and more aggressive about documentation and getting this information entered into court records.

Since 1985, the National Coalition on Television Violence and B.A.D.D. have sent their information on the deaths related to fantasy role-playing games to the Federal Trade Commission's Bureau of Consumer Protection, its associate director for advertising practices and its associate director of labeling. We do not advocate banning of fantasy role-playing games and materials, but we have asked for an impartial committee to review, study and evaluate the materials in relationship to the tragedies.

To date, nothing has transpired. There have been no congressional hearings on this or related subjects. (If you share our concern, please write a letter in support of our request and mail it to: Associate Director of Labeling, 411 11th Street. N.W., Washington, D.C. 20580) In the event that a committee is appointed to evaluate this problem, and in the event such a committee did determine that fantasy role-playing games have the potential for harmful effects, we would ask only for a warning label to advise parents of this potential since these games are sold in toy stores which most parents assume means the games are safe.

Are Your Local Schools Promoting Dungeons & Dragons?

Some readers may be aware of so-called "gaming clubs" in the schools in their localities. Gaming clubs are organizations of students (and sometimes school employees) who meet to play Dungeons & Dragons or other fantasy role-playing games. The game is also played in the classrooms of many schools in this country.

Since school systems are independent and are run by independent guidelines depending on the political structure of the communities that support them, the position of an individual school system regarding fantasy role-playing games depends on the attitudes of the citizens of that community.

While there are school systems that still promote the use of these games and sanction gaming clubs, many have refused to do so. Still others have discontinued support and sanctions after being made aware of the potential dangers. A number of schools have removed the game because of its religious content (the occult). Some of the school systems which have removed the game, or refused to sponsor its use include those of Alamogordo, New Mexico; Arlington, Virginia; and Heber City, Utah.

One school board member stated that studies she had made of the game "Dungeons & Dragons" showed that the negative effects far outweighed any benefits. "I have enough information on my own," she said, "that I can confidently say I don't want it in the schools."

A number of other fantasy role-playing games exist, and most are imitations of "Dungeons & Dragons." Some of the most popular ones are "Tunnels and Trolls," "The Arduin Grimoire," "Runequest," "Empire of the Petal Throne," "Nuclear Escalation," "Traveller," "Boot Hill," "Demons," "The Court of Ardor," "Melee & Wizard," "Metamorphosis Alpha," and "Gamma World."

In England, a fantasy role-playing game is being played by mail. A news article headline reads, "Kids sent murder in the mail."

The game is called "It's A Crime," and details have been mailed to homes all over England.

According to the game's promotional materials, "The game is set in New York in the 1990's where the citizens are in a life-and-death struggle with the ever-increasing number of drug-crazed street gangs."

Players become ruthless gang chiefs and can order their gangs to commit assaults, sell and/or use drugs, bomb buildings and murder their enemies.

Another popular fantasy-by-mail game in England is "Further Into Fantasy" which was the game played by Michael Ryan, the "Rambo-maniac."

In another case of a game-related homicide, a 20-year-old man armed himself with a crossbow and knives and dressed in a camouflage jacket. He killed his girlfriend's mother and seriously injured two more people before he was apprehended.

Several macabre drawings were presented in evidence at his trial. The drawings were of mythological characters similar to those found in fantasy role-playing game manuals. One of the drawings depicted a decapitation which came very close to being an accurate representation of the body of his victim. It was noted during the trial that the young man had a fascination with a number of fantasy games as well as violent movies.

Another area of concern is the young white supremacist movement, what some call the neo-Nazi movement in this country. I am often asked about this group by police officers who attend my seminars. They report that they are seeing a mixing of occult symbolism in the vandalism and graffiti of some of these young people.

There Must Be a Public Outcry

I recall a case involving the vandalizing of a Jewish temple in the South. Graffiti had been spray-painted all over the temple, both inside and out. The graffiti at first appeared to be that of young dabblers. There were pentagrams, a ritual circle drawn on the basement floor and red and black candle wax drippings. However, a closer look revealed racist comments such as "F--- the Jews." It became clear to me that some white supremacist groups are combining their ethnic hatred with satanic symbolism.

In 1987, I received a newspaper in a brown envelope in the mail. At the top of the newspaper was typeset "paper undated." It was in regular newspaper format and one of the articles was titled "Dungeons, Snakes and Toads [Heavily Forbidden Tales of Fiction from the White Racial Underground]."

The article read, "I play a kind of Dungeons & Dragons. My status is fighter. I do not play on a game-grid. I participate directly in the big cities of the powers that be. I am a fighting machine. Reality is my battleground. I am aligned with White racial good. My quest is to destroy White racial evil.

"Now you know me, understand the twelve terms I use before I account to you my fantastic adventure into the big city that I call the 'Dungeons of Illusion.'"

1. Niggers — Are Toads
2. Mexicans — Are Roaches
3. Asians — Are Snakes
4. Halfbreeds — Are Mutants
5. Faggots — Are Faggots
6. White Traitors — Zombies
7. Police — Are Pigs
8. Government — Great Sorcerer
9. Big Business — Conglomerate
10. Cities — Are Dungeons
11. Television — The Box
12. Jew — The Mind Bender

The scenario then described the most hate-filled propaganda in almost a satirical manner, mocking and mimicking every ethnic group. All of the groups listed above were spoken of in extremely racist and negative manners.

Near the end of this hate-filled "adventure," the author described the killing of a Jewish leader as follows: "Later, a Toad ambulance loaded the still corpse of the Mind Bender, Shlomo Ratstein, into the meatwagon. A piece of paper laying on the ground caught the Toad's eye. Reaching down, the Toad picked up the flyer and began to read it. The message said, 'White Students! Unite under the common banner of revolutionary racism. Have fun hunting down, killing and robbing Mutants, Roaches, Snakes, Toads, Faggots, Mind Benders and other low life filth while doing your own race a favor. Our goal is to create a network of White youth gangs and wolf packs across the nation in order to insure our racial survival. With one single determination of the racial will, one million White students, with four members in each group, could form overnight a quarter of a million wolf packs ... Listen for the cry of the wolf. Find three other Whites you can trust, build weapons and prepare for action as total race war approaches.' The Toad knew that after reading the White Power flyer and witnessing what had been done to the Mind Bender, that no matter how hard his fellow Toads tried, they would not be able to jump out of this kettle of boiling oil once the lid came down."

This story was followed by an editor's note which read, "Aryan Youth Movement-White Student Union salutes the wolf pack of John Lester, age 17, Scott Kern, age 17, Jason Ladone, age 16, as well as twelve other Aryan youths for hunting down and causing the death of Negro Michael Griffith, and for physically beating with baseball bats Negroes Cedric Sandiford and Timothy Grimes in the Howard Beach area of New York on the date of December 20, 1986. This story is dedicated to their revolutionary efforts."

The three supremacist young men mentioned in this dedication were found guilty recently in the death of Michael Griffith and the beating of Cedric Sandiford. Scott Kern was sentenced to 2 1/2-7 years in prison; John Lester was sentenced to 10-30 years; and Jason Ladone was sentenced to 5-15 years.

Needless to say, it disturbs me that this questionable "organization" is using the "Dungeons & Dragons" game to promote antisocial, racist propaganda.

Some people who have seen this paper have said, "Oh, it's just a joke." If it is a joke, it is a very sick one, and I, for one, do not believe it is a joke.

How many teenagers have experienced emotional problems as a result of fantasy violence? How many crimes have gone undetected? How many suicides were related to entertainment violence and fantasy role-playing games, but that relationship was never discovered? I don't know that we ever will have the total count or the complete answers to these questions. The public will have to exhibit a level of concern high enough to stimulate the interest and research to provide definitive answers.

Parents must be made aware of the controversy surrounding fantasy role-playing games and make their decisions only after they have enough information to make those decisions based on solid understanding of the game in question. Most parents that I have met who advocate fantasy role-playing games have absolutely no understanding of the game dynamics or anything about the characters or even of what a role-playing game is. A great many parents whose children play have never grasped the concept that this is not a board game; apparently, they are fooled by the dice. It is sad to see uninformed parents defend an issue when they do not know the subject matter but only that the idea or product under discussion makes their child happy.

Finally, we offer here a comprehensive guide for parents to use when determining whether a child has a problem or is headed for trouble where fantasy role-playing games are concerned.

Profile of Participants

1. Usually very intelligent
2. Creative
3. Ninety-five percent of the players are male with the majority being Caucasian.
4. Imaginative, adventurous
5. Academically interested in history and computer science with a high math aptitude and/or an interest in drama
6. Physically either fairly slight build, clean-cut or possibly overweight and sloppy appearance (generally not the muscular, sports-oriented type)
7. Usually socio-economically from a middle- to upper-middle class family
8. Generally, the adolescent D & D player is not involved with drugs; at most, there may be some use of marijuana. However, if he becomes heavily involved in satanism, the likelihood of more serious drug use is increased.
9. Adolescents who become heavily involved generally are "good kids" with no prior behavioral problems.
10. The majority of serious players are in the 12-20 age group.
11. Manufacturers estimate 4-million-plus active players.
12. Possibly science fiction fan and/or horror film hobbyist
13. Some are loners, but many are not as this is a group-oriented game.

Observed Symptoms of Obsessive Involvement

1. Loss of interest in other activities
2. Excessive time spent playing fantasy games
3. Drawings depicting cartoon-type figures of gross mutilations, monsters, and/or violent scenes.

4. Drawing occult symbols such as pentagrams, 666, triangles, swastikas, etc.

5. Recurring nightmares

6. Difficulty sleeping, insomnia

7. Change in eating habits

8. Writing poetry with themes of death and dying

9. Written work with themes about supernatural occurrences with dark themes

10. References to a multiplicity of gods

11. Exhibiting a belief in his/her ability to possess psychic powers

12. Speaking in riddles

13. Falling grades

14. Collecting artifacts such as talismans, animal bones, weaponry

15. Fascination with magic, collecting herbs, etc.

16. Threatening to kill others, especially parents

17. Suicidal talk or talking about death; preoccupation with themes of death

18. Deterioration of personal hygiene

19. Hearing voices

20. Obsession with weapons, especially knives

21. Obsession with paramilitary, "Rambo-like" mentality and/or a pre-occupation with war and the violence thereof simply for the sake of the violence

22. Making "pacts" with the devil or, in some cases, suicide pacts

Parents, family members, teachers, friends and police officers should consider the following when a homicide or suicide has occurred which is possibly related to fantasy role-playing games or some other form of entertainment violence:

1. Look for game materials such as books, miniatures (small metal figures in the form of dragons, warriors, etc.), drawings on graph paper, composition books, written notes, etc.

2. Make a check list of interests and hobbies.

3. If victim or suspect played fantasy role-playing games, ask relatives and friends to name the Dungeon Master or group leader.

4. If suspect was a Dungeon Master, in his/her possessions would be a vast amount of written materials on other game players. If these are missing, something is wrong.

5. If victim or suspect is just a player, character sheets by him/her should be in personal belongings.

6. Everyone who plays fantasy role-playing games has a group leader or Dungeon Master. When a crime has occurred which is related to gaming, there is a great deal of denial of involvement by other players.

Fantasy role-playing games are just one of the many subjects about which today's parents must become knowledgeable. These games can be very dangerous. They also are representative of the many subtle ways in which occult influences can prey upon the minds of children.

SEVEN

HEAVY METAL AND BLACK METAL MUSIC

Music has been a popular medium of expression for thousands of years. It is a means of communicating feelings of both great joy and great sadness. Waltzes make us feel dreamy, marching tunes fill us with pride, contemporary music encourages listeners to tap their feet in rhythm.

The power of music has not escaped the world's great thinkers. The philosopher Plato said, "When modes of music change, the fundamental laws of the state change with them." Aristotle, a contemporary of Plato, believed so strongly in the power of music that he felt all music for the young should be regulated by law.

Vladimir Lenin, the father of the Russian Revolution, said, "One quick way to destroy a society is through its music."

Psychologist Dr. George Stevenson said in his book *Music and Your Emotions*, "The widespread occurrence of music among widely distributed peoples in varied cultures is evidence that in music we have a great psychological force."

Life magazine's October 2, 1969 issue quoted the late rock musician Jimmy Hendrix: "Music is a spiritual thing of its own. You can hypnotize with music, and when you get people at the weakest point, you can preach into the subconscious what [you] want to say."

Hendrix apparently was satisfied that he could control minds with music.

When we talk about the ways in which teens open the door to the occult and we mention heavy metal music, many people say, "Oh, no, here we go again."

Parents traditionally have complained about teenagers' music, and many view this as typical of the gaps in taste that always have existed between generations. These well-meaning individuals have little knowledge of the changes that have occurred in the world of music since the 1950s.

The sexual innuendoes of Elvis shaking his hips and the then-shocking appearance of those long-haired Beatles were mild by comparison to the explicitly violent and sexual lyrics of some heavy metal music and the blatant glorification of drug use, murder, suicide and, yes, satanism in some of today's most popular songs.

A few years ago, there was a great deal of discussion about "back-masking," or the intentional recording of backward messages on some records and tapes. Whether this practice actually was used in the recording industry, we no longer have to try to play albums backward to hear songs praising Satan.

We now have an offshoot of heavy metal music known as "black metal" which has the sole purpose of paying tribute to and encouraging youngsters to honor Satan. An increasingly large number of the adolescents with whom we work report having developed an interest in the occult as a direct result of this brand of heavy metal music. The black metal offshoot glorifies violent sex, antisocial acts against women and children, sex with the dead, suicide and murder, and satanic worship.

Heavy metal music has been defined by Darlyne Pettinichio, a California probation officer, as follows: "Heavy metal cultivates a macho image with black leather, chains, and spikes or studs attached to leather wrist bands, belts and jackets. When you think of heavy metal, you think of power. Women are sometimes portrayed in degrading situations. Heavy metal album covers and videos sometimes show women being dragged around by the hair, caged or being walked on leashes like dogs. The main focus of the heavy metaler is drugs, sex and rock 'n roll. The most alarming aspect is its preoccupation with the occult. There are some subtle and not so subtle 'satanic' overtones [black metal] in this type of heavy metal. Album covers include such things as illustrations of devils' heads, crucified figures, demonic babies, skeletons, pentagrams, black candles and the occult number 666."

Many parents as well as professionals have passed off the growing popularity of heavy metal and black metal music as "just a fad." This presumption has proven deadly in many cases. In some cases where the suggestion has been made that there is a relationship between the homicide or suicide of a young person and the music listened to by the perpetrator and/or the victim, professionals have expressed the opinion that those involved were predisposed to the act, were already inclined toward violence and the music had no influence. Laymen have made such comments as, "He would have killed himself anyway," or, "She was already weird."

Such opinions reveal a dangerous lack of knowledge of the cases under discussion and the violent aspects of heavy metal and black metal music. We could accept, perhaps, the "fad" theory if suicide and murder among adolescents had remained relatively stable over the last few decades, but it has not.

Professionals and parents who have not yet recognized the relationship between the increases in teen devil worship, murder and suicide and the heavy metal/black metal music culture would do well to examine the issue of music as it relates to their patients and children.

Punk Rock and Self-Punishment

Pettinichio also provides the following definition of punk rock: "Music which began in England as a revolt against the economic, education and political systems. Shabby clothes, spiked hair, Mohawk haircuts, shaved heads and outlandish makeup represented the British youth rebellion. When punk came to America, the issues faded, but the anti-establishment statement was the same. Whatever society cherishes — religion, law and tradition — punkers denigrate. Punkers tend to be angry, alienated kids who follow punk rock groups and view themselves as society's victims. Punkers' ultimate goal is to live recklessly and to die young and fast. The punk rock dance called the 'slam dance' involves slamming into someone else, kicking them and punching them. Many punkers seem bent on self-destruction, and it is not unusual for them to wound themselves with razor blades, knives, cigarettes or cigarette lighters (from Press Enterprise, Riverside, Cal., May 7, 1986)."

As you can see, so-called punk rock has many of the same dangerously violent overtones as those types of music labeled heavy metal and black metal; it also has its related homicides and suicides.

Nancy Spungeon, a 20-year-old heroin addict, was found stabbed to death in her New York hotel room in October 1978. Her boyfriend, Sid Vicious of the rock group Sex Pistols, was charged with her murder. Vicious died of a drug overdose four months later. It would be irresponsible to say that the deaths of these two punk rockers were caused by the music around which their lives revolved, but the whole subculture of drugs and self-punishment mixed with music that glorifies death and destruction most certainly influenced their attitudes toward life and its relative worth.

If we accept the concept that adolescence and young adulthood are years of transition during which a young person may move back and forth among a variety of values systems searching for his own niche, then we also must accept that he may be influenced by lyrics such as these from a song by the punk rock group known as the Nihilistics: "*So you're looking for an anthem for a brand new age/It's not a fad, but it's a rage/This method is effective, tried and true/It's the only solution left for you./Kill yourself, kill yourself/It's about time you tried/Kill yourself, kill yourself/It's about time you died./Kill yourself—heed my advice/Kill yourself—take your life/Kill yourself—it's all for the best/Kill yourself—it's time for a rest.*"

Ozzy's Song of Death

Several heavy metal rock bands have been named as defendants in lawsuits brought by the distraught families of suicide victims. In one highly publicized case, heavy metal rocker Ozzy Osbourne, several of his associates and the company that produces his albums were sued by a couple who claimed that at least one of Osbourne's songs drove their teenage son to suicide.

The 26-page bill of complaint stated that the defendants "were the authors, writers, creators, producers, composers, directors, singers, musicians and disseminators of music and lyrics that aided or advised or encouraged another person to commit physical harm or suicide."

The parents of 19-year-old John McCollum alleged that their son's thinking became distorted as a direct result of his listening to Osbourne's outrageous and violent music and that the boy eventually shot himself in the head while listening to one of the musician's recordings.

The plaintiffs also contended that Osbourne, his associates and the production company should have known that the lyrics to the song entitled "Suicide Solution" would encourage impressionable adolescents to kill themselves, and therefore were negligent in producing, marketing and distributing the recording.

Osbourne made a statement to the press in London in which he said that he was sorry about the boy's death, but that he himself was not to blame in any way. "It's absolutely ridiculous to suggest that I'm responsible for their son's death," he said. "He was obviously deranged."

There is the presumption as mentioned earlier that a victim or perpetrator of a suicide or homicide already was predisposed to violent acts and the music with which he entertained himself was incidental.

John Anderson, the McCollums' attorney, countered by saying that he was sorry for Osbourne. "He's ill," the lawyer told reporters, "and I feel sorry for anyone who is ill. Unfortunately, he spreads the venom and bile of his illness ... through his music."

Osbourne, whose stage shows are renowned for their explicit sexuality and violence (he once bit off the head of a live bat to entertain an audience) claims that he wrote "Suicide Solution" as a memorial to fellow rock star Bon Scott who died of alcohol intoxication.

The problem is that Ozzy forgot to include an explanation of this in the album on which the song appears; in other words, he failed his young listeners by neglecting to tell them what he *now* claims to have really meant.

Consider how you might perceive the lyrics to "Suicide Solution" if you were a teenager and did not know about Ozzy's later "interpretation":

> *Wine is fine, but whiskey's quicker/Suicide is slow with liquor/Take a bottle, drown your sorrows/Then it floods away tomorrows.*
>
> *Evil thoughts and evil doings/Cold, alone, you hang in ruins/Thought that you'd escape the reaper/You can't escape the Master Keeper.*
>
> *'Cause you feel life's unreal and you're living a lie/Such a shame, who's to blame, and you're wondering why/Then you ask from your cask is there life after birth/What you sow can mean Hell on this earth.*
>
> *Now you live inside a bottle/The reaper's traveling at full throttle/It's catching you, but you don't see/The reaper is you and the reaper is me.*
>
> *Breaking laws, knocking doors/But there's no one at home/Make your bed, rest your head/But you lie there and moan/Where to hide, Suicide is the only way out/Don't you know what it's really all about?*

Another critical aspect of this case involved allegations that there were subliminal messages in the chorus which included the words, *"Ah, no, people, you really know where it's at ... you got it! Why try, why try? Get the gun and try it! Shoot ... Shoot ... Shoot,"* followed by laughter (subliminal means below the threshold of consciousness; in other words, the listener does not consciously hear such messages).

The Institute for Bio-Acoustics Research, Inc. (IBAR) was hired to evaluate "Suicide Solution." IBAR's normal function is to study the effects that sounds have on the human mind and body and to find commercial uses for the results of their research. This company has produced a tape entitled "Sounds of Oregon" which takes the listener on an "audio walk" along a forest stream and along the beach. Designed to induce relaxation, the tape incorporates a subliminal heartbeat that is gradually slowed, a technique which tends to slow the listener's own heartbeat.

"It's the same basic principle as going into a high-action scene in a movie," says one of the tape's producers. "If you concentrate, you'll hear a heartbeat moving quite fast. That's designed to key into your own heartbeat and have it move faster."

The IBAR producers examined Osbourne's recording and stated that they found lyrics on the record that were not included in the copyright "lead sheet" for the song "Suicide Solution." Their findings suggested that, during a 28-second instrumental segment which calls for "vocal fills and ad libs" on the published lyric sheet, the alleged subliminal messages are sung at one and one-half times the normal rate of speech and are "not readily intelligible" to the first-time listener; however, according to the complaint, these subliminal lyrics "are audible enough that their meaning and true intent becomes clear after being listened to over and over and over again. The existence of these words is intentionally concealed from any person who reads the album jacket or the copyright version of 'Suicide Solution.'"

The lawsuit also cites results of IBAR's analysis of a low-pitched hum that appears in portions of the recording. The analysis states that evidence was found of Hemisync tones "which result from a patented process that uses sound waves to influence an individual's mental state. The tones have been found to increase the rate at which the human brain assimilates and processes information." The suit alleged that the Hemisync tones made young McCollum more susceptible to the lyrics sung by Osbourne.

The McCollums' attorney told reporters that he had received "at least twenty phone calls from parents indicating their kids committed suicide —not just listening to heavy metal but specifically to Ozzy Osbourne."

One of the IBAR representatives stated in an interview, "We all know that music has a great power and a great influence. People all over the world love music and always have. We're starting to get to the point where we can actually analyze from a psychological and biological perspective just why it is we're moved by music, how we respond to music and what our level of awareness is."

In spite of the efforts of the McCollums, their attorney and the IBAR representatives, the case against Ozzy Osbourne was thrown out of court by Superior Court Judge John Cole who said that holding the musician and his associates responsible for John McCollum's death would inhibit the First Amendment right of free speech. Apparently, Judge Cole did not have a thorough understanding of the concepts of subliminal messages and Hemisync tones used *in conjunction with* violent lyrics. His decision seems to have been based solely on the freedom of *speech* which would apply only to the lyrics.

Science Probes Psychological Effect of Music

Audio cassettes with subliminal messages deliberately implanted to help the listener break a variety of bad habits (smoking, overeating, etc.) and relieve stress and anxiety are widely available in book and music stores and through mail-order catalogues. A double-edged philosophy appears to be operating in our society which holds that it is acceptable to use subliminal messages to influence a person's thinking when there is money to be made, but if this issue is raised to hold a company responsible for its actions, we are inhibiting freedom of speech.

While the frequency waves of music may sound like mumbo jumbo to the average person, it should be noted that the conscious control and use of sound waves is not new to the United States military.

According to Lt. Col. Michael A. Aquino (an avowed satanist and high priest of the Temple of Set) who has studied the effects of sound waves and resonance, "ELF [Extremely Low Frequency] waves [up to 100 hz] are once more naturally occurring, but they can also be produced artificially [such as for the Navy's Project Sanguine for submarine communication]. ELF-waves are not normally noticed by the unaided senses, yet their resonant effect upon the human body has been connected to both physiological disorders and emotional distortion. Infrasound vibration [up to 20 hz] can subliminally influence brain activity to align itself to delta, theta, alpha or beta wave patterns, inclining an audience toward everything from alertness to passivity. Infrasound could be used tactically, as ELF-waves endure for great distances; and it could be used in conjunction with media broadcasts as well."

What all of this means to us is simply that scientific research now supports the widely held theory that sound waves produced by music can affect the listener both psychologically and physiologically. The military research in combination with the studies conducted by IBAR and similar companies should leave no doubt in anyone's mind that music can be used to manipulate and distort the thinking of listeners and that, when combined with violent and/or satanic lyrics, it represents a serious threat to the psychological, emotional and physical well-being of children, teenagers and young adults.

"I Didn't Have Any Control"

Another case involving the suicide of a teenager resulted in a lawsuit against the heavy metal rock group Judas Priest. Eighteen-year-old Raymond Belknap shot himself in the head in December 1985, after he and a friend listened to a Judas Priest album for about six hours in Belknap's bedroom.

Belknap's mother brought the legal action against the rock group, the production company and the writers of the music on the 1978 album entitled "Stained Class."

The bill of complaint stated, "The suggestive lyrics combined with the continuous beat and rhythmic non-changing intonation of the music combined to induce, encourage, aid, abet and otherwise mesmerize the plaintiff into believing the answer to life was death."

It also stated that the boy was encouraged to take his own life by the "lyrical instructions of the music he was listening to just before his death and at the time of his death that created an uncontrollable impulse to commit physical harm to oneself or suicide."

Belknap's mother said that her son and a friend, James Vance, had destroyed Raymond's bedroom during the marathon heavy metal session, then left the house through a window, taking a shotgun with them. They went to a nearby church playground where Belknap put the shotgun to his head, pulled the trigger and died instantly. His friend followed suit, but survived the severe injury to his face.

The friend said in a written statement that the two had become convinced (after hours of listening to the album) that "the answer to life is death." This belief led them to form a suicide pact.

Attorney Kenneth McKenna said, "They just literally obeyed the commands of the music, and the lyrics ... are very, very suggestive to influence someone to commit suicide."

The production company was ordered by the court to turn over the master tape for the album "Stained Class," but reported that the 24-track tape could not be found. For this and a number of other reasons, the case is still in litigation. However, Vance offered some insight into the motives behind the teen suicide pact.

James Vance had been the "new kid in town," and, not being a particularly good student or athlete, he quickly was accepted by what he calls "the fad people." He and his new friends, who included Belknap, drank heavily and used drugs, engaged in promiscuous sex and frequently listened to heavy metal music by the hour. He reported that, on one occasion, "we started rocking out, you know, and we started getting really involved in the music. The music has as much power as a drug or alcohol." He said that he and his friends enjoyed "rushes of power" when listening to heavy metal music.

Vance and Belknap formed what they referred to as a "brotherhood" and often took oaths on this relationship that were considered sacred. On the day of Belknap's death, the two had been listening to the Judas Priest album and trying to interpret a song entitled "Beyond the Realms of Death." One of them suggested, "Let's find out what's next" (meaning after death, according to Vance), and the two took an oath on their brotherhood to follow through.

As Belknap lay dead on the playground, Vance prepared to remain true to the oath. He said, "There was just tons of blood. It was like [the gun] had grease on it. There was so much blood I could barely handle [it], and I reloaded it and then, you know, it was my turn, and I readied myself. I was thinking about all that there was to live for, so much of your life is right before your eyes, and it was like I didn't have any control ... my body was compelled to do it and I went ahead and shot."

As mentioned earlier, Vance survived the gunshot wound, but the story does not have a happy ending. James Vance slipped into a coma on November 28, 1988, and died a few days later.

According to the expert witnesses who analyzed the "Stained Class" album, both subliminal messages and backmasking were used in producing the recording. The analyses indicated that the lyrics to the song "Better By You Better Than By Me" are Oedipal in meaning, that is they convey the message that the singer has failed his mother, causing her great pain and suffering, and that the only way to stop hurting his mother is to end his own life.

"You will find my blood upon your windowsill" is one line from this song.

The analyses also indicated that this song has the subliminal message "Do it" which is repeated at least six times in the song.

"Red Hot White Heat" contains the over message *"The devil is coming to earth and amassing his army,"* according to the music experts and, when played in reverse, becomes *"Sing my evil spirit"* followed by *"F--- the lord and f--- all of you."*

Whether or not the court finds that a relationship existed between the music and the deaths of Belknap and Vance, it appears that the teenagers tragically perceived that at least some of the messages on the album were directed at them.

In another case, 16-year-old Dewey Overman died in 1986 after jumping from an overpass onto an interstate highway. A note found in his car read, "I'm tired of life. I'm tired of school. I'm tired of this world. I really don't belong in this world. I belong in a world full of mystic powers, rainbows in crystal raindrops. I wouldn't mind if someone would write the Scorpions [a West German heavy metal rock band] and tell them their No.1 fan has left. Tell them that I've flown to the rainbow."

The note also made reference to a girl Overman was scared to approach for a date. According to friends, Overman was a quiet young man who made excellent grades without much effort.

In a Wisconsin case, an 18-year-old military school cadet hung himself in his dormitory room. Near the body of Phillip Morton were a human skull, a burning candle and a tape recorder playing continuous heavy metal music (the album "The Wall" by Pink Floyd).

The chief medical examiner was quoted as saying, "My personal feeling is that this type of music is going to add to [a person's] depression. If [he] is depressed, this music is going to send [him] deeper.

And if [Morton] wanted to change his mind sometime during this, the music wouldn't help."

"The Wall" contains songs with the titles "Is There Anybody Out There?," "Good-bye, Cruel World," and "Waiting for the Worms."

Real life dramas

Two 19-year-olds were charged in 1986 with the murders of Terrence and Marie Duffy, parents of Patrick Duffy of "Dallas" fame. One of the young men was Sean Wentz, a troubled youth who had attempted suicide on one occasion and apparently was in despair over the death of his mother.

According to his girlfriend, Wentz listened obsessively to an album entitled "Kill 'Em All" by the heavy metal rock group Metallica. He told her, "It's the only way I can separate myself from all the problems coming down. I'm putting myself into oblivion."

Members of the California-based heavy metal rock group Agent Steel were charged in 1987 with child abuse and aggravated assault in an incident in which they reportedly taped firecrackers to the chest of a 17-year-old boy and then set them off.

While chanting, the band members then poured alcohol on the juvenile (who was referred to as a "willing victim") and urinated on him.

They told investigators that the satanic ritual they were performing was part of their stage act. Fortunately, the "willing victim" was not injured.

Probably one of the most widely publicized cases in which heavy metal music appears to have been an influencing factor is that of Theron (Pete) Roland, Jim Hardy and Ron Clements (all 17-year-olds) of Missouri. The three juveniles were charged in 1987 with the savage bludgeoning death of 19-year-old Stephen Newberry whose body was found in a cistern. According to one investigator, Newberry had suffered 40 to 50 blows to the head.

When I first saw the headlines regarding this incident, I had no way of knowing that I would be invited by one of the defense attorneys in the case to act as a consultant. The case is by far one of the most complex with which I have ever been involved due simply to the large number of teenagers and others who had to be interviewed.

It appeared then (and we believe to this day) that many local residents were aware of the self-styled cult activities of the boys involved in this incident and of other teenagers in the area who practiced occult rituals. I am convinced that the teen occult activity in the large county of Jasper did not end with the arrests of Roland, Hardy and Clements. It appears that most of this activity was ignored by residents and passed off as "a fad" prior to the murder of Newberry; since that murder, the continued activity has been "hushed up" with the "maybe it will go away if we ignore it" attitude.

According to the evidence in this case, the four teenagers were part of a satanic cult which practiced animal mutilations and committed acts of vandalism in the area. Jim Hardy was the group leader, and the boys' increased distancing from reality followed the typical pattern of obsession with occult entertainment, the use of drugs and alcohol, vandalism, animal mutilation and, finally, human sacrifice.

On the night of the murder, they had listened to the songs "Crash Course in Brain Surgery" and "Damage, Inc.," both by Metallica, to set the mood for ritual activity. After the sacrifice of a cat (in which the victim also participated), the boys turned on Newberry and beat him to death. After Newberry was dead, and stating that "This is for Satan," the boys bound the victim's right side with twine and threw him into the cistern which they called the "well of hell."

One particularly interesting aspect of this case is that, on the day of the killing, Jim Hardy told the others not to take any drugs because this would reduce the power of Satan.

Here are the words to "Damage, Inc.," one of the songs the boys listened to prior to the sacrificing of the cat and, ultimately, Stephen Newberry:

> *Dealing out the agony within/Charging hard and no one's gonna give in/Living on your knees, conformity/Or dying on your feet for honesty./Inbred our bodies work as one,/Bloody but never cry submission./Following our instinct, not a trend/Go against the grain until the end.*
>
> *Chorus: Blood will follow blood/Dying time is here/Damage incorporated.*
>
> *Slamming through, don't f--- with Razorback/Stepping out? You'll feel our hell on your back/Blood follows blood and we make sure,/Life ain't for you and we're the cure./Honesty is my only excuse,/Try to rob us of it but it's no use/Steamroller action, crushing all/Victim is your name and you shall fall.*
>
> *Chorus: We chew and spit you out./We laugh, you scream and shout./All flee. With fear you run,/You'll know just where we come from.*
>
> *Damage incorporated./Damage jackals ripping right through you./Sight and smell of this, it get me goin'/Know just how to get just what we want./Tear it from your soul in a nightly hunt/F--- it all and f---ing no regrets/Never happy endings on these dark sets./All's fair for damage incorporated, you see./Step a little closer if you please.*
>
> *(Chorus)*

Heavy Metal and Black Metal Music

I examined interviews, statements, the autopsy report, evidence from the ritual killing of the cat and the words to "Damage, Inc." I also conducted my own interviews with defendants and witnesses.

Pete Roland and Ron Clements were extremely honest and helpful in their statements, but none of the boys showed any remorse or fear. They appeared to have no understanding of the seriousness of their crime. These teenagers are, in my opinion, victims of the occult philosophies they *chose* to pursue as well as being perpetrators of a horrible crime. I have no doubt that their occult involvement was influenced strongly by heavy metal music.

One of the most blatantly violent songs to be released in a while is "Bodily Dismemberment" by Rigor Mortis (copyright 1988, by Dirt Head Music):

> *Welcome to my home my dear/I'll show you a good time/*
> *It's too bad that you never heard/My fetish is a crime/There's*
> *no need to worry b----/Just lay there and relax/And as you*
> *reach your climax/I'll be reaching for my ax.*
> *Chorus: With five easy slices/You're in six lovely pieces/*
> *Bodily dismemberment/As passion increases.*
> *So you wanna play games do ya/Well just who do you*
> *think you're f---ing with/You see I learned everything the*
> *hard way/Yes I've been through hell and back.*
> *I believe the time has come/To show you why you're here/*
> *You see the weapon in my hands/And know your death is near/*
> *When I tied your hands and feet/You thought it was exciting/*
> *But now you know you cannot stop/Your body's disuniting.*
> *Chorus*
> *Who's laughing now you fool/You had your chance and*
> *that's it/Expect no mercy from this maniac/Well you're f---ing*
> *history b----/First I'll slice your tender leg off just above the*
> *thighs/Then I'll remove your slender arms/My passion run-*
> *ning high/Last I will decapitate your/pretty little head/A*
> *masterpiece of blood and flesh lies twitching on my bed.*
> *Chorus*
> *Why do you make me do these things/When you know I*
> *never wanted to hurt you/But no you wouldn't listen would*
> *you/Well you stupid f--- look at you now.*

I often am asked for some black metal song titles and the names of the groups that record them. There are so many musicians performing this type of music (and new groups being formed all the time) that keeping up with them is difficult. However, here is a sampling of what is available in the way of satanic music:

114

"Holy Hell" by Possessed (copyright 1985, Combat Records)

Holy Hell, death to us/Satan fell, unholy lust/Devil's water, starts to flood/God is slaughtered, drink his blood.

Our bonding trust is at hand/Go we must, to Satan's land/Pray for death and cry for life/Reaper's breath will breathe new life.

Satan's child, he is born,/And to death, he is sworn,/Days of hate and days of pain/Endless term of Satan's reign.

Endless dreams, in the night/Eternal sleep, eternal fright/Defiled crosses, Oh Black mass/Satan's reign. me at last.

All of heaven, all of earth/You'll meet your God/Chained to torment, chained to pain/Like a dog

Evil days and evil nights/are black as death/Hearts of sinners, hearts of stone/Reaper's breath.

There was blood and there was pain/Ecstasy/Rage of magic, rage of witches/Sorcery

Feel the power, feel the heat/Down below/Kill the people, kill them dead/Take their soul.

Blackened masses, blackened crosses/Ritual/Cut the heads, cut the throats/Take the fall.

"Bad Omen" by Megadeth (copyright 1986, Capitol Records)

Down fell the stars, as they/Splashed in the sea./"Minomine Baphomet,"/Come dance with me./Sacrifice the virgins,/Spiritual rites./Their Master's time has come,/The moon is full tonight.

Drinking, dancing,/They worship, and toast/The Devil, who's watching,/With demons remote./Fire, rising,/Racing in your blood./Possessed, naive,/His service is done.

Bloody blasphemy.

Sinister's the word,/As the demons take their fill./An orgy's taking place,/Human blood will spill./An act of worship,/ As they conceive the ghouls,/Satan has their souls,/They sing pagan tunes.

The ceremony/is sure to be cursed./They wait for his blessings,/But, down comes the worst./Their bodies, soulless,/A corpse from the grave,/Their minds are helpless,/And, no one can save,/No one can save them.

Titles of others include "Suffer Not the Children" (by Venom), "Possessed" (by Venom), "Altar of Sacrifice" (by Slayer), "Into the Coven" (by Mercyful Fate), "The Antichrist" (by Slayer), "Evil Has No Boundaries" (by Slayer), and "No Will to Live" (by Possessed).

The Role of the Industry

Should the music industry share in the responsibility for some of the bizarre and often tragic behaviors of adolescents? I believe they should. Consider the following:

The American public spends approximately 15 billion dollars a year on rock and roll (not just heavy metal) music.

"The average teen listens to 4-6 hours of music per day. On an average, this constitutes 11,000 hours of rock from the 7th to 12th grades which equals the entire amount of classroom time from 1st grade through high school (*Teen Vision*, PMRC videotape "Rise to the Challenge")."

"Nearly half of all music videos contain violence or suggestions of violence. The visuals contain three times as many acts of violence as the lyrics" (Dr. Thomas Radecki, M.D., National Coalition on Television Violence.)

In a study conducted by Hannelore Wass, Ph.D. and published in *The Influence of Media on Adolescents*, the findings were as follows: "90% of the students [surveyed] reported being rock fans. Altogether, the students listed 1,761 items of rock music. Of these students, approximately 17% [n = 116] were found to be HSS [homicide, suicide, satanic practices] fans. 9% of the urban middle school students, 17% of the rural and 24% of the urban high school students were identified as HSS fans. Slightly more than 72% of the HSS group were male and about 96% were white. Nearly three-fourths of the HSS fans listed more than five materials in the HSS categories almost exclusively ... 41% of the HSS group compared to 25% of the general rock fans said they know all the words of their favorite music. About 47% of both groups said they know many of the words. About 40% of both groups reported that they agree with the words often, and 20% reported that they agree always."

If those facts and figures haven't convinced you that music is powerful enough to influence a teenager's behavior and that, therefore, the music industry should be required to institute and uphold new standards of record production, take a look at the following quotes by heavy metal performers:

"The one thing I got from Hitler was the idea of the Nazi youth. I believe in the motley youth. The youth of today are the leaders of tomorrow. They're young, and they can be brainwashed and programmed (Nikki Sixx of Motley Crue, *Faces* magazine, 1984)."

"Hey, we love controversy. Yeah, there's a song called 'Crucifix.' There's also one called 'Wayward Son' and another called 'Exterminator.' If people want to pick on us as a bad influence, there'll be plenty of reason for them to do it, but we don't care (David Wayne of Metal Church, *Power Metal* magazine, July 1988)."

"We really don't give two sh--s about what people think about us. You don't think a band that features guys standing on stage bleeding is looking for critical praise, do you? We know we're not for everyone, but what we do is different. We're a band that's really into violence and death. We're going even more in that direction on our second album. We know that we're never gonna be on American Bandstand, but who'd want to be? We just want to be known as the sickest band on earth (RH Boeckel of E-X-E, *Power Metal* magazine, July 1988)."

"I love to drink. I love to be f----d up ... But I'm not going to drive anymore. And I think we should tell our fans ... don't drink and drive, not don't drink. Do whatever you want to do, man. Shoot up heroin, I don't care. Do it. Have fun. It's your life." (Vince Neil of Motley Crue, *Kerrang* magazine, February 1986.)

Desensitizing Our Youth

"Manipulation of children's minds in the field of religion or politics would touch off a parental storm and a rash of congressional investigations. But in the world of commerce, children are fair game and legitimate prey (from a slip inside the album "Welcome to the Pleasuredome" by Frankie Goes to Hollywood)."

"The rack is back, but it gets better. The song after we use the rack, I'll cut the girl down, throw her over my shoulder, take her to the center of the stage and drop her in this contraption. It's like a meat grinder. It'll spray her all over the audience. We'll even pass out raincoats. The sicker they get [the audience], the sicker we'll get (Blackie Lawless of W.A.S.P., *Circus* magazine, November 87)."

"We're not playing for a bunch of record executives. We're playing for the kids. It's the kids that are the hellraisers. We're Hellion, and we're playing for hellions (Ann Boleyn of Hellion, *Metal Mania* magazine, Issue number 8)."

"I like to drink blood and torture females on stage (Blackie Lawless of W.A.S.P., *Rockline* magazine, April 1985)."

It is both unrealistic and dishonest to say that the behavior of children and teenagers is not influenced by the music they listen to and the other forms of entertainment which occupy their time. The evidence is overwhelming. A large number of crime scenes are littered with the symbolism of heavy metal/black metal rock groups. Much of the graffiti at crime scenes as well as on overpasses, bridges and walls of every kind, is heavy metal/black metal: the names of the bands, their logos and sometimes the lyrics of their songs. The ideas of murder and mayhem are the themes around which the stage performances of these bands are designed.

Do we honestly believe that our children can leave the concert halls or turn off their tape players and remain unaffected by scenes of and songs about torture and bloodshed?

I do not believe that every teenager who listens to heavy metal music is going to become a deranged killer or even a devil worshiper. However, we as parents and professionals involved in and concerned about the welfare of children must educate ourselves regarding the wide variety of music that is available and accessible to youngsters. Then we must teach them what we have learned. In order to be selective in the forms of entertainment they choose, children must know the kinds of music that are being marketed to their age groups and what values (if any) certain groups represent. In other words, we must help our children become knowledgeable consumers.

Should Parents Speak Up?

It often surprises me that some parents who are otherwise diligent in supervising their children's purchases (cosmetics, food, clothes, automobiles, etc.) pay little or no attention to the record albums and tapes those same children buy. Some parents may feel uncomfortable in or even intimidated by local music stores. The weird lighting and loud music used to lure the teenagers into the store tend to make us tell the kids to go on in and make their purchases while we window shop in the mall.

What we really need to do is go in with them, look at what they are looking at and listen to the music that interests them. Speak up if you find a particular song or album offensive. We do not have to allow obscenity and violence in our homes just because they come wrapped in a colorful package of cardboard and cellophane. Children who are old enough to shop alone should have guidelines regarding the types of musical recordings they are allowed to bring home.

We know that adolescents are vulnerable to peer pressure and their identities and moral values are not yet solidified. Mental health professionals who specialize in developmental psychology and the psychology of adolescence tell us that it is normal to rebel against authority during these tumultuous years. Let's be honest. Most of us can recall sowing a few wild oats ourselves. But, as our children tell us, things really are different today, and it is up to us to channel the normal teenage rebellion onto the least dangerous paths.

To say that a child who gives in to violence, perversion, criminal activity and suicide was "already disturbed" is a cop-out in most cases. While there is the occasional child who seems bent on self-destruction from an early age, the vast majority of children in treatment today began life as healthy, happy children.

Of the teenagers I have come in contact with who are involved in occult activities, as many are from two-parent families as single-parent ones; some have used drugs, and others have never touched them. Some have gone to religious services every week of their lives, and some have never been inside a church or synagogue. The common factor in almost every single case has been an obsession with entertainment violence.

One of the most touching mailings our office has ever received was a simple, straightforward letter from a mother. It is reprinted here in its entirety with the mother's name deleted to protect her privacy.

Dear Sirs,

My son died in April of 1983. He was a teen suicide. He was six weeks away from high school graduation in the top 5% of his class. He took 4 years of math, science, French, English and other requirements to get into a top-notch college. He was accepted at the college of his choice. His math teacher told us he had the finest mathematical brain the teacher had worked with in 10 years. He was the only student in his high school of over 2,000 recommended by his chemistry teacher to participate in a [major university] summer work-and-learn program. He was the only photographer in the area to have an award-winning photo [that he took and developed] selected by the Photographers' Society of America Young Photographers' Showcase traveling display throughout the U.S.A. for one year. He had perfect attendance in school every year since 7th grade. The autopsy showed no trace of any alcohol or drugs of any kind. He did not use drugs or smoke anything.

When my husband and I were going through his papers after he died, we found the words to a rock song, "Suicide Solution." We asked his girlfriend about the words, and she told us it was his favorite song. I feel that these words opened up a tragic alternative to him that he would not otherwise have considered. I blame rock music for the loss of a fine young man. I think the cost in loss of young persons is too great to ignore. How many others have been lost?

My son was not perfect. He had to be told several times to take out the garbage, etc., but he did have a bright future ahead of him. If the control of this type of rock music prevents even one loss, one family from this devastating grief, then is it not worth the effort? I hope other parents wake up and listen to the words before it is too late. I only wish I had.

Sincerely,

Is Your Child Involved in the Occult

Probably the most frequently asked question at my seminars is, "*How do I know* when my child is in danger?" Here are the answers.

A child is in trouble when he/she has an obsession with one or more of the following: fantasy role-playing games, magic and other occult sciences, black metal music, "slasher films" like "Friday the 13th," and movies with occult themes like "Poltergeist." A true obsession (involvement to the exclusion of other types of entertainment) with any of these indicates that a child is in trouble and needs help and intervention.

Parents also should be concerned if they observe the following in any combination in their children: the collecting of occultic jewelry (inverted pentagrams and crosses, goats' heads, the number 666, swastikas and the like); the wearing of black clothing with or without occultic symbols and/or names of black metal rock bands; falling grades; secrecy within a small circle of friends or a sudden, drastic change in friends; lack of personal hygiene; irritability with family and friends; nightmares; change in eating habits and sleeping patterns; lying about where they are going and who they are with; drawings with themes of mutilation, dismemberment, demons and symbols of the occult; poetry/essays about death, mutilation and/or demons; and self-mutilation (cuts, burns, etc.).

The next most frequently asked question is, "*What do I do* about it now that I recognize that my child is in trouble?"

Get outside help, preferably with a therapist *and* a clergyman of the family's faith (your child is in psychological and possibly physical danger as well as spiritual danger). **Do not pass it off as a fad and do not listen to others who pass it off as a fad.**

We do not recommend that you automatically tell your child to stop listening to his favorite music or to cease doing whatever activity indicates his involvement; more often than not, the child will simply comply with the rules when at home and begin lying in order to continue the activity away from home.

It is far better to have an open discussion with the child, not an argument. If he or she talks openly and does not become belligerent, then you probably do not have a child in trouble. But if the child becomes hostile and tells you "it's none of your business" or verbally assaults you with threats and curses, you have cause for concern. This is a child who needs outside help. Fast.

Occasionally, there even can be a problem finding competent outside help since many professionals are not well-informed in the area of teen occult activity, and some refuse to accept that heavy metal/black metal music can present any dangers; they insist that a child's interest in these things (even if it approaches obsession) is a passing one and nothing to worry about. If you encounter this type of approach, do not hesitate to end the relationship with that professional and find one who will evaluate the situation with a less-biased attitude. Better still, interview prospective therapists, counselors and even clergy before choosing to find out how informed they are in the area of your family's concerns.

Remember that a great many professionals themselves subscribe to New Age philosophies of "anything goes," "there is no right and wrong," and "let children do what they will." Unfortunately, many families have had to go through a trial-and-error process to find competent therapy for their children. This can result in the loss of precious time, a loss which is detrimental to the welfare of all concerned.

Parents should use common sense and the God-given intuition that most parents have. If all the indicators are go, but you get a bad feeling about a situation, trust the bad feeling. "Most of the time, you will not regret it."

Some professionals will say that is hardly a scientific approach. My reply to them is, "It works."

Remember, parents, these are your children. If something happens to them, you will suffer more than you can imagine. Do not be intimidated by well-meaning people who try to give you advice on how to raise your children. This means even those people who have walls filled with degrees and years more education than yourselves. Listen to what they have to say, certainly; then weigh all of the facts carefully, consider what you know about your own child that no one else can possibly know or understand, and trust your instincts.

Fantasy role playing manuals and gaming masks.
(Photo by Frank Parham)

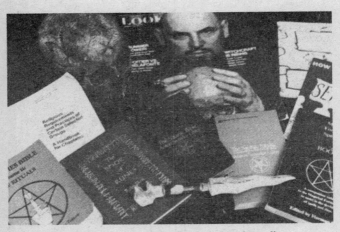

Occult books, jewelry and other paraphernalia.

Ritualistic mutilation of a dog found at ritual circle in Mississippi, thirteen similar mutilated animals were found at the location.

Mutilated cat, dipped in wax and feet cut off, ritual site in Virginia.

Left to right: Pat Pulling, Henry Lee Lucas,
Irving Lee Pulling—Death Row, Oct 1988.

Sean Sellers, Death Row—1988.
Photo compliments Carlos Lindley,
Sean's grandfather.

Investigator Pat Pulling points to the nganga, cross, cigars and body parts found in the sacrificial "Shed of Death" at Matamoros, Mexico.

The "Shed of Death" where Mark Kilroy and many others were sacrificed in Matamoros, Mexico.

A "close-up" view of the nganga—it contains feathers,
some gold, pieces of skulls and brain tissues—all still
visible to the investigators at Matamoros, Mexico.

Melissa Ann Meyer murdered and sacrificed
by John Wayne Rose and his accomplice.

Inverted Pentagram below
the number 666.

Satanic graffiti in storm drain:
Upside down cross, anarchy symbol, ankh,
inverted pentagram, 666, broken cross.

Graffiti "Satan is God"
with inverted cross.

Lt. Jim Gaertner, Sedalia, MO.
Police Dept. — Satanic graffiti.

Left to right: Chief Gary Starke, Sedalia, MO.,
Pete Rowland convicted murderer, 1988.
(Photo compliments *Sedalia Democrat*)

Center: Jeffrey Meyers, convicted
murderer now on Death Row.
(Photo compliments of *Fayetteville Times*)

EIGHT

OTHER FORMS OF ENTER-TAINMENT VIOLENCE

Those who have not noticed the increase within the last few years of mayhem and gore in many, many forms of entertainment have not been paying attention. A large number of children and teenagers are being entertained by unbelievably violent music videos on television, occultic movies, T.V. series, games and toys, and records and tapes while their parents are at work or sleeping soundly.

We at B.A.D.D. have paid attention and, along with other concerned organizations and individuals, have tracked this trend in an attempt to answer three questions: *who is promoting it; why are the kids buying into it with their hearts, minds and dollars; and is it leading children into devil worship?*

During a recent interview, Bill Ruehlman of the *Virginian Pilot* newspaper asked me if I am concerned about the entertainment industry marketing such quantities of violence (much of it with occultic themes) to young audiences. I told him that my more specific concern is why this market exists at all. The children and teenagers obviously are maintaining their end of the supply-and-demand principle. To learn the answers to our questions, we must look not only at the eager and receptive market furnished by the kids, but also at the larger society and its role models.

Dr. Thomas Radecki, M.D., chairman of the National Coalition on Television Violence, has helped me become far more sensitive to the gratuitous violence I had grown accustomed to seeing on television and to put it into perspective. A paper written and published by Dr. Radecki, entitled "Entertainment Violence: A Major Cause of

Anger and Aggression in Modern Society," is condensed here with the author's permission.

"Over one thousand research studies and reports are now available focusing on entertainment violence. Thirty-three studies look at cartoon violence, ten at violent toys, more than fifty at sexual violence, forty-eight at sports violence, etc. Several dozen carefully done field studies are available over one- or more year periods of time and some covering 22 years. Roughly three-fourths of all studies have found some harmful impact on viewers. The average size of this impact has been a 25% higher level of aggressive attitude or behavior in the violence viewing group ...

"The violence of television and film entertainment is highly unrealistic. In eighteen episodes last year, the two heroes of 'Miami Vice' killed five times as many people as the entire Miami police force in the previous year. The kill ratio of these two fictional, trigger-happy police officers was more than 12,000 times higher than the kill ratio of the average American big-city officer. ... Whereas real violence is almost always senseless loss of temper triggered by alcohol intoxication and aided by gun ownership, and frequently occurs [among] family, friends and acquaintances, television violence pits cunning, middle-aged businessmen against equally cunning and violent detectives or wild vigilante officers ...

"... whereas 50% of real-life violence is committed under the influence of alcohol, only 1% of television violence falls into this category. Instead of teaching the realistic message that the way towards peace in society is to get away from violence and alcohol abuse, television teaches that heavy alcohol consumption, a quick temper and a ready gun are the best avenues to peace.

"An even more frightening recent development is the increasing sadism of popular Hollywood entertainment. Major corporations like Time-Life, Inc., Coca-Cola and Gulf & Western now massively promote extremely sadistic and gruesome horror-slasher entertainment to children and adult viewers. Studies from the U.S. and Australia show that films of extreme and brutal sadism have become a standard part of growing up in modern western 'civilization.' A recent study by the Junior League found that 25% of middle-class children had seen 'Nightmare on Elm Street' during the first month of its release on cable. Even more shocking was the fact that the average child who saw the film saw it an average of four times each.

The Devil's Web

"NCTV research has documented a major increase in the proportion of violence on prime time T.V., children's T.V., rock music lyrics, sports violence, children's toys, pornography and even best-selling books in the past twenty to thirty years. The average American by the age of twenty-one will have enjoyed 10,000 hours of violence on his or her home television set. The first television generation has grown up to be the most violent generation in recorded American history. The second television generation is now being raised on much stronger stuff ..."

Let's examine some of the films with occultic overtones.

7 Doors of Death — A movie about a New York woman who inherits a Louisiana hotel located near the gate to hell. The woman and a doctor are taken over by satanic spirits; many brutal killings. Murder with chains, boiling acid, victims nailed to walls, spikes driven into wrists, tarantulas, woman's throat ripped out by dogs, and many shootings.

Friday the 13th, The Final Chapter — A supernatural psychopathic killer continues to murder people, often while they are committing some sexual indiscretion. The film begins with highlights of murders from the first three films, encapsulizations of the most gruesome scenes, then continues the slashing and hacking. Several characters are shown committing adultery, and others are graphically stabbed with knives and machetes, hacked with axes and hatchets, disemboweled, impaled, strangled with chains, choked, hung, and cut up in tiny pieces. One scene depicts the crushing of a skull (audible).

Gremlins — A cute little gremlin is given as a gift to a young boy ... it is discovered that when (the gremlin) feeds after midnight, it reproduces into many ugly, green, violent little monsters. Soon there are hundreds of gremlins terrorizing the town. Virtual warfare exists between the gremlins and anything in their path. They stab, strangle, bulldoze a house and people, bite and eat people, intentionally cause traffic accidents, chase people, fire guns and hit people with objects while the townspeople use a microwave oven, trash compactor, knives, fire, a baseball bat and more to kill them.

Evil Dead — Five young people rent a cabin in rural Kentucky for a weekend. A Babylonian curse causes them, one at a time, to turn into demons and attack their companions. Violence is extremely gory and includes a man hacking a demon's head with an ax, a demon stabbing a man in the back, a demon beheaded with a shovel, a woman grabbed by vines, torn clothing, pending rape, and lots of bloody fighting.

124

Deathstalker — Deathstalker is challenged by a sorceress. He must take a sword, medallion and a chalice from Monkor. Violence is extremely gory and includes two graphic rapes, some sexual assault, women being grabbed, their hair pulled, women are tied up and chained in numerous scenes with the threat of pending rape, torture, choking, a man decapitated, a man crushed, knifings, man beaten by a crowd, man torn apart by crowd, and more.

Revenge of the Ninja — A martial arts film, the plot of which serves only as a transition tool between fight scenes, many of which are gory. Underlying theme seems to be the inevitability of violence and killing even when one desires to avoid them. Stabbing, kicking, attempted rape, restraint with chains, drowning, kidnapping, poison darts thrown in eyes and face, and more.

What about sexual violence to women? Is this having an effect on our children? A few years ago, a video game came on the market called "Custer's Revenge." At first, it seemed to be just another video. In "Custer's Revenge," Custer is wearing only boots and a hat and his intentions toward an Indian maiden are not those of an officer and a gentleman. The player earns points by coupling the male figure with the naked Indian maiden as many times as possible without being hit by an arrow. According to an AP wire story, Stuart Kesten, president of American Multiple Industries, makers of the game, stated, "Our object is not to arouse. Our object is to entertain ..."

According to a September 15, 1982, press release by the NCTV, "The researchers report that 35% of American and Canadian college and adult males admit at least some chance that they would rape a woman if assured of not getting caught ..." Dr. Ed Donnerstein of the University of Wisconsin and Dr. Neil Malamuth of UCLA presented the research at [an] annual meeting of the American Psychological Association in Washington, D.C. The studies compared the effects of four types of films on male viewers: sexually violent, violent but not sexual, explicitly sexual but not violent, and neutral. The researchers found no increase in violent or sexually violent attitudes toward women caused by either the neutral or the explicitly sexual films. However, both the violent and ... the sexually violent films resulted in major increases in the willingness to administer pain to women and to report an increased likelihood of raping a woman. If the men were angered beforehand, the readiness to violence caused by the violent film was even greater."

In 1988, the Rhode Island Rape Crisis Center conducted a *survey* that resulted in the following statement: "A majority of sixth through ninth grade students felt that a man had the right to rape a woman, particularly if he had spent money on her (PMRC and Teen Vision videotapes, "Rising to the Challenge, July 1988)."

Some have argued that the term "rape" may have been unfamiliar to some of the younger readers who were surveyed but, even if they interpreted "rape" to mean "make love to," a very serious issue exists here that requires further study, and we have to wonder to what extent these children's attitudes have been influenced by the sexually explicit television shows, movies and advertisements they have seen.

Grim Reaper As Entertainment

An issue which is even more frightening to many is that of movies which depict *real* death scenes, often called "snuff films." The most popular on the market are *Faces of Death, Parts I, II and III*. These films contained actual footage (according to accompanying blurbs and comments from promoters) of various types of death including an execution, accidents and, in one case, a human sacrifice that was allowed to be filmed. Whether these death scenes were real is still being debated, but the significant element here is that the films were advertised, marketed and distributed as films of real death scenes.

The incidence of "copy cat" criminal activities has risen in proportion to the popularity of slasher and snuff films. In one case, a 15-year-old boy in Dedham, Massachusetts, beat a 14-year-old classmate to death because he "wanted to find out what it was like to kill someone." The youth, who was found guilty of the murder and is eligible for parole in 15 years, had told friends of his desire to kill someone. He showed the body to two of his friends after the killing.

An anonymous tip allowed investigators to arrest the boy a month later. He told a psychiatric counselor that he had made the decision to kill someone after viewing the *Faces of Death* videotape.

In another incident in Portsmouth, Virginia, a man who repeatedly had watched the movie *Revenge of the Ninja*, donned black Oriental combat gear, armed himself as a Ninja warrior, and murdered two people before killing himself.

A 6-year-old boy in Michigan hung himself after copying, detail-for-detail, a hanging scene in a "Scooby Doo" cartoon. His parents sued the network and the makers of the cartoon, and collected an undisclosed amount of money on the condition that no information would be released to the press. Still, Hollywood and the television networks tell us that viewers do not imitate what they see.

Why am I coming down so hard on television and movie violence in a book on teen devil worship and other occult activities of children? Because numerous case studies and other research data have shown that young people who are obsessed with either violent themes or occult themes almost always are influenced by or, at the very least, receptive to the other.

Consider the case of young Jason Wayne Rose.

Jason, age 20, was charged with the 1988 murder of 19-year-old Melissa Ann Meyer. In a videotaped reenactment of the crime, Jason described how he killed Melissa. He stated that he hit her on the back of the head with a machete after choking her to unconsciousness, then stood with another young man, John Ray Jones, on opposite ends of a wooden spear that lay across her neck.

Jason said that he killed Meyer after being instructed to do so by the casting of rune stones (a fortune-telling device). He further stated that the killing was a sacrifice to the god Arioch (a Babylonian god of chaos and evil listed in the "Dungeons & Dragons" book entitled *Deities and Demigods*).

Jason was involved heavily with many forms of entertainment violence as well as the occult. He had a number of "Dungeons & Dragons" materials and admitted having been involved with that game for some time. He listened to heavy metal and black metal music almost exclusively. During cross-examination, his attorney referred frequently to the book *Necronomicon* which includes occult spells and rituals.

In addition, Jason watched extremely violent movies which included *Faces of Death, Parts I and II* (graphic videos about death, dismemberment, autopsies, etc.).

I testified as an expert witness for the prosecution in this case, explaining to those in the courtroom the effects of adolescent involvement in satanism and other occult activities.

The trial ended and the verdict was given on May 16, 1989. After nearly two days of deliberation, the nine-woman, three-man jury unanimously found that Jason Rose, 21, killed Melissa Meyer intentionally and without provocation, and that Rose is a continuing threat to society. He was sentenced to death. Jason Rose is the first person in 62 years to be sentenced to death in Oregon.

Rose's attorney told reporters that testimony during the trial regarding Rose's activity in the occult and satanism was inappropriate. He said that while the murder probably was unprovoked, it was spontaneous.

The prosecutor, Mr. Brian Barnes said Gough's claim (Rose's attorney) was "attorney talk." Claims that the crime wasn't connected to satanism is "simply not borne out by the evidence," Barnes said.

Meyer's killing was the result of a "unique combination of a social deviant involved in cult activities," he said.

What About the Victim, Melissa Meyer?

In the video re-enactment, it was quite clear that young Melissa Meyer fought for her life with her fist, her feet, and her screams, begging

The Devil's Web

to be let go. It obviously was very difficult on her parents to not only listen to the testimony but to hear how their daughter suffered and struggled.

I think some of the saddest parts of trials and the work that is involved in theses crimes is to watch the pain of the families. Jack Meyer and his wife Nancy had comments to make to the press after the verdict was given. (Taken from the *Register Guard*, May 17, 1989.)

The Meyers described Melissa as an adopted child who came to them at the age of 5 with two left tennis shoes, wide brown eyes and jet black hair that hinted of her Indian heritage.

"She was sexually and physically abused as a child before her adoption. She distrusted strangers but at the same time gravitated toward them, her parents said. She often kept to herself as she grew up, they said.

The Meyers said that as a child, Melissa cried when she saw someone "die" on television. And she talked to her grandmother on the telephone several times one day to make sure she wasn't dead after her grandmother had told her that she, too, would die some day.

The couple said they have removed their daughter's pictures from the living room wall because emotionally they can't reconcile the small smiling girl in the photographs with the image of the body found on a Springfield hillside nearly a year ago.

Unlike Jason Rose, Melissa Meyer was not involved in the occult, her parents said. She was intelligent and strongwilled and "one of her last possessions was her Bible," her mother said.

Melissa Meyer liked to jazz dance and ride horses and loved the feeling of her hair flying in the wind, her family said. She was an exceptional secretary and clerical worker, and family photos show her smiling, dressed in carefully selected clothing, posing like a model. ... The Meyers often talk about their daughter in the present tense. However, time for grief has been little.

The couple have dogged police for information, tracked court dates and been actively involved in finding out what happened to their child. They've also joined a support group for families of victims of violent crimes in Seattle.

"... they tried to take her spirit. That is the big thing. They tried to take her spirit at the time of death," Nancy Meyer said, referring to Rose and Jones chanting to an occult god in the course of the slaying."

It is obvious that this kind of pain permeates every such tragedy and we must not forget the victims.

This case is only one of many I have investigated and/or studied in which obsessions with occult themes as well as violence go hand-in-hand.

Dorothy Singer, Ph.D., a researcher of children's toys, television programming and music videos at Yale University, says, "We desperately need parental and child education. We are seeing children exposed to the ugly, disgusting and violent at younger and younger ages. It starts when you are young. ... It leads into more heavy-duty material and behavior problems later in life. For fifteen years, we have been giving our research findings to the networks and now the toy industry. I'm so discouraged. Nobody listens. They're making so much money."

Consider the following wire service reports: "With stunning frequency, new stories appear about one of the most perplexing of all crimes, that of homicides committed by children, some as young as seven and eight-years-old, against other children and teenagers. Statistics compiled by the Federal Bureau of Investigation show that 9.88 per 100,000 Americans were arrested for homicide in 1982, but the rate among 17-year-olds, for instance, was more than double the rate for all ages: 22.6 per 100,000 (from the *New York Times* News Service)."

"A Justice Department survey shows teenagers are twice as likely as adults to be the victims of violent crime, and their assailants are often casual friends or relatives (from UPI)."

Steven Schlesinger, director of the Bureau of Justice Statistics, said in an interview with the *Cedar City Spectrum* (Utah) that a survey conducted by his department revealed that from 1982 through 1984, young people 12- to 19- years-old were the victims of approximately 1.8-million violent crimes and 3.7-million thefts annually. Those crimes were 2.2-times more frequent than for persons 20-years-old or older.

I do not believe that all violent crime involving teenagers and children is related to entertainment violence, but we must recognize the potential for entertainment-related violence and explore the possibility that a relationship exists between an individual crime and the entertainment preferences of those involved.

Certainly child abuse and drugs play a major role in motivating young people to commit violent acts, but we would be taking the easy way out if we ascribed all the ills of society to these two factors. We must examine all social factors when trying to understand an individual's actions in order to assist in correcting negative behaviors.

Toys, Cartoons, and Agression

A question often comes up in seminars related to toys and cartoons. I always try to accentuate the positive rather than preaching a doomsday philosophy. There are many excellent toys and games on the market, and there are many delightful and educational cartoons and other television programs for children and adolescents. Television can be a wonderful teaching tool, but we must remember that if good programming can teach our children good things, then it follows that bad programming can teach our children bad things.

According to statistics compiled by the National Coalition on Television Violence, the sales of war toys have climbed by 350 percent since 1982 to create a record $842 million per year market. Many of these toys are promoted to young viewers via Saturday morning cartoon programming, some of which is extremely violent and based upon themes of war. A very disturbing aspect of this type of programming is the heavy emphasis on intense battles between "good" and "evil," battles which escalate rapidly and end only when the enemy is totally obliterated.

NCTV also reports that the average American child sees approximately 800 advertisements per year which promote violent toys.

Dr. Radecki comments, "This repeated teaching of seeing your opponent as someone despicably evil who can only be dealt with through combat is very harmful. The research of cartoon violence and violent toys is quite clear. These programs and their violent war toys are teaching children to be more violent and desensitizing them to the real horrors of war and military combat. We have found thirty different scientific research studies relevant to the cartoon violence issue. Twenty-eight of these found at least some harmful effects while only two did not. These studies covered over 4,300 children from six different countries on four continents. Although the research on violent toys is less extensive, it gives exactly the same answers. The cartoon and violent toy studies show that these materials cause children to hit, kick, choke, push and hold down other children. They have found increases in selfishness, anxiety, and the hurting of animals. Sharing and school performance have been found to decrease."

NCTV notes a recent survey of U.S. psychiatrists which found that 81 percent think violent entertainment has a harmful effect on viewers while only 8 percent think it has a beneficial effect.

Dr. Leon Eisenberg, M.D., a leading Harvard psychiatrist, says, "War toys are likely to prepare children for a world that accepts war as commonplace. I would guess that most clinicians would agree that war toys are bad for children and should not be bought or supported. These are not the kinds of things that parents ought to encourage."

Dr. Ron Slaby, Ph.D., of Harvard's Center for Research on Children's Television agrees, saying, "From research findings on the effects of playing with toys with aggressive themes, we can say that playing with these war toys is likely to stimulate higher levels of aggression. When children play actively with toys that have aggressive themes, they are more likely to show higher levels of aggression. T.V.

and movie programs of a violent nature are also likely to stimulate the viewer. Ads or programs depicting toys in war-type combat are likely to cause high levels of aggression even in normal children as well as children who already have problems with violence. These toys and programs can teach healthy, nonviolent children new ways of behaving aggressively, besides increasing violent behavior in problem children."

A report prepared by the National Institute of Mental Health and condensed in a *New York Times* article offers four theories to explain the link between violent television programming and increased aggression in children and teenagers revealed by the study:

1. Observational learning—The theory is that violent behavior is acquired from television much the way that cognitive and social skills are learned from siblings, parents and friends.

2. Arousal process—This theory examines physiological arousal resulting from witnessing violent episodes.

3. Justification processes—This holds that persons who are already aggressive find justification for their behavior by watching favorite television characters.

4. Attitude change—Studies show that children who watch television heavily are more suspicious and distrustful and tend to think there is more violence in the world than do others.

Any time we begin to discuss a variety of ways in which television programing might be regulated in order to protect children, we are met with a great deal of suspicion and, occasionally, hostility. Indeed, any time any person or group tries to educate the public regarding harmful children's entertainment, they are accused of promoting the violation of the constitutional right of freedom of speech of the creators of the entertainment. In open discussions, the conversation usually digresses and becomes a verbal confrontation revolving around the issue of censorship.

It is at these times that I feel it necessary to take a strong stand on what I believe the real issue to be. We are talking about children and adolescents, and, yes, we do have the responsibility to ensure their safety. We have determined the ages at which people may be licensed to drive cars, purchase pornography, purchase and consume alcohol and enter into binding contractual agreements.

To protect our children from the proven influences of violent entertainment seems no less critical to me than protecting them from these other dangers. Children need and deserve to be allowed to mature to the point where their values and attitudes are solidified before they are bombarded with confusing, obscene and violent entertainment. Children have rights, and the parents of children must have the right to protect those children.

Let's consider other non-occult-related violent films which also affect young people.

By far the most controversial to date has been the *Rambo* series of movies. *First Blood* and *First Blood, Part II*, the first films in the series, started a nationwide weapons fervor that some have called "Rambomania."

Soon after these two films were released, a California cutlery store reported that sales of survival knives of the type used by the Rambo character (with hollow handles and sawtooth blades) had jumped from one sale per week to more than eight per week. These knives cost between $60 and $220 apiece.

One of the owners of a Nevada machine gun firing range said that his business had increased by 50 percent since the Rambo movies were released. He added that customers also were showing interest in crossbows of the type used in the films.

Younger Rambo fans were enticed with Rambo high-energy candy bars, walkie-talkies, trading cards, cap guns and other toys.

A licensing agent for Rambo products said shortly after the release of the first two movies, "The licensing for Rambo is going to be very successful. We are just at the beginning of it."

Quite a few Rambo-related incidents have been reported by the media.

In a California case, two prep school students, both age 17, were arrested and charged in the stabbing death of a transient. A local newspaper reported that a "Rambo film" was expected to be an issue in the case. The two youths allegedly had "sharpened a military knife and practiced attack maneuvers."

In an Iowa case, two 14-year-olds from a prestigious Sioux City neighborhood broke into a home and stole weapons from a collection. Several nights later, the boys dressed in camouflage gear, armed themselves with knives and the stolen guns and broke into a local hardware store. They were apprehended after their movements triggered an alarm.

The *Sunday Nonpareil* (Council Bluffs) reported that the boys "went on a raid, going it the way they imagined Sylvester Stallone's 'Rambo' character or Chuck Norris movies commandos might have done it." A juvenile officer said to reporters interviewing him about this case, "Kids have a belief that there is a personal magic that protects them. All their thoughts are correct and nobody understands them. This magic will protect them. They can drink a case of beer and not get drunk, have intercourse and not get pregnant, and drive 100 miles an hour and not get hurt."

USA Today reported that a 20-year-old man was found guilty of the murder of a 15-year old boy. The article stated that Mark Johnson stabbed Thomas Schroeder seventy-two times "while playing Rambo."

Other violent movies which apparently have overstimulated some youngsters include *Gremlins*, *Road Warriors*, and the seemingly endless Ninja films.

A pair of fourth graders in Los Angeles pretended they were on a treasure hunt, resulting in one child becoming trapped in a chimney. One of the boys told his mother that they were playing at being "Goonies [from the movie of the same name]."

An Oklahoma man was killed when two teenagers hurled a rock from their truck through the windshield of his vehicle. The youths made written statements in which they admitted to having been inspired by the movie *Road Warriors*.

Susan Cabot Roman, a former actress who, at one time, was linked romantically to Jordan's King Hussein, was beaten to death by her 22-year-old son who was "into" Ninja "stuff," according to a police officer. Before confessing to the murder, the young man had claimed a burglar outfitted as a Ninja warrior had committed the crime.

In Lexington, Kentucky, a sniper carrying a samurai sword and dressed in black martial arts gear opened fire with a rifle from a building at the University of Kentucky.

The list goes on.

Parents often ask me about "war games" like "Killer," "Assassin" and "Laser Tag." I cite specific incidents for their consideration.

A California deputy sheriff shot and killed a 19-year-old man who was playing "Laser Tag" at an elementary school around dusk. The young man had fired "flashes of light" from his toy gun at the deputies who had responded to a report of prowlers at the school. The deputy sheriff was described as "anguished" and required intense counseling following the incident (yet another victim?).

In Salem, Oregon, police officers rushed to a building in the downtown area where a gunman reportedly was crouching on the roof. The subject quickly dropped his "weapon" and surrendered to police. It was determined later that the 16-year-old youth, armed with a cap gun, had been playing the game "Killer." He represented a character called "The Saint" and was waiting on the rooftop for "The Spectre." A symbolic killing of "The Spectre" by "The Saint" would have meant points toward winning the game for the latter.

One police officer commented, "Some strange things are happening in the name of fun ... Will people try to stop this or will they accept it? And if they do, what will be the repercussions? This one turned out for the best, but you just wonder what the next one is going to be."

These represent only a few of the many war-game-related incidents in police files around the nation, making it clear that this type of entertainment has, at the very least, some very serious potential for danger and death. Don't be fooled. These games are a far cry from the once-popular childhood games of "Cowboys and Indians" and "Cops and Robbers."

All entertainment violence, even that which is non-occultic, desensitizes the young viewer to death and pain, making him a vulnerable target for those who would ensnare him in the web of devil worship. Criminal satanists love violence, and "turning on" young people to themes of death and destruction is one way of breaking down a child's resistance to occult influences.

Be a Guiding Light

Where, then, do we draw the line on our children's entertainment? A good place to start is with family values. As parents, we have both the right and the responsibility to be informed about our children's activities. If the entertainment being enjoyed by a child in any given family is in contrast to that family's moral standards, the adults in that family must not remain silent. Our children are precious gifts from God; He has entrusted them to our care and protection. We are duty-bound to speak up and take appropriate action when we believe that their sensibilities have been violated; minors are not capable of giving "informed consent." It may seem like an obvious statement, but simply by virtue of the fact that they **are** children, they do not always make wise and safe decisions.

I have used the example before, but it bears repeating: we don't let them drive when they are still children; by law, children cannot drink alcohol, buy pornographic materials or enter into contracts. How, then, can we justify ignoring the games they play and the movies and videos they watch when some of those games and films have been proven to negatively affect their behavior?

Open the lines of communication with your children regarding the forms of entertainment they enjoy. State your case firmly but calmly when the values represented by certain forms of entertainment are in conflict with your family's religious, ethical and moral beliefs and standards.

If your child tries to shut down those lines of communication and/or becomes hostile and belligerent, you should consider enlisting the aid of a competent therapist or trusted member of the clergy to counsel and advise.

Whatever your course of action, do not throw your hands up in the air and give up the issue. Saying, "Forget it! We can't get through to him!" is taking the easy way out. If **you** can't talk to him, find someone who can. More important, find someone who will **listen** to him and to you. Most communication failures are the result of too much talking and too little listening.

Many of us also need to become more sensitized ourselves. Most parents reading this book are themselves members of the first "television generation." In many cases, our own sensibilities have been violated, and we really need to work at reversing the effects of those violations. Stop and think about the kinds of television programs and movies you watch, sometimes mindlessly, often oblivious to senseless violence and obscenity. If you find (as I did) that you are surprised at your own viewing habits, consider making a conscious effort to choose more carefully the programing to which you commit your valuable time.

Additionally, we need to involve our children as much as possible in family activities. This isn't easy for any of us these days. We all seem to be going in so many different directions that some families even find it difficult to sit down together for a meal, much less schedule an evening when everyone can enjoy a movie, ball game or concert together; but can we really afford not to make every effort to steer our children in the direction of positive and rewarding leisure activities? We must first educate ourselves about violent forms of entertainment and examine the alternatives. Then we must educate our children. In spite of what they may say, they're counting on us.

EPILOGUE

No family is immune to the threat of occult activity or ritual crime simply by virtue of their religious beliefs, moral standards or the locks on their front doors. Almost without exception, the children whose cases have been discussed in this book came from "good families" with loving parents who had taught their children well. The children are victims of Satan's web, and the people who love them also are victims.

Much needs to be done to stem the tide of occult, ritual-related criminal activity in this country. Parents must continue to encourage their children in the family's religious faith, to keep close watch on their activities, the friends they choose, the music they listen to, the movies they watch and the games they play.

Mental health professionals and physicians must take occult involvement seriously, learn to recognize signs and symptoms, learn interviewing techniques and not pass such involvement off as a fad.

Likewise, law enforcement officials must take occult activity seriously and learn the proper investigative procedures with which to approach crime scenes, suspects, surviving victims and the families of all involved.

Members of the clergy also must educate themselves and prepare to counsel victims and their relatives and friends.

Teachers and other school officials also bear a responsibility to be alert to signs of occult involvement in children and teens so that the proper individuals can be notified, appropriate steps taken and the children protected.

For the continued protection of our children, families and school systems should discourage the wearing of occult-related clothing and jewelry and the playing of games with occult themes.

We must document all information relating to occult activity even if it does not appear relevant at the time. Police officials must document "satanic graffiti" in incident reports rather than "graffiti" and look closely for other indications such as wax drippings from candles that often go unnoticed.

Teachers who observe children behaving in bizarre fashions that may indicate ritual or occult activity should document such observations as well as graffiti on walls and lockers, occult drawings, phrases and words on composition books, and essays and poems with themes of death, mutilation and devil worship.

School counselors also can be effective in this area by bringing such activity to the attention of principals and parents.

Parents also should document symptomatic behaviors.

I remember a case in which a mother and father were disturbed about their son's activities. In addition to his use of drugs, they were concerned about his attitudes and behaviors which signaled some occult involvement. While charting a course of action with therapists and other helping professionals, they kept a diary of their son's activities. This became an invaluable tool for the therapists and juvenile authorities when they made recommendations concerning the youth's need for specialized help.

Keep an open mind. Too often people who become involved with ritualistic crime carry with them their personal feelings, beliefs and backgrounds. While we certainly do not want to imagine occult activity where it does not exist, it is equally important not to overlook symptoms that are there and are relevant.

On occasion, a crime scene is so bizarre that those who must examine it will say that the occult signs are not "real," but rather evidence of "kids fooling around." This is not to say that we should not have a healthy degree of skepticism, but we also must not rule out the possibility of certain events having taken place just because we can't conceive of them happening.

Remain objective. This is difficult advice to take when dealing with a subject like occult activity, but the least effective people working in this field are those who allow their personal beliefs and value systems to impair their ability to evaluate a given situation objectively.

When criminal activity is suspected or the possibility exists that a child is in danger, the authorities must be notified. Parents must not hesitate to make such notification themselves, and school personnel and therapists also must be willing to speak up in cases where this type of activity is suspected.

Never assume that an individual is acting alone until all other information surrounding a case has been investigated fully. Too often, those who don't know any better will say, "Johnny is just a lone, self-styled teen devil worshiper."

Ask yourself how many people you know who practice a belief system by themselves. If Johnny is a child from a Judeo-Christian background or another mainstream religious denomination and suddenly converts to "devil worship," we must dig to find out when his conversion took place and how.

If an individual is involved in "satanic criminal activity," he may deny a great deal in order to protect others as well as the belief system to which they adhere. Adolescents often will confess readily to avoid incriminating friends. This is a fairly typical teenage behavior pattern, but it can be very serious in cases where children are truly afraid of the other group members and what they might do to him if he "snitches." In these cases, it becomes even more likely that the child being questioned will "take the fall."

Have a team approach. Work with a therapist, a clergyman and other helping professionals. Don't forget that law enforcement officials are helping professionals, too. Everyone must work together to help a young person recover from an experience with a destructive cult or philosophy.

In some cases, helping professionals will refuse to discuss religious beliefs with these children, either because they do not have belief systems of their own or because they do not feel qualified to do so. Since many of these children are confused and have questions they need answered which pertain to religion, it is imperative that a trusted clergyman who has experience in this specific area of counseling be brought into the team. This is not an area in which all members of the clergy are knowledgeable or able to work effectively.

Educate the community so that tragedies can be prevented. Few scenarios are more discouraging than the ones in which cases go to court and are presented to juries whose members do not believe that occult and ritual-related crimes take place. We cannot expect the public to care or to react appropriately to problems if they don't know or believe that the problems exist.

Use the following tips to educate community groups:

1. **Use the media to get the message to the public.**
   A. Have a specific goal.
   B. Identify specific problems in your area.
   C. Educate media personnel.
   D. Maintain good media relations.
   E. Clearly explain the facts. Do not sensationalize this subject.
   F. Maintain your own credibility.

2. **Have specific targets of education.**
   A. Churches
   B. School PTAs
   C. Law enforcement agencies
   D. Social service agencies
   E. Mental health organizations
   F. Local prosecutors
   G. Community action groups
3. **Have specific programs designed for each group.**
4. **Plan a continuing education program which is progressive.**

To be effective, begin with educating the various groups with the simple facts about ritualistic involvement including a basic overview and definition of the problem.

If necessary, progress to deeper levels of ritualistic involvement. Develop a list of credible speakers who are willing to address the groups in the community. Check their references carefully. Find out how much experience they have in this field and whether they actually have worked on cases of occult activity or with individuals.

Avoid labeling your speakers as "experts" unless their expertise is undeniable. Always allow for question-and-answer periods. Even if your speaker does not know the answer to every question (and he probably will not), this is a good time for interaction with the audience. Beware of speakers who do not allow for questions and answers.

Remember to use a team approach to educating the community. Involve police officials, mental health professionals and community groups well-versed in ritualistic activity. If necessary, create a community task force or an organization with the goal of educating the public.

We have prepared the following checklist for survivors of occult-related criminal activity and/or suicide. This applies to those who have lost a loved one, those whose children have been victimized, and friends and relatives of those involved.

1. It takes time to recover from a tragedy. Do not expect to feel like yourself too soon.
2. Allow yourself time to grieve.
3. At the time of the tragedy, you probably will be in shock. Your most difficult times may come later, particularly at holiday times, anniversaries, birthdays and other favorite family occasions.
4. Talk with others who have had similar experiences.
5. Take time to cry, move through the pain, and know that grief is not a weakness, but a relief valve.

6. Be grateful for friends, but don't allow yourself to be put on a pedestal. Let your friends know when you are hurting. Talk about your grief.

7. Recognize your needs. If you need to talk to a professional, do it. Don't be ashamed to ask for help.

8. You will be able to serve others once your healing begins. You will know when you are ready.

9. Try to get out and do something enjoyable, something that makes you laugh. Laughter can be a great healer.

10. There is light at the end of the tunnel. Don't become bitter, and don't blame God. Realize what has happened, but know that the tragedy was caused by human beings.

People often ask me, "Isn't this topic depressing? When do you think you will burn out?"

All I can say is that we look for what good we can bring out of every tragedy. We count the wins, and we don't dwell on the losses.

Sean Sellers is an excellent example. He has created an organization from his prison cell called Radical Teens for Christ. His grandfather, Carlos Lindley, and other family members in Oklahoma help run the nonprofit organization. So, you see, much good can result from tragedy if we only work together to make it happen.

Does community education really work? You bet it does.

I received a letter from a police officer which is reprinted here with his permission. His name and state of residence have been deleted to protect his family's privacy.

Dear Patricia Pulling,

... I am a police officer in a small community in (state). Recently I have come across what I believe is "satan worship" in our school system. One particular incident involved a 15-year-old who was heavily involved in Dungeons & Dragons, heavy metal, and eventually "satanism." This youngster had written on a calendar in his room that he was going to kill his parents. The boy's mother found the calendar three days before the killing was to take place. At this time, our department was called in and a shotgun was found in the boy's room.

I went to the home to take the boy to a mental home as a result of the mother fearing for her life. Before I took the boy, I looked in his room and found heavy metal posters, 666, upside-down crosses carved on a table, and also a pentagram carved on the table.

This boy told me that there are about thirty others that are involved in this ...

Oh, I forgot to mention that the boy I took to the mental hospital I later led to Christ.

Thank you for your help ...

This is a case where a double homicide was prevented through awareness, caring people, and someone who took this teen "fad" seriously.

Here is another letter, this one from a mother who recognized her son's need for help:

My name is Cheryl ... my son's name is Ricky and he is thirteen-years-old. Ricky has never been a fighter or trouble-maker, but when he reached seventh grade, he started hanging around with kids who were [not good influences]. His grades were terrible, and his attitude changed for the worst. I really never thought anything about it. I thought he was going through a phase. Then I started hearing about "satanism." I watched a tape about it, and I also went to a seminar. After watching the tape and seeing the attitudes these children had and all the signs they drew, I started to get a little worried. I also noticed all of these people were into heavy metal music. My son just craved that kind of music. So I decided to go through his papers and room one day when he wasn't home. I couldn't believe the things I found. There were poems, drawings and Nazi signs with tanks and guns.

I had talked to my brother who had seen all the seminars and he said he would help all he could. I decided to talk to [a friend] and we both decided I should call our pastor, and I did. He was really understanding and helpful. He asked me if he could see the tapes, poems and drawings, so I took them to him. I also mentioned to him that my son stopped going to church. He looked through the things and said he really didn't think my son realized what he was getting into, but was headed in that direction. He said he would talk to the youth administrator about my son ...

The youth administrator talked to my son, which I thought was great because my son really looks up to him ... Our pastor suggested I get my son away from these kids who were doing this. In a school of 900 kids where you can't sit with [your child] all day long, this is hard to do. So we decided it would be better to change schools, and we did ...

Ricky's grades have improved, he plays basketball on the team at school, his attitude is better and he now listens to music other than heavy metal. Everyone is so proud of Ricky. He has improved so much.

I thank God every night that we have a pastor and a youth administrator who care about people the way they do. With their help, we were able to stop it before it was too late ...

Sincerely ...

Children are our greatest hope, and they rely on us to guide them. Their successes depend upon our willingness to instruct and lead them, and we must never give up. Our own futures and the future of this great nation ultimately will be in their hands.

When I first became involved in ritualistic research and investigation, I read a quote which has become my inspiration for everything that I do. The English philosopher Edmund Burke said, "All that is necessary for evil to triumph is for good men to do nothing."

My sincere wish is that all readers will feel compelled to do something even if it is only to remain alert and pay attention to signs of ritual activity in the communities in which they live.

Those who have more time may wish to volunteer a few hours a week to serving the educational needs of their communities on the subject of ritualistic activity.

If this subject does not concern you or if you are convinced that your community doesn't have a problem in this area, perhaps you will consider giving a few hours of time to some other social issue involving children and teenagers.

Please find the time to help out in some critical area so that we can put the wheels of destructive and dangerous influences into reverse.

Monetary contributions are helpful, but we need personal involvement and caring individuals even more. Together we can make a difference. Together we can save our children from *The Devil's Web*.

APPENDIX A

HISTORY OF
THE OCCULT

Man has always sought to understand and explain the forces in nature, to discover the purpose of his own existence and to determine whether there is a life beyond this one.

Archaeologists have uncovered cave markings and burial sites in western Europe and the Middle East that indicate our earliest ancestors recognized a power greater than themselves and prepared their dead for a life in the hereafter.

The ancient Greeks and Romans developed elaborate mythologies and hierarchies of gods and goddesses to explain the unseen powers that control man and the world around him.

American Indians worshiped a number of nature spirits in ritual ceremonies.

Virtually every culture and organized religion has generated a system of beliefs based on faith in one or more deities, the leadership of revered prophets and teachers, and a deep and abiding conviction that this life has real and positive meaning which survives the earthly grave.

During the evolution of man's spirituality, a darker side of his character also emerged, a side which sought not simply to understand and worship, but to harness, manipulate and control the forces that determine his destiny and the destinies of those around him. While many of the earliest practitioners of what we now view as magic and other so-called occult sciences were engaged in sincere attempts to reconcile their mystical beliefs with contemporary religious views, others had far less honorable intentions.

It is this darker side of human nature and those who have succumbed to it to which we owe the current proliferation of destructive cults and other harmful influences which can and do affect our children. A working knowledge of man's past involvement with magic, witchcraft and demonology is critical to an understanding of today's occultic sects and the dangerous consequences of violent games, books, movies and music.

The world's earliest written records tell of "magicians," men who claimed to possess great stores of secret knowledge and to have special powers. The Acts of the Apostles in the New Testament relates the story of Simon Magus (Simon the magician) who could perform miracles, but who finally was defeated by a prayerful Apostle Peter. Others considered to be among the early magicians were the Gnostics, a sect of Christian heretics who denied that Christ had existed in physical form and who claimed exclusive ownership to the secrets of salvation.

The *cabala*, a system of Jewish mysticism which may predate the time of Christ, purported to teach the industrious student the secrets of the universe and of life itself. A complex diagram called "the tree of life" was supposed to describe man's relationship to God and exists as an example of one of the first attempts to reconcile opposing religious views. While never a part of mainstream Judaism, the *cabala's* influence is still evident today in some forms of numerology and other mystical systems used by occult practitioners.

The Testament of Solomon, which appeared in the 2nd century A.D., explained the binding of devils and demons into slavery, and later versions included listings of demons which could be so bound and made to attend to the fortunes of magicians.

The Key of Solomon, which did not appear until the 14th century A.D., relied heavily on a mystical system using pentacles or five-pointed star diagrams which could be used to invoke various demons to wreak havoc upon the earth and its inhabitants at the discretion of the magician.

The Lesser Key of Solomon further details the demons and devils available for this type of work. The Testament and Keys of Solomon are significant in that they represent some of the earliest connections drawn between magic and demonology.

Belief in a multiplicity of demons was fairly widespread among religious leaders as well as the general populace during the Middle Ages. Near the end of this period, Martin Luther, the German theologian and leader of the Protestant Reformation, wrote extensively of his physical battles with the demons who tried to interfere with his work.

It was during the Middle Ages that the first secret societies alleged to worship one or more demons began to appear. The Knights Templar originated in the 11th century with a group of eight knights who assigned themselves the task of policing the roads to the Holy Land.

They were held in great favor by the nobility early on and became quite wealthy, their ranks swelling to 30,000 by the end of the 12th century. However, allegations arose which hinted at evil doings in the order, and the membership was investigated by the Church. Many confessed under torture to such heretical acts as worshiping the devil and defiling the crucifix during their rituals as well as to committing unnatural sexual acts. They were burned to death, the only means acceptable to the Church for permanently eliminating heretics.

Another group frequently associated with early devil worship was the Cathars, a 12th century French sect who believed that Lucifer and his devilish horde of followers created this world and that the Church and all of mankind were basically evil. The Cathars were branded heretics by the Inquisition, and many confessed under torture to worshiping the devil in the form of an animal and to kidnapping and murdering children whose bodies were later used in their rituals. The Church had completely eliminated the sect by the late 1300s.

While the Knights Templar and the Cathars may have been the first secret societies suspected of occultic practices, they certainly were not the last. Secret societies in general have flourished throughout history; the more elaborate and secretive their rituals, the more people flocked to join them. Some societies, like the 17th century Rosicrucians and the 18th century Egyptian Freemasons, have been linked to occultic practices due to their claims of esoteric and powerful knowledge that only could be shared with the faithful. Most others were little more than groups of outcasts who banded together for the purpose of extorting huge initiation fees and engaging in orgiastic rituals. Many of today's destructive cults are secretive societies of this latter type.

The Renaissance, a period which saw the vigorous pursuit of all things intellectual and artistic, was also a period of renewed interest in things mystical which we now equate with the occult. Many 15th- and 16th-century religious scholars studied the ancient *cabala* and the works of Solomon as well as what were then believed to be the sciences of alchemy (a fervently sought-after chemical process that would change base metals into gold), astrology and numerology. The majority of these scholars sincerely attempted to discover a rational line of thinking that could bring the religious views of the day into harmony with ancient mystical beliefs, but most died discredited by their contemporaries.

Those who still practice ancient forms of magic are not to be confused with today's stage magicians. These flamboyant showmen are masters of illusion and sleight of hand and are eager for audiences to understand that their skills are the result of countless hours of study and practice rather than any supernatural powers or dealings with demons. Although some stage magicians may dabble in the occult, the acts of most are more closely associated with those of jugglers and other dexterous performers than with any of the ancient systems of magic.

Before moving into the area of modern occultic practices, we also need to look at the concept of witchcraft or, as believers prefer to call it, *wicca* which means "craft of the wise." Witchcraft dates from pre-Christian times and is based on ancient pagan fertility rituals. The most obvious difference between the old systems of magic and witchcraft is that the female was the most important figure in witchcraft as opposed to the dominant male sorcerer or wizard who practiced magic. Today's covens (groups of witches, usually numbering 13) are as likely to include men as women, although some are still predominantly female.

Witchcraft is mentioned in the Bible in Exodus 22:18 which states, "Thou shalt not suffer a witch to live," and again in Deuteronomy 18:12 which calls witchcraft "an abomination unto the Lord."

Witches appear in earlier literature in the mythologies of the Greeks and Romans. Homer's Circe was an enchantress whose magical potion turned men into swine. Medea was a sorceress who married the legendary Jason and assisted him in obtaining the Golden Fleece. The lamias were female monsters of classical mythology who drank the blood of children.

The early Christian fathers appear to have tolerated so-called witches and issued mild statements urging them to refrain from un-Christian activities and behavior. By the 12th century, witches were pretty much accepted by the Church as harmless peasant women who relied on herbal medicines to attend to the ailments of villagers. Around the year 1300, the Church issued the *Canon Episcopi* instructing local religious leaders to teach their followers that the more lurid and frightening suspicions beginning to be associated with witchcraft were totally without basis. The document dismissed the idea that witches had any supernatural powers whatsoever.

The "witchcraft craze" that eventually spread throughout Europe and the New World and which resulted in the persecutions of between 200,000 and 300,000 people began during the 14th century with the Crusades against the Cathars and with the publication of the *Malleus Maleficarum* ("Hammer of Witches"). Heinrich Kramer and Jacob Sprenger, two theology professors, expressed in this book their conviction that the supernatural aspects of witchcraft were real and dangerous threats to the Church and to all decent folk. The work of these two inquisitors detailed the methods to be used in trying and torturing persons suspected of witchcraft. In virtually every case, accusation was tantamount to conviction, and the great witch-hunt was on.

The ancient and widely accepted belief that certain women had special healing powers and the gift of foresight led naturally to acceptance of the *Malleus Maleficarum* as fact. Any woman who lived alone, especially in an isolated setting, suddenly was suspect, as were those women who were poor, handicapped or considered odd in any way by their neighbors. A child who became ill, a crop that failed, a business deal that fell through—all were reasons to assume that witchcraft was involved.

Outstandingly successful women also were mistrusted and Joan of Arc, the French heroine who led the siege of Orleans, brought about her own downfall when she confessed to taking her orders from mysterious voices that only she could hear. She was convicted by the English of witchcraft and burned at the stake in 1431.

Did the widespread belief in witches have any factual basis? Certainly every age has produced both men and women who have engaged in acts of perversion, cruelty and murder. It appears that at least some of those convicted and executed as witches were indeed sick and evil people. The most significant fact, however, is that the great majority of witchcraft confessions were extracted under horrible tortures. Many of the accused reportedly confessed after learning that they would be hung to death before being burned, a marginally better alternative to being burned alive as were those who refused to admit to the practice of witchcraft.

Some of the most famous trials that gave credence to the belief in real witches involved women who used poisons to murder their husbands. Dame Alice Kyteler, the first accused witch in Ireland, was suspected in 1324 of trying to kill her fourth husband by poisoning. She fled to England, but a young maid she left behind allowed that her mistress was a witch and that she herself had engaged in sexual relations with the devil. The maid subsequently was burned to death.

In another case, a number of spouse-murderers in 17th-century France began to suffer from guilt and confessed to their priests. The police learned of these confessions and began an investigation which led to the arrests of five people who were providing poisonous mixtures to those who wanted to do away with their husbands or wives. When names of members of the nobility began to appear on the customer lists, Louis XIV created a commission known as the *Chambre Ardente* ("lighted chamber") to determine the extent of the situation. Thirty-six persons were convicted of witchcraft and sentenced to death, and nearly a hundred more were imprisoned or exiled.

The witchcraft craze reached its American peak in Salem, Massachusetts in 1692 when a West Indian slave named Tituba began to entertain several local children (including the minister's daughter) with occult stories and the telling of fortunes. When the girls began to have strange episodes of crying, throwing themselves on the floor and thrashing about, they were asked by examiners to tell who it was that afflicted them. The children began "the naming of names," the identification of local witches. Just as the naming of names had indicted thousands of innocents in Europe, the practice led to the execution by hanging (except in one case where the victim was pressed to death with stones) of 20 men and women in Salem.

Fortunately, cooler heads began to prevail in the colonies and in Europe following the madness in Salem and after the appearance of several documents (one published anonymously by a priest) which may be viewed as the birth certificates of modern psychiatry. These documents set forth the reasonable theories that the accused, rather than being witches, were for the most part the mentally deranged and other unfortunates who needed medical treatment, and that anyone might confess to anything if enough torture were applied. These tracts also suggested that the witch-hunters themselves were far guiltier than those they persecuted. People paid attention to these commonsense arguments, and by the end of the 18th century, the witchcraft craze had quite literally burnt itself out.

To fully understand modern occultic practices and the dangers they hold for children and teenagers, it is important to note that a great many of the confessed witches and sorcerers (as the men were called) admitted to hurting children with curses of illness and death, and others were suspected of having intercourse with demons and even Satan himself which relations were believed to result in the birth of monstrous children who required the flesh of other children for survival. These stories resulted from the convictions of the earliest pedophiles (child molesters) and child murderers.

Gilles de Rais, a 15th century European nobleman preoccupied with alchemy and other occult sciences, was also a sexual deviant and sadist who murdered nearly 300 children before he was arrested, tried and sentenced to death. Other evidence suggests that the earliest practitioners of demonic worship did indeed sacrifice small children during their ritual ceremonies.

One 17th-century record describes a Black Mass (a high ceremony in homage to Satan) during which an infant was sacrificed over the body of a noblewoman.

The innocence of children always has been considered a powerful force in the ancient black arts, a force that could be used to the advantage of the celebrant if properly released through real or mock sacrifice. According to the oldest satanic beliefs and practices, children were pure, infants were the purest of all, and Satan demanded the sacrifice of these innocents as proof of devotion.

Most modern-day witches disavow any traffic with the devil and claim no relationship whatsoever to those who worship Satan in their services. Most of those who openly discuss their practice of witch-craft today contend that they practice only "white magic," specific rituals designed to bring about desired and positive changes. Some, however, don't seem to mind dabbling occasionally in "black magic" if the need arises to get even with an unfaithful lover or someone else who has done them wrong.

A popular handbook for witches is *The Modern Witch's Spell-book* which purports to teach the reader "Everything You Need to Know to Cast Spells, Work Charms and Love Magic, and Achieve What You Want in Life Through Occult Powers." This book by Sarah Lyddon Morrison includes a section titled "Hate Magic" which gives specific instructions for the casting of spells "To Cause a Lot of Agony" and "To Maim and Kill."

As we look at modern cults and other harmful influences on chil-dren and teenagers, it is important to realize that this and similar books on witchcraft and other occult subjects are widely available to youngsters in bookstores throughout the country and in many school libraries.

The practices of witchcraft and satanic worship, while very differ-ent occult areas, enjoyed a renewed interest during the 19th century. Gerald Gardner, called by many the "king of the witches," is largely responsible for much of the confusion that exists today in separating witches from satanists. Gardner, born in 1884, was a sadomasochist who published *Witchcraft Today* in 1954 when he was 70-years-old. The book informed readers that witchcraft was alive and well and that he belonged to a coven (a group of witches) whose rituals revolved around flagellation and copulation.

The rituals of practicing satanists of the 19th and 20th centuries also have involved nudity and/or sexual acts, hence the confusion between witchcraft and satanism. From this point on, it becomes necessary to look at individuals who, by the sheer force of their per-sonalities, have drawn followers into their occultic circles.

Aleister Crowley is the first and most notorious of the 20th-century occultists and probably is responsible more than any other person for the enormous popularity of the black arts today. Despite a puri-tanical upbringing, this Englishman began what would become a lifelong obsession with the occult shortly after he left Cambridge University around the turn of the century. He joined the Hermetic Order of the Golden Dawn, a group of intellectually sophisticated occultists which at one point counted among its members the poet William Butler Yeats. After a number of quarrels with the group's leaders, Crowley was dismissed from the Order.

He and his wife Rose traveled extensively, and Crowley reportedly discovered his "true identity" as the Antichrist when the two visited the Boulak museum in Cairo in 1904. It was here that Crowley was drawn to the exhibit numbered 666 which was a statue of the Egyptian sun god Horus. He noted that the number was the same as that of the Great Beast in the Bible, and Crowley identified with the principal antagonist of Christ for the rest of his days.

He and Rose collaborated on *The Book of the Law* which proclaimed that Crowley was "Lord of the New Aeon" and that the whole of the law was "Do what thou wilt. ..."

He formed a new order called the Astrum Argentinum which appears to have been based on little more than some dubiously interpreted Egyptian philosophies, the use of cocaine and other drugs, and the practice of "sex magic" which he claimed was the way to enlightenment.

Crowley died in 1947, but his voluminous written works and many followers inspired a number of other occult orders including the California sect known as the Ordo Templi Orientis, a group which is considered a mystical and magical group. The O.T.O. remains an active organization today with branches worldwide.

Another prominent occultist of the 20th century whom many historians have failed to link to the black arts was Adolph Hitler. Hitler was a superstitious man who engaged in the pouring of lead to foresee the future and other means of fortune-telling. He was known to fall into lengthy periods of depression when his readings of the future were discouraging and to use drugs to alleviate his black moods. Hitler was fascinated by many occult subjects, and select S.S. troops met regularly at Wewelsburg Castle, a mountaintop retreat, to perform occult rituals in secret.

A 1987 videotape entitled "The Occult Experience" (available in most video stores) tells of Black Mass rituals performed at the castle for the purpose of creating a master race. Hitler's troops adopted the skull and lightning bolt as symbols and the wearing of black uniforms, occult influences which are seen frequently today in the jewelry and dress of many heavy metal rock bands as well as those adults and youngsters involved in the neo-Nazi movement. Many occult investigators view Hitler's slaughter of millions of Jews as a mass human sacrifice. Hitler himself certainly believed that the annihilation of those he viewed as enemies would increase his chances of worldwide domination, a conviction not unlike the tenets of some cult leaders today.

One of the most infamous of the modern-day satanists is Anton Szandor LaVey who founded the Church of Satan on April 31, 1966 (a significant date in that it corresponds to Walpurgis Night, a pagan holiday of feasting and sacrifice). The Church of Satan is headquartered in San Francisco, and membership estimates range from 5,000 to 10,000.

Born in 1930, LaVey was a gifted musician who played the oboe in the San Francisco Ballet symphony orchestra when he was 15. He dropped out of school in the 11th-grade and joined the Clyde Beatty Circus as an assistant to the lion trainer. He later became the regular calliope player after demonstrating his musical talents.

LaVey left the circus at age 18 and joined a carnival as a stage hypnotist's assistant. His already considerable interest in magic and the occult grew in this atmosphere, and the theories he would later formulate into the philosophies of the Church of Satan began to take shape.

LaVey worked as a photographer for the San Francisco Police Department after leaving the world of sideshow magic, but abandoned that career after several years to delve more deeply into his occult studies. He began to teach classes on occult subjects in the San Francisco Bay area. His students learned to perform rituals based on those of the ancient Knights Templar and the Hermetic Order of the Golden Dawn. The philosophy of the Church of Satan evolved from these meetings, a doctrine which states that Satan is only that part of man that longs for the fulfillment of lustful desires, that to give in to these desires is good, and that true evil exists in and results from denial.

The Church of Satan does not view Satan as evil, but rather a symbol of the carnal satisfaction to which man should submit lest true evil erupt. However, LaVey and his followers are not above placing curses upon those who cross them. In one famous instance, LaVey himself cursed an attorney by the name of Sam Brody who also happened to be the lover of Jayne Mansfield, the blonde bombshell of the 1960s. Mansfield was one of LaVey's most devoted followers, and Brody had tried unsuccessfully to draw her away from the Church of Satan. After placing the curse on Brody, LaVey warned Mansfield not to ride in a car with her lover/lawyer. Mansfield and Brody died in an automobile accident on July 29, 1967.

LaVey remains to this day a master showman, and some occult researchers as well as leaders and members of other satanic cults insist that he is not a true satanist, but only a gifted performer whose main interest is in media attention. Indeed, LaVey has invited members of the press to his home to witness Black Mass rituals during which a naked woman serves as the altar, LaVey the celebrant, and the congregation is sprinkled with their own unique brand of holy water from a phallus-shaped container.

The High Priest of the Church of Satan appeared as the devil in the movie *Rosemary's Baby* and worked as a technical advisor on the film *The Devil's Rain* with actors Tom Skerritt and John Travolta. The Church of Satan numbers among its current followers many professionals in the fields of the arts, science, law and education.

LaVey appears in the videotape "The Occult Experience," and the following is his own explanation of The Church of Satan's philosophy from that videotape: "It occurred to me for many years that there was a large gray area between psychiatry and religion that was untapped, and no religion had ever been based on man's carnal needs or his fleshly pursuits. All religions are based on abstinence rather than indulgence. And all religions, therefore, have to be based on fear. Well, we don't feel that fear is necessary to base a religion on. The fact that religions for thousands of years have been telling people what they should do and what they shouldn't do according to the basic whims of a person who might be running the show is very understandable. We are realists, we are satanists, but we also feel that a person has to be good to themselves before they can be good to other people. This is a very selfish religion. We believe in greed. We believe in selfishness. We believe in all of the lustful thoughts that motivate man because this is man's natural feeling."

Perhaps LaVey is best known for his publication of *The Satanic Bible* and its companion manual *The Satanic Rituals* in 1972. An explanation of some of the Church of Satan's beliefs appears on page 25 of *The Satanic Bible* where the author lists nine Satanic statements:

1. Satan represents indulgence, instead of abstinence!
2. Satan represents vital existence, instead of spiritual pipedreams!
3. Satan represents undefiled wisdom, instead of hypocritical self-deceit!
4. Satan represents kindness to those who deserve it, instead of love wasted on ingrates!
5. Satan represents vengeance, instead of turning the other cheek!
6. Satan represents responsibility to the responsible, instead of concern for psychic vampires!
7. Satan represents a man as just another animal, sometimes better, more often worse than those that walk on all fours, who because of his divine spiritual and intellectual development has become the most vicious animal of all!
8. Satan represents all of the so-called sins, as they lead to physical or mental gratification!
9. Satan has been the best friend the church has ever had, as he has kept it in business all these years!

Its loosely defined dogma and frequently laughable psycho-dramas have caused many to dismiss The Church of Satan as any kind of a serious threat to mainstream religious communities.

Whether one believes LaVey's claims that he can place death curses, several areas of significant concern deserve our attention.

The Satanic Rituals includes a rite of baptism for infants and children which reads in part, "In the name of Satan, Lucifer, Belial, Leviathan, and all the demons, named and nameless, walkers in the velvet darkness, harken to us. ... Welcome a new and worthy sister/brother, *(child's name).* ... Welcome to you, sorceress/sorcerer, most natural and true magician. Your tiny hands have strength to pull the crumbling vaults of spurious heavens down, and from their shards erect a monument to your own sweet indulgence. Your honesty entitles you to a well-deserved dominion o'er a world filled with frightened, cowering men."

While it is generally acknowledged that parents have the right to introduce their children to the family's religion of choice, and while no obviously criminal or physically dangerous activity takes place during these ritual "baptisms," many child advocates fear for the long-term emotional and psychological stability of children raised in an atmosphere of immediate gratification and total self-indulgence. The long-term physical health and safety of these children is also a legitimate concern.

The Satanic Bible and *The Satanic Rituals* are widely available in bookstores and libraries throughout the country. One manager of a store that is part of a nationwide chain said recently that, while many stores no longer stock these books, employees frequently order copies for teenagers who request them.

The Church of Satan also published a monthly newsletter entitled *The Cloven Hoof* which reportedly had a circulation of several thousand. It is likely that copies of this publication find their way into the hands of thousands more, including impressionable children and teenagers.

Another satanic church is the Temple of Set founded by Michael Aquino in 1975, also in San Francisco. Aquino had risen through the ranks of The Church of Satan, then left the organization due to philosophical differences with LaVey. Aquino claims to have summoned Satan who appeared to him as Set, an ancient god of destruction. Set proclaimed Aquino the "Second Beast" (Aleister Crowley maintaining his position as the "Great Beast") and leader of a new age of enlightenment.

The Temple of Set teaches its followers that Satan is a figure of literal substance rather than a symbol and that believers can achieve the highest intellectual levels by advancing to various planes of consciousness through a carefully outlined system. Temple members engage in the practice of rituals to invoke various deities for the purpose of accomplishing whatever goals the celebrants have determined.

The Temple of Set and the Church of Satan officially denounce the sacrificing or harming of any animal or human during rituals, and the Temple of Set refuses to consider for membership anyone under the age of 18. However, Aquino was investigated by the San Francisco Police Department in 1987 in connection with a case of child molestation. At last report, no charges had been filed and Aquino had instituted legal action against the city of San Francisco for defamation of character. The Temple of Set has never had more than a few hundred members at any one time, but its message may be more widespread due to its newsletter, *The Scroll of Set*.

The most recently organized satanic church is the Church of Satanic Liberation founded by Paul Valentine in 1986, and based in New Haven, Connecticut. Valentine was inspired to found his organization after reading LaVey's *The Satanic Bible*, and many of the rituals practiced by this satanic high priest and his followers are taken directly from that publication and *The Satanic Rituals*. However, Valentine's organization differs greatly from other satanic churches in its emphasis on "sex magic," rituals based on the belief that powerful forces are released during orgasm, forces that then are available to carry out the will of the celebrant.

Valentine's beliefs are more openly anti-Christian and more vehemently blasphemous than those of LaVey and Aquino which, though decidedly un-Christian, are mild by comparison. During a guest appearance on the Sally Jesse Raphael show in May 1988, Valentine stated, "The rotting corpse of Christianity is stinking so bad. It's not going to be too long before it just totally dissolves."

Later, during the same taped interview, he said, "My goal in life is to start the wheels of the eventual destruction of Christianity through education."

He claims to have fathered 33 children by 19 women (at last count), admits that his congregation is predominantly female, and announces that he has every intention of founding his own "dynasty."

The organizations of LaVey, Aquino and Valentine are well-known due to extensive media coverage of their activities and philosophies. Their leaders appear frequently on nationwide and local talk shows and speak openly with journalists and authors. Their willingness to share their extraordinary views with a curious public is, according to many occult investigators, evidence that they present little real or immediate danger.

Far more dangerous, child advocates and law enforcement officials contend, are the hundreds of small, poorly organized cults and a few larger and better-organized groups which operate in total secrecy. It is these groups which often go undetected until one or more suicides, homicides or other grisly incidents put them on the six o'clock news and on the front pages of newspapers around the country.

This brief introduction to the occult can be concluded best with a statement made by Sally Jesse Raphael in closing the show on which Valentine appeared in 1988: "A lot of what we have heard frightens me. It frightens me more for the kids than for anything else. We have de-emphasized God in the schools, in our lives and in places that we go. Maybe this is the product of that de-emphasis. And that's scary, isn't it?"

CRIME SCENE INVESTIGATIONS

Clues Unique to the Black Occults in General

1. Mockery of Christian symbols (inverted cross, vandalized Christian artifacts)
2. Use of stolen or vandalized Christian artifacts
3. Discovery of candles or candle drippings
4. Unusual drawings, symbols on walls/floors (pentagram, etc.)
5. Non-discernible alphabet
6. Animal mutilations, including removal of specific body parts (anus, heart, tongue, ears, etc.)
7. Use of animal parts (feathers, hair, bones) to form signs and symbols on the ground
8. Absence of blood on the ground or in animal
9. Altar containing artifacts (candles, chalice, knife, etc.)
10. Effigies like voodoo dolls stuck with pins or otherwise mutilated
11. Bowls of powder or colored salt
12. Skulls with or without candles
13. Robes, especially black, white or scarlet
14. Rooms draped in black or red
15. Books on Satanism, magic rituals, etc.

APPENDIX C

FORENSIC ASPECTS OF RITUAL CRIME

Because ritual crimes are relatively new to most police agencies, a revision in the way certain crimes are investigated and the manner in which certain crime scenes are handled has become necessary.

To develop a technique for handling this type of crime and its related effects, it is necessary to develop a working knowledge.

Homicide Investigations

1. Any missing body parts may be used in additional rituals or ceremonies. If the body is found in a location other than where the offense took place, body parts may be stored at the suspect's home and should be included on any search warrants.

2. The location of any stab wounds or cuts may indicate that this occurred during a ritual and may be in a precise pattern.

3. Any burn marks, tattooing or branding may also indicate a ritual murder.

4. Wax drippings, oils or incense found on or near the body may give indications as to the ceremony conducted and may match items located in additional searches.

5. Be sure to look for human or animal feces either consumed or smeared on the body.

6. A stomach content analysis should be done, especially for urine, drugs, wine, feces (animal/human), foreign blood types, human flesh which may have been consumed.

7. You should look for boundary markers around the site such as pieces of string on trees.

Look for a circle nine feet in diameter (which may or may not contain a pentagram) and a second circle one foot inside the larger one. NOTE: If in a house, the circle may be smaller if the ritual room does not lend itself to the traditional nine-foot circle. Also, there may be only one circle. The south end of the star is an observation point. Each point holds symbols. The south point should be the main point and pentagram faces the south point. If it faces the north, make note of this.

West point of the circle is area of the altar (usually).

If a fire ring is present, dig down three feet and use a bomb screen to collect the earth.

Look for a trail leading from the circle towards water. Search for stakes, etc., used to place victims in a spread-eagle position (head towards water).

Look for cages for animals and limbs, lumber, etc., from which animals may have been hung.

Words of Warning

Do not enter the perimeter unless advised to do so.

Do not enter the circle unless the entire perimeter and any vantage points of observation are secure.

Look for painted rocks, symmetrically placed rocks, bones, feathers or pennies.

Inside Crime Scene

Search for the same clues sought at an outside crime scene as well as the following:

Check refrigerators for bottles or vials of what might appear to be blood.

Look for hypodermic needles (these may be used for removing blood from animals/humans).

Check under mattresses for occult books, and do a thorough check of the inside looking for items specifically listed on the search warrant. If there are any strange items that appear which have not been listed on the search warrant, make note of them.

Since books are part of the search warrant, look for any writings, particularly student composition books, essays, poetry and hand-made drawings.

CRIME SCENE PROCEDURES WERE COMPILED BY B.A.D.D. FROM INFORMATION OBTAINED FROM LAW ENFORCEMENT OFFICERS.

Items Which Should be Listed on a Search Warrant

1. Occult games, books (I Ching, Ouija board, Tarot cards, crystal ball, fantasy role-playing games)
2. Ashes from fire pits, including fireplaces and wood stoves
3. Robes, detachable hoods
4. Gongs, drums, bells
5. Wooden stand for altar, marble slab, crosses
6. Chalice, goblet, cruet
7. Phallus
8. Heavy wooden staff, sword, knives
9. Small velvet pillow, scarlet in color
10. Bull whip, cat-o'-nine-tails, ligatures
11. Mirror
12. Animal mask, possibly of papier mache
13. Black satin or velvet glove for right hand
14. Large ruby (or other red stone) ring, worn on first finger of right hand
15. Flash powder, smoke bombs
16. Incense
17. Body paint/face paint

CASE PROBLEMS

1. Investigators disregard original statements regarding rituals and satanism, therefore they only document the sexual abuse.

2. No evidence is found at alleged crime scenes to substantiate statements made by victims.

3. Crime scenes are never found.

4. Crime locations are found but do not fit descriptions given by the victims.

5. Your administrators want proof of these crimes within ten days (time set for all other investigations).

6. The child victims are interviewed together, by parents, by foster parents, or in the presence of parents.

7. The suspects are made aware of the investigation prematurely.

8. The press becomes aware of the details of the investigation.

9. The District Attorney wants the case wrapped up quickly.

10. The District Attorney says to go only on the sexual abuse and ignore the satanic aspects.

11. In light of the above, the victims continually talk about the ritualistic aspects during interviews.

12. The District Attorney says that if the ritualistic statements come out on the stand, he will say the kids were under the influence of drugs and hallucinated that part of the story (what does this do to the child's credibility?)

13. Parents/therapists refuse to allow testimony by the children because of the increased traumas.

14. Only one parent is supportive of proceeding with the investigation.

15. Though homicides are reported, no bodies are found.

16. Though children say they saw other children there who were kidnapped, no record of these children can be found with the National Center for Missing/Exploited Children or the F.B.I.

17. No ritualistic/pornographic photographs have turned up.

18. Children are allowed to remain in the home. Investigations later reveal that family member(s) may be involved.

19. Parents begin to feel everyone around them is suspect, including one of the police officers involved in the investigation.

20. The daycare center is well-known and well-respected in the community.

21. Parents take investigation into their own hands and begin to conduct interviews of the children and surveillances of the suspects' homes.

MATERIALS ABOVE FURNISHED BY SANDI GALLANT, SAN FRANCISCO POLICE DEPARTMENT.

SIGNS AND SYMBOLS OF THE OCCULT

The following are signs and symbols commonly used by adolescents who are into devil worship. These do not include all alphabets and signs, but only those used with the greatest frequency. Parents and all other adults whose work concerns the safety and well-being of children should become familiar with these signs and symbols as they often signal a child who is "dabbling" and, in some cases, may indicate more serious involvement.

PENTAGRAM: The five-pointed star is an important symbol in magic. It represents the four elements surmounted by the Spirit. It is more commonly used by witches for "White Magic."

INVERTED PENTAGRAM: The five-pointed star inverted is associated with evil or "Black Magic." It is symbolic in that it forms the goathead which typically represents Satan.

HEXAGRAM: Also referred to as the Star of David or the Crest of Solomon. This symbol was used by the Egyptians long before the Israelis adopted it. The Jews began using the Star of David during their Babylonian captivity, and it now has a Jewish significance. However, when used by occultists, it is regarded as having considerable magical power.

CROSS OF NERO: In the '60s, this was known as the "peace symbol," but today it is being used by some heavy metal fans and occultists to represent a broken cross—the defeat of Christianity.

SWASTIKA: Also known as the Sun Wheel. An ancient religious symbol used long before Hitler came on the scene. In sun god worship, it is supposed to represent the sun's course in the heavens. It has become a modern symbol of evil. Nazis used the counterclockwise symbol to depict movement away from the "godhead."

ANARCHY: Denial of authority. Many adolescents are using this sign when they are involved in the occult to show contempt for authority. It has been seen in many scenes of vandalism where satanic graffiti is spray-painted on buildings.

THAUMATURGIC TRIANGLE: Used for magical purposes such as spell casting and demon summoning.

UDJAT: Also known as the "all-seeing eye."

SCARAB: A design based on the dung beetle, this is the ancient Egyptian symbol of reincarnation. It also is associated with Beelzebub, Lord of the Flies.

LIGHTENING BOLTS: Also referred to as the "Satanic S." This symbol was used by Hitler's Nazi troops.

666: Represents the number of the Great Beast or the Antichrist. The last book of the Bible (Revelations 13:18) states, "Let Him that has understanding count the number of the Beast; for it is the number of a man; and his number is six hundred, three-score and six."

ANKH: This is an Egyptian symbol of life and often is associated with fertility.

INVERTED CROSS: Upside-down cross often referred to as the "Southern Cross." This symbolizes mockery and rejection of the Christian Cross. This is painted in graffiti, on some album covers and made into jewelry such as necklaces and earrings. Some teens will use this symbol in tattooing themselves.

BLACK MASS INDICATOR: Both symbols can be used to indicate a Black Mass. A Black Mass is a satanic practice deliberately parodying the Catholic Mass. During a Black Mass, holy items are defiled and forbidden activities performed including the alleged sacrifice of unbaptized infants and the reciting of the Lord's Prayer backwards.

EMBLEM OF BAPHOMET: Note the inverted pentagram forms the head of the goat. This symbol is indigenous to Satanists. Found in graffiti, on notebooks and in jewelry such as necklaces. This is considered a demonic deity symbolic of the devil.

CHURCH OF SATAN: This is the symbol of the Church of Satan in San Francisco. It can be found in *The Satanic Bible* above the "Nine Satanic Statements." Adolescents are using this on their notebooks, in graffiti and sometimes in self-made tattoos.

CROSS OF CONFUSION: This symbol was first used by Romans who questioned the truth of Christianity.

Adolescents also will write words, sentences and sometimes entire letters backwards. Some typical examples follow:

    NATAS/SATAN
    NEMA/AMEN
    REDRUM/MURDER
    EVIL/LIVE
    MAD DOG/GOD DAM
    SUSEJ/JESUS

Occult Alphabet

A = ![symbol]   B = ![symbol]   C = ![symbol]   D = ![symbol]

E = ![symbol]   F = ![symbol]   G = ![symbol]   H = ![symbol]

I = ![symbol]   J = ![symbol]   K = ![symbol]   L = ![symbol]

M = ![symbol]   N = ![symbol]   O = ![symbol]   P = ![symbol]

Q = ![symbol]   R = ![symbol]   S = ![symbol]   T = ![symbol]

U = ![symbol]   V = ![symbol]   W = ![symbol]   X = ![symbol]

Y = ![symbol]   Z = ![symbol]

The commonly called "Witches Alphabet" omits the letters J, U, and W. However, adolescents typically use the alphabet above and refer to it as the "Witches Alphabet."

GLOSSARY OF OCCULT TERMS

A A: The abbreviated form for Argenteum Astrum, the magical order founded by Aleister Crowley in 1904.

ABADDON: A Hebrew word meaning "Destruction"; in context in the Old Testament the idea seems to be "Destruction Personified."

ABRAXAS: A Gnostic term for their supreme deity (in a few Gnostic sects the name of a minor deity); using the Greek number system, "Abraxas" as a numerical value of 365, representing a cycle of divine action (also the number of days in a solar year)

ABYSS: To the Egyptians, the abode of the dead; to the Babylonians, the chaos from which the universe came into existence.

ACOLYTES: Initiates

ADEPT: One who is skilled in the magical arts; in Theosophy, a spirit being who sends messages to this world.

ADRAMMELECH, ANAMMELECH: Sepharvaite Gods brought to Samaria, II Kings 17:31-34.

AEROMANCY: Observation of air (one of the original four "elements"), sky, clouds, shapes, or other atmospheric phenomena for purposes of divination; weather forecasting, of course, is not considered divination

AGRIPPA: A grimoire written in black or purple pages, and shaped like a man.

ALCHEMIST: Practitioner of alchemy. Middle Ages primary goal was to transform base metal into gold.

ALCHEMY: Any seemingly magical power or process of transmuting.

ALECTRYOMANCY: Divination by observation of a bird picking grains from a circle of letters.

ALEUROMANCY: Possible answers to questions are placed in balls of dough and baked. One is chosen at random, and will presumably be the correct answer. Modern "fortune cookies" come from this practice.

ALOMANCY: Divination by salt.

ALPHA: Main ritual room.

ALPHITOMANCY: Divination by means of special cakes, which are presumably digestible by a person with a clear conscience but are distasteful to others.

ALTAR: Ritual table used to hold artifacts during rituals. Can be made of wood, stone, or earth. In Anton LaVey's form of Satanic religion, a "nude woman" is used as the altar.

AMENON: Ruler of the spirits of the East.

AMULET: An ornament or charm used to ward off spells, disease, etc.

ANACHITHIDUS: A stone used for calling up demons.

ANACHITIS: A stone used for conjuring water spirits.

ANARCHY: The letter A drawn in a circle meaning all out attack (usually by punk Rockers and now sometimes being used by heavy metal followers).

ANCIENT ONE (S): The officiating priestess at a black mass is sometimes known as "the Ancient One" regardless of her age; evil Gods who wish ill for mankind, counterparts to the Elder Gods.

ANIMISM: Worship of the spirit that presumably animates all things.

ANKH: Egyptian symbol resembling a cross with a loop at the top. The Ankh is a symbol of life and every major Egyptian deity is depicted carrying it. It has been suggested by some that the symbol has a sexual origin, combining the penis and vagina in one motif; however, Egyptologist Willis Budge regards this interpretation as "unlikely." The Ankh is also known as the crux Ansata.

ANOLIST: In ancient times, someone who conjured demons at an altar for divination.

ANTHROPOMANCY: An ancient form of human sacrifice.

ANTHROPOPHAGY: The practice of eating human flesh, particularly by witches at Sabbat.

ANTICHRIST: Enemy of Christ.

APANTOMANCY: Divination based on seemingly chance meetings with animals or creatures; for instance, Mexico City was founded on the spot where Aztec priests saw an eagle on a cactus holding a live snake; black cat superstitions may come from this practice.

APOTROPAION: A charm that protects someone against evil spirits or the Evil Eye.

APOTROPAISM: Defensive or protective magic.

APPORT: The sudden appearance of an object in or from other objects, usually in seances or other spiritistic practices.

ARCANA: A secret process or formula; in Tarot, twenty-two pictorial cards comprise the Major Arcana and fifty-six (or fifty-two) cards divided into four suits are the Minor Arcana.

ARCHETYPE: A symbolic idea that comes from the overall experience of mankind and is present in each person's subconscious; the concept has been developed by Jung and others.

ARCHFIEND: A chief or foremost fiend (Satan).

ARCHONS: According to Gnostic thought, deities less powerful that God but hostile to Him or unaware of Him, who rule the world.

A.R.E.: Association of Research and Enlightenment founded by Edgar Cayce which promotes reincarnation.

ARITHMANCY: Divination by numbers; usually by attaching significance to number relationships such as birthdates, "lucky numbers," or number values given to letters.

ASCENDANT: The astrological sign rising on the horizon at the time a subject is born.

ASHERAH: A Canaanite mother-goddess of the sea, or an image made for her.

ASHTEROTH, ASHTORETH, ASTAROTH, plural for ASTARTE: Canaanite goddess of fertility and war. Judges 2:13; 10:6, 1 Samuel 7:3-4; 12:10; 13:10.

ASMODEUS: In demonology, the evil spirit who was king of the demons and who filled men's hearts with rage and lust. Asmodeus angered King Solomon by preying on one of his wives; and it was not until the arch-angel Michael intervened, offering King Solomon a magic ring, that this mighty demon could be conquered. Asmodeus was credited with a knowledge of geometry and astronomy and could also locate buried treasure. Sometimes identified with Samuel.

ASTRAL PROJECTION: A person's spirit travels outside the natural body. Sometimes great distances, and operates on a different level of consciousness.

ASTROGYROMANCY: Divination with dice bearing numbers or letters.

ASTROLOGY: The practice of telling the future by reading the stars. The whole practice of astrology claims to have basic questions asked about life. These are known as "horoscopes."

ATHAME: A ritual sword or dagger used by a priestess or witch in a magical ceremony. It has a black handle and magic symbols engraved on its blade.

"ASTAB" ETSEB OTSEB: A Hebrew word for an idol whose service is laborious, or is a cause of grief.

AUGURY: Observing the flight of birds as a means of divination, or any interpretation of the future based on signs and omens.

AURA: An energy field that presumably surrounds all living things.

AUSTROMANCY: Divination by studying the winds.

AUTOMATIC WRITING: Writing done while in a trance—ostensibly containing supernatural and prophetic messages. The pen is held in the hand but is directed by spiritual forces. The finished product is often in a hand-written style or language other than that of the one holding the pen. For an example read "Dialogue with a Demon" by Lona Kay, an El Paso, Tx. author.

AVERSE: Black or evil.

AXIOMANCY: Divination by observation of the quivers of an ax or hatchet.

BAAL: The chief god of the Canaanites.

BAAL-BERITH: "Lord of the Covenant"; A Canaanite God

BAAL-PEOR: "Lord of the opening"; A Moabite god of uncleanness; also referred to as "Peor."

BAALZEBUB: A Hebrew name that means "Lord of the Flies"; in the Old Testament, the God of Ekron (see Beelzebub).

BAALZEPHON: In demonology, captain of the guard and sentinels of hell.

BACULUM: A witches wand, staff or broom stick.

BAHIR: A source book of the Cabala; presents some of the basic teachings of Judaic mysticism.

BALEFIRE: Ritual coven fire.

BAPHOMET: For centuries has had a curious and highly secret following among humans. Appears to humans as a goat-god. In this form has been worshiped by inner circles of several occult brotherhoods. Appeals to sadomasochistic tendencies of his followers by representing himself as the scapegoat for all forces of evil in the body. Probably also the mysterious "bearded demon."

BARROW: An Elven or Celtic burial mound.

BASILISK: A legendary dragon, serpent, or lizard whose breath or look was considered fatal.

BEELZEBUB: Traditionally one of the most powerful demons; ranking in importance with Lucifer, Ashtaroth, Satan. Thought of as a demon of decay.

BEL: The chief Babylonian deity.

BELIAL: Without a master.

BELL: Rung to begin and end rituals.

BELOMANAY-RABDOMANCY: Divination by tossing or balancing arrows.

BELTANE: Celtic, pre-Christian spring festival, celebrated on May Day. One of the major witches' sabbaths.

BIBLIOMANCY: Divination by books.

BIND: To cast a spell on someone or something.

BLACK DRAGON: A popular grimoire attributed to Honorius, an occultist of the 15th century.

BLACK MASS: Satanic practice, deliberately parodying the central ritual of Catholicism, in which the host (representing the body of Christ) is stolen from a church, consecrated by an unfrocked priest, and desecrated. The desecration can include defecating and urinating upon the vessel. The ceremony includes activities forbidden by the Church, including the alleged sacrifice of unbaptized infants and the recitation of the Lord's Prayer backwards.

BLACK PULLET: A grimoire that probably dates from the late 1700's.

BLACK WIDOW SPIDER: Mark of death.

"BLESSED BE": Phrase used by witches both as a greeting and as a farewell. Note: "So Moot it be" may be used.

BLOOD: The part of man which survives death. In drinking it you acquire his divine quality.

BOLLINE: An Athame, often sickle-shaped.

BOOK OF (THE) DEAD: An Egyptian handbook for guiding the souls of the dead through the underworld.

BOOK OF ENOCH: An extra-Biblical work, apparently written in the 2nd century B.C. which forms the basis for much of the mythology associated with witchcraft.

BOOK OF MOSES: The standard magician's code of the Middle Ages; it contains a complicated ritual for the induction of neophytes.

BOOK OF TOTH, THOTH: A book containing the wisdom of the Egyptian gods; possibly the origin for the Tarot.

BOTANOMANCY: Divination by burning tree branches and leaves.

BOUL: Ruler of the West.

BRIGID: A witch festival held on February 2nd Eve.

CABALA, KABBALAH: Occultic material that apparently originated in Chaldea and Mesopotamia and was incorporated into ancient Jewish works and traditions; also refers to practices of magic that are derived from those works.

CALF WORSHIP: Calves and bulls figured prominently in Egyptian mythology and the Israelites in demanding a golden calf may have been recalling Egyptian idols or perhaps were just adopting a well-known god-symbol. Every king after Jeroboam carried on sacrifices to the golden calves that Jeroboam made.

CANCER: An astrological sign. (In the month of June and July)

CANDLEMAS: See brigid.

CANDLES: Used in all rituals and ceremonies the color reflecting the type ritual black is the color associated with the devil.

CANNIBAL: A person who eats the flesh of human beings.

CANTRIP: A spell cast by a witch.

CAPNOMANCY: Divination by observing smoke as it rises from a fire, such as from a burnt sacrifice or from incense.

CARTOMANCY: Divination or fortunetelling by means of cards.

CATHARI: From the term "cat" whose posterior they kiss and in whose form Satan appears to them.

CATOPTROMANCY: Divination by means of gazing at a mirror tilted towards the sun.

CAULDRON: Like a cup, Medieval witches were said to stir their magical concoctions in a cauldron.

CAUSIMOMANCY: Divination by observing how an object placed in fire burns or fails to burn.

CELEBRANT: The presiding priest at a ceremony.

CEPHALOMANCY: Divination by using the head or skull of a donkey or goat.

CERANUOSCOPY: Observation of thunder and lighting for signs or omens.

CEROSCOPY: Melted wax is poured into cold water, and the resulting shapes are interpreted as a means of divination.

CEREBERUS: Three headed dog that guarded the entrance of hell.

CHAKAM: A Hebrew word for "wise."

CHAKKIM: A Hebrew word for "wise one."

CHALDEAN ORACLES: Oracles and mystical sayings allegedly deriving from the Chaldean Magi and Zoroaster, but transcribed and translated by the Neoplatonists. Commentaries on the Oracles were written by Psellus, Pletho, Iamblicus, and Porphyry. The Oracles have much in common with Gnosticism.

CHALICE: Cup or goblet symbolized woman in ritual use; can contain sacrificial blood, wine or water.

CHAMMANIM: Images of the sun.

CHAPTERS: Branches of church organization.

CHARM: In magic, an incantation or object believed to have special super-natural power. The word derives from the Latin carmen, meaning "a song." Compare with Talisman.

CHARTOM, CHARTUMMIN: A Hebrew term derived from Egyptian, meaning "men learned in sacred writings, rituals, spells."

CHEMOSH: A national idol of the Moabites and the Ammonites, has been identified with Baal-Peor, Baalzebub, or various Greek or Roman gods by some sources.

CHILD SACRIFICE: Worship of Moloch included child sacrifice; other instances not specifically related to Moloch-worship are listed in the Old Testament. (Note: Moloch is a god also included in demonology and child sacrifice appears in various books on the occult as it relates to a "Black Mass.")

CHIROMANCY: Divination from studying the lines of the head.

CHIROGNOMY: The study of the general shape or formation of the hand.

CHRESMOMANCY: Determining the future by the utterances of one in a frenzy.

CHRIST FAMILY: The Christ Family started in the 60's by using transient type people. (late teens - early twenties) They (allegedly) harbor runaway kids. Their mission is to let us know that this is the end of times. They wear white sheets, army blankets and have bare feet. Men will wear diapers on their heads for bandannas. They appear to be into transportation of drugs. Vehicles by the Christ Family will have Star of David with lightning bolt through it. If the leader of the group is inside the vehicle, his arch angels will be armed with small caliber hand guns and knives. If a single person of the Christ Family is found; and he or she is hurt or injured, it is because the group left them behind. They believe anyone hurt is possessed.

CHRISTIAN SPIRITUALIST CHURCH: An organization that promotes mediums and spiritists.

CHURCH OF SATAN: Headed by occultist Anton LaVey. It encouraged the development of the animal instincts, self-indulgence, and free sexuality; and included in its rituals a satanic "mass." Male and female participants in the ritual wore black robes with the exception of a naked woman who volunteered to be the "altar." Reports indicate the Church ceased functioning in 1975 and has now been replaced by the Temple of Set, headed by Michael Aquino. (Note: Anton LaVey was a former lion tamer and police photographer).

CHURCH OF THE SATANIC BROTHERHOOD: Founded in 1972 by ex-members of the Church of Satan.

CIRCLE: Physical or imaginary drawn or placed on the floor during the calling of demonic powers or spirits. Usually 9 feet in diameter, magic is done on the inside for protection and concentration.

CLAIRAUDIENCE: The ability to hear sounds made in the spirit realm, such as voices, etc.; or the ability to hear things distant in space or time.

CLAIRVOYANCE: The ability to see people or events distant in space or time.

CLEROMANCY: Casting lots using pebbles or other objects, often of different colors.

COLORS: Colors are symbolic of various meanings. Black: evil, devil, sorrow, darkness; Blue: pornography, sadness, water; Green: nature, soothing, restful, cleansing; Red: blood, sex, energy; White: purity, innocence, sincerity; Yellow: power, glory, wealth, perfection; Orange: adaptability, desanctification; Purple: progress, ambition, power.

CONE OF POWER: Will of the coven or group focusing the power or energy released in blood or sexual sacrifice to a particular goal or task.

CONJURATION: The act of summoning a demon.

CORD: Used in magic and to cinch the waist when wearing robes, usually 9 feet long in cotton, silk or wool. The color is symbolic or rank or of the ritual performed. (Note: there may be variations when working with self-styled groups).

CONSECRATING: To make, declare or set apart as sacred.

CONSULTER WITH FAMILIAR SPIRITS: Consulting the supposed spirits of the dead.

COVEN: A group of witches who gather together to perform ceremonies at esbats and sabbaths. Traditionally, the number of members in a coven has been assumed to total thirteen. The earliest reference to this is the claim of Isobel Gowdie in 1662 that the Auldearne witches had "thirteen persons in each coven."

COVENATOR: Minister of lowest rank.

COVENDOM: The area within three miles of the Coven's domain.

COVENSTEAD: Place where the coven meets.

CRESENT: The shape of the waxing moon, symbolic of fertility and abundant growth.

CRITOMANCY: Observation of barley cakes for possible omens.

CROSS: Ancient pre-Christian symbol interpreted by some occultists as uniting the male phallus (vertical bar) and female vagina (horizontal bar). It is also a symbol of the four directions and a powerful weapon against evil.

CROWLEY, ALEISTER: Probably the most famous and notorious occultist of the 20th century. Crowley founded a new Order, the Argenteum Astrum and claimed exclusive contact with magical Egyptian forces.

CRYSTAL BALL READING: Determining the future by gazing into a fire.

CRYSTALLOMANCY: Gazing into a crystal ball or other object.

CULT: A group strongly committed to a cause or obsessively devoted to a person.

CURSE: A spell or charm invoked against someone or something.

CYCLOMANCY: Divination from a turning wheel.

DACTYLOMANCY: A dangling ring indicates works and numbers by its swings.

DAEMON: From the Greek, Diamon: A spirit, an evil spirit or demon. Also used as a term for beings at an intermediate level between God and people.

DAGON: The national God of the Philistines.

DAIMONIAN (DAIMON): Greek words that mean "demon" or "devil."

DAIMONIODAS: A Greek word meaning "from the devil" or "of the devil."

DAIMONIZOMAI: A greek word that means "demonized"; although usually translated "demon-possessed." "Daimonizomai" can refer to a wide range of demonic influence.

DAPHNOMANCY: Listening to branches, particularly laurel branches, burning in a fire; the louder the crackle, the better the omen.

DEMON: A non-human spirit; according to the Bible, they are angels who rebelled against God.

DEMONCRACY: Worship of an evil nature.

DEMONOLOGY: The study of demons and evil spirits, and the rites and superstitions associated with them. Many deities associated with Middle Eastern and Egyptian religions (e.g., Baal, Ashtarogh, Bel, Apophis and Set) have become associated either with demonology or the gods of black magic and the left-hand path.

DENDROMANCY: Divination utilizing oak or mistletoe.

DERASH: A hebrew word for "one that inquires of the dead."

DEVIL: Synonymous with demon; the devil refers to Satan or Lucifer.

DIABLERIE: Dealing with demons or the Devil; sorcery or witchcraft.

DIABOLUS: Two morsels, kill body and soul.

DIAKKA: Spirits that communicate with or materialize for mediums or spiritists.

DIRECTIONS, FOUR: In Western magic, the four directions are symbolized in ritual, representing the elements air, fire, water and earth, respectively.

DISCIPLE: Lay member.

DIVINATION: The attempt to gain information about people or events by supernatural means.

DIVINER'S STAFF: Refers to a staff used for divination.

DOWSING, DOWSER: A person skilled in locating underground sources of water by means of a divining rod. The dowser uses a Y-shaped rod that is generally made of hazel, but is sometimes made of metal or substitute woods like rowan or ash. As the dowser walks above the location of the underground water, the rod jerks in an involuntary and spontaneous manner, indicating to the dowser both the location and depth of the supply.

DRAGON: In Revelation 20:2, Satan is identified as "the dragon."

DRUIDS: Celtic priests in pre-Christian Britain and Gaul. Skilled in astronomy and medicine, they worshiped the sun, believed in the immortality of the soul, and in reincarnation.

DUNGEONS & DRAGONS: A fantasy role-playing game which uses demonology, witchcraft, voodoo, murder, rape, blasphemy, suicide, assassination, insanity, sex perversion, homosexuality, prostitution, satanic type rituals, gambling, barbarism, cannibalism, sadism, desecration, demon summoning, necromantics, divination and many other teachings. There have been a number of deaths nationwide where games like Dungeons & Dragons were either the decisive factor in adolescent suicide and murder, or played a major factor in the violent behavior in such tragedies. Since role-playing is used typically for behavior modification, it has become apparent nationwide (with the increased homicide and suicide rates in adolescents) that there is a great need to investigate every aspect of a youngster's environment, including their method of entertainment, in reaching a responsible conclusion for their violent actions.

ECTOPLASM: A substance that supposedly comes from a medium during a seance.

EIDOLEION: A worshiper of idols.

EIDOLOLATREIA: A Greek word for idolatry.

EIDOLON: An idol

EIDOLOTHUTON: Something that is sacrificed to an idol.

EIKON: An image, in Revelation 13, an image of the beast is made, which people are required to worship.

EL: A generic name for god or gods; also used of God.

ELAEOMANCY: Divination by observation of a liquid surface.

ELAH: God, or a god; an object of worship used by pagans in reference to their various duties.

ELEMENTAL: A familiar, or one of four classes of demons.

ELEMENTS: The early Greeks considered Earth, Air, Fire and Water to be the four elements.

ELF FIRE: Fire produced without the aid of metals, used to light a balefire.

ELIL: Literally an empty or vain, worthless thing.

ELIZEN: Ruler of the spirits of the North.

EMAH: Idols that impress terror on their worshipers.

ENOCH: According to Genesis, Enoch was a man who "walked with God," and was taken to heaven without suffering death; occultists attribute various special powers and abilities to him.

EQUINOX: The time at which the sun crosses the equator. This takes place on March 21 and September 22, and on these days the length of day and night are equal.

ESBAT: Coven meetings held on a regular basis usually at least once a month at the full moon. It is at these meetings "work" is performed such as healing and magic.

ESOTERIC: Term applied to teachings that are secret and only for initiates of a group; mysterious, occult, "hidden."

ESOTERIC DOCTRINE: Occultists claim that there exists mystical teaching known to the most highly evolved adepts, parts of which can be found in various religions, but is wholly contained in no single one; this doctrine is presumably given by seers to the world in times of great need.

ETSEB (ATSAB, OTSEB): A Hebrew word for an idol whose service is laborious or is a cause of grief.

EVIL EYE: A superstition which credits certain people with the ability to dispense bad luck with a gaze; people hope to counteract it by wearing charms or amulets.

EXORCISM: The act of removing demonic control from someone who is demonized; in witchcraft, purifying something from alien influences.

EYES: The "evil eye" is feared.

FAMILIAR SPIRIT: A demonic spirit who serves a witch or medium, or an animal that it may inhabit.

FASCINATION: The act of charming or casting a spell on someone nearby by a projection of power through the eye, etc.

FETISH: An inanimate object presumably inhabited by a spirit.

FINGER: Holds spiritual powers. Index finger is known as "poison, witch or cursing finger." Must not use it to touch a wound or it will never heal.

FIRE: Symbolizes Satan.

FIREWALKING: Supernatural ability to walk over hot coals without feeling pain.

Glossary of Occult Terms

FLOROMANCY: Determining the future by study of flowers.

FREYA: Scandinavian Goddess of Love, Queen of Lower Regions. Frey's sacred day was Friday. Witches held weekly assemblies on Friday.

FULL MOON: Greatest magical power.

GASTROMANCY: An ancient form of ventriloquism; prophetic utterances were delivered in this way.

GELOSCOPY: Divination from the tone of someone's laughter.

GENETHLIALOGY: Observation of the position and influence of the stars at a person's birth to predict their future.

GEOMANCY: Interpretation of figures or dots drawn on the ground, or perhaps on paper, according to accepted designs.

GHOSTS: According to occultists, the spirit of a dead person; most Christians consider them to be demons masquerading as the dead person.

GLAMOUR: A fascination.

GNOME: An elemental who lives in the earth.

GNOSTICISM: A religious and philosophical system which seeks after hidden mystical knowledge.

GOAT: Believe Satan appears in form of a goat.

GOAT'S HEAD: Sixteenth century symbol for Satan. (Note: This appears to still hold true in present practices.)

GOETIA: Tradition of black magic, including incantations, ceremonies and techniques of sorcery, often provided practical instructions for contacting demonic spirits. (Note: Also known as the lesser key of Solomon.)

GRAPHOLOGY: A psychic analysis of someone's handwriting.

GREAT BEAST: The name for the Anti-Christ in the Book of Revelations, and the name popularly associated with the magician Aleister Crowley.

GRIMOIRE: A book of spells that belongs to a witch or a coven.

GYROMANCY: Use of a person spinning in a circle and then falling to the ground to determine the future.

HAIR: Holds character. In witch hunt times, it was believed sorcerers magical potency was in his hair.

HALLOWEEN: A November Eve witches holiday; considered to be the day of the year most suitable for magic or demonic activity. (Oct. 31, also a time when the souls of the deceased revisited their former homes and once again enjoyed the company of their kinsfolk.)

HAND OF DEATH: A cult which allegedly sacrifices people and have rituals that are satanic. They are allegedly into cannabalism. Lucus and Toole allegedly were part of this group. Very little is known about this group.

HAND OF GLORY: In witchcraft, a lighted candle positioned between the fingers of a dead person's hand - usually that of a criminal condemned to death.

HARUSCOPY, HEIROMANCY, HUROSCOPY: Various names for observation of cuts, cracks, or markings in very old object and drawing prophetic conclusions.

HEAD: Central powerhouse of the body believed to contain all magical powers.

HEART: Symbol of eternity. Some groups believe that by eating the heart of another, you acquire the characteristics of the victim and obtain all of his power.

HEAVY METAL ROCK: "Heavy metal cultivates a macho image with black leather chains and spikes or studs attached to leather wrist bands, belts and jackets. When you think of heavy metal, you think of power. Women are sometimes portrayed in degrading situations. Heavy-Metal album covers and videos sometimes show women being dragged around by the hair, caged or being walked on a leash like dogs. The main focus of the heavy metaler is drugs, sex and rock'n'-roll. The most alarming aspect of heavy metal is its preoccupation with the occult. There's some subtle and not so subtle Satanic overtones in Heavy Metal. Album covers include such things as illustrations of devil's heads, crucified figures, demonic babies, skeletons, pentagrams, black candles and the occult number 666." (Quotes by Darlyne Pettinicchio, Probation officer from Orange County, Calif., Director of the Back in Control Center, News Article, the Press Enterprise, Riverside, Ca., May 7, 1986).

HECATE: Goddess of Lower Regions and Patroness of Witchcraft.

HEXAGRAM: A six-point talismatic star.

HIPPOMANCY: Divination from the neighing and stamping of horses.

HOODOO: Practices in Voodoo, Black Magic. One that brings bad luck.

HORNED GOD: Symbol of male sexuality in witchcraft, part man; part goat.

HOROSCOPE: A chart showing a person's destiny as determined by astrology practice.

HOST: In Christianity, the sacred bread regarded as the "body" of Christ in a Communion service. It symbolized Christs' personal sacrifice on behalf of humankind (from the Latin hostia, meaning "a sacrificial victim"). In various accounts of black magic and the Satanic Mass, the host is desecrated.

HYDROMANCY: Observing any number of several aspects of water, including its color, ebb and flow, or ripples caused by pebbles dropped into a pool.

I CHING: Also known as the book of changes, chinese book of divination dating from at least 1000 B.C., Confucius and the taoist sages valued it highly, and in recent times it has again become popular as a method of divination. The I Ching is said to gauge the flow of yin and yang energies and offers the seeker an appropriate course of future action based on the interplay of positive and negative forces that shape our destinies. Usually a heap of fifty harrow sticks is used- —some short and the other long. The stalks are divided in heaps until a combination of stalks provides an arrangement that can be identified as one of the lines in a hexagram. The lines are built up from the bottom to the top, and the hexagram is formed from six lines. When the hexagram is completed, the meanings are read in the I Ching itself. A system of divination from coins can also be used. In modern times, the noted psychoanalyst Carl Jung and the translator of buddhist and taoist texts, John Blofeld, have both expressed their belief that the I Ching seems to work infallibly.

ICONS: Sacred ornate frames decorated with red cloth.

INCANTATIONS: Repetitive use of words, phrases or sounds to produce a magical effect.

INCUBI, INCUBUS: A demon or wraith in male form sent for sexual purposes.

INITIATE: New Member.

INVERTED CROSS: Mockery of Christian cross. (Note: Cross is turned upside down)

INVERTED PENTAGRAM: Five pointed star with single point downward.

INVOCATION: Calling power in general or calling a demon.

I.P. MESSENGER: Minister of lowest rank.

IPSISSMUS: Highest order held in Satanism. Rarely attainable during a lifetime.

KARMA: The idea that our station in this life is a result of good or bad things done in previous lives.

KASHAPH, KESHAPHIM: To practice magic or use incantations, usually with the intent to deceive, pervert, or do mischief; "KASHAPH" refers to the person and "KESHAPHIM" refers to the magical practice.

KATEIDOLOS: Full of idols.

KEMARIM: Idolatrous priests.

KEY OF SOLOMAN: Probably the most famous grimoire ever written; some legends hold that it was written by demons and hidden under Solomon's throne. Various versions in different languages survive today.

LADY: Female leader of a coven.

LAMMAS: August witch celebration. [August 1, Great Sabbat]

LAMPODEMANCY: Observing lights or torches for omens.

LAVEY, ANTON SZANDOR: American Satanist of Romanian-German-Gypsy parentage, who is the founder and present head of the Church of Satan in San Francisco, Calif. Earlier in his career, LaVey played oboe in the San Francisco Ballet Orchestra, worked as a lion-trainer, assisted in hypnotism shows, and became a police photographer. He began holding an occult-studies group, which included filmmaker Kenneth Anger, and in 1966 he shaved his head and proclaimed himself high priest of the Church of Satan. LaVey claims an affiliated membership of nine thousand members in the United States, France, Italy, Germany, Britain, and South America, and has been an advisor on several occult feature films, including, The Mephisto Waltz and Rosemary's Baby — where he appeared on screen as the Devil. LaVey's books include the Satanic Bible (1969) and the Satanic Rituals (1972).

LETHE: Stream of forgetfulness in Hell.

LEVITATION: The act of raising an object or a person from the ground and causing them to float in the air through supernatural power.

LIGATURE: A spell which prevents a person from doing something.

LILITH: In Talmudic tradition, Adam's first wife who bore him demons.

LINKING: A mental identification with a person or spirit; usually as part of a practice of magic.

LITHOMANCY: Divination using precious stones, possibly colored beads; usually stones are thrown on a flat surface, and whichever reflects the most light is considered the omen. Blue means good luck, green means realization of a hope, red means happiness in love or marriage, yellow means disaster or betrayal, purple means a period of sadness, and black or grey means misfortune.

LUCIFER: The archangel cast from heaven for leading a revolt of the angels: Satan.

LUCIFERANS: A medieval Satanic sect prevalent in the 13th century. They sacrificed to demons. They worshiped Lucifer and believed him to be the brother of God wrongly cast out of Heaven.

LYCANTHROPY: The assumption of an animal form by an occultist. [Note: such as werewolf]

MAGIC: The attempt to influence or control people or events by supernatural means.

MAGIC, BLACK: Magic performed with evil intent. The "Black Magician" or sorcerer calls upon the supernatural powers of darkness—devils, demons and veil spirits—and performs ceremonies invoking bestial or malevolent forces intended to harm another person.

MAGIC, CEREMONIAL: Magic that employs ritual, symbols and ceremony. Ceremonial magic stimulates the senses by including in its ritual ceremonial costumes, dramatic invocations to the gods or spirits, potent incense, and mystic sacraments.

MAGIC, CIRCLE: Circle inscribed on the floor of a temple for magical ceremonial purposes. Believed to hold magical powers within and protect those involved in the ceremony from evil.

MAGICK: Science and art causing change to occur in conformity to the will.

MAGIC, WHITE: Magic performed for a spiritual, healing or generally positive purpose, as distinct from black magic which is performed for self-gain, to inflict harm or injury, or for other evil purposes.

MAGISTELLUS: An elemental servant or familiar.

MAGISTER: Male leader of a coven.

MAGUS: A male witch.

MAIDEN: Title sometimes conferred upon a Lady's daughter.

MANDRAKE: A Eurasian plant, Mandragora officinarum; thought to resemble the human body. This plant was once believed to have magical powers.

MANTEUMAI: A Greek word that means divine, prophesy, or give an oracle.

MARE: A demon which sits on the chest and causes a feeling of suffocation.

MARGARITOMANCY: Divination using pearls which were supposed to bounce upward beneath an inverted pot if a guilty person approached.

MASKIN: Seven subterranean demons.

MASKITH: An image usually painted or carved.

MASS: Ceremony.

MASSEKAH: A statue or image made from a mold.

MASTER: Top Leader.

MATERIALIZATION: Physical manifestation of a spirit being.

MASTEBAH: Something that sits upright, like a statue or pillar.

MAY EVE: Festival Roodman.

MEDIUMS: In spiritualism, one who acts as an intermediary between the world of spirits and discarnate entities and the everyday world or normal reality. Spirits are summoned during a seance and their influence may be perceived through materializations, through Ouija board communications, through an agreed code of rappings and knocks, or through automatic writing or automatic painting and drawing. If a discarnate entity takes over the body of the medium during a seance, that being is known as the control.

MENDES, GOAT OF: Form in which the devil is said to manifest during the witches' sabbath.

MENTAL TELEPATHY: The use of mental images to receive and transmit messages.

MENTOR: Senior brothers and sisters.

MERODACH: Regarded for a time as the supreme deity of the Babylonians; sometimes associated with Bel (Bel-Marduk) [Marduk is in the D & D Manuals].

METAGNOMY: Divination by viewing events while in a hypnotic state.

METEOROMANCY: Observing meteors or similar phenomena for omens.

METOPOSCOPY: The reading of character from the lines on a person's forehead.

MIDSUMMER: Festival of Beltane. [May 1]

MINOR LUMINARY: Lieutenants to leaders.

MISSAL: Book with rituals and teachings.

MOLYBDOMANCY: Divination by observing the hissing of molten lead.

MYOMANCY: Drawing prophetic conclusions from rats and mice, particularly their cries or the destruction they cause.

NECROMANCY: Communication with the supposed spirits of the dead, usually with the use of bones or some part of a corpse.

NECROPHILIA: Sexual intercourse with the dead. This sometimes arises with psychopathic murderers who believe their victims to still be alive. Necrophilia seems to be a feature of the more debased forms of black magic.

NEO-AMERICAN CHURCH: Their symbol appears to be a three-eyed frog. The Neo-American church recruits children into their activities; and also hinders the finding of missing children. The Neo-American church people usually drive vans with gun racks located behind the driver's seat. They will show up with Rainbow tribe, and also, associate themselves with other groups.

NEOPHYTE: One who is a candidate for initiation.

NOVEMBER EVE: October 31 (Halloween)

NUMEROLOGY: Use of numbers associated with a person's name and birthdate as a means of divination.

NUDITY: Believed essential to raising forces through which magic works.

OCCULT: Beyond the realm of human comprehension, mysterious, inscrutable secret.

OCULOMANCY: Divination by observing a person's eyes.

ODIN: Norse mythology; supreme deity and creator of the cosmos and man.

OFFICER: Third leader in a coven, after Magister and Lady.

OLINOMANCY: Looking for omens from wines.

OMEN: A prophetic sign.

ONEIROMANCY: Interpretation of dreams.

ONOMANCY: Finds meaning and omens in the names of persons and things; onomancy is seldom used today, except for interpreting a person's proper name.

ONOMANTICS: Onomancy applied to personal names.

OOMANTIA, OOSCOPY: Ancient practice of divination by eggs.

OPHIOMANCY: Divination from serpents.

O. P. MESSANGER: Student Ministers.

ORDO TEMPLI ORIENTIS O.T.O.: Sexual magic order formed by Karl Kellner around 1896. After Kellner died in 1905, leadership passed to Theodor Reuss, and then in 1922 to Aleister Crowley. There are now two organizations that bear the name OTO. The first of these is headed by the tantric occultist Kenneth Grant in England, and the second by Grady McMurtry in California. Members of the OTO arouse sexual energy during their magical ceremonies and identify with the gods and goddesses who personify this principle.

ORIENS: Ruler of the Spirits of the East.

ORNISCOPY, ORNITHAMANCY: Observation of the flight of birds for omens.

OUIJA BOARD: Board with letters and numbers with which supposed spirits can communicate.

OVOMANCY: A type of divination from eggs.

OWL: Bird associated in many cultures with evil powers, death, and misfortune.

PACT: A vow of secrecy given by a witch who joins a coven.

PAGAN: One who is not a Christian, Jew, or Moslem. The term is used derogatorily to describe a heathen or "unbeliever," but has now assumed a new currency among practitioners of witchcraft and magic. The so-called New Pagans are dedicated to reviving the old religion and reestablishing the worship of Nature and the lunar goddess.

PAGANISM: A practicing pagan.

PALMISTRY: The interpretation of lines and formations of the hand.

PAN: "In ancient Greek mythology, the son of Hermes and Dryope. Pan was the god of flocks and shepherds, but also had a more far-reaching role as lord of nature and all forms of wildlife. He was depicted as half-man, half-goat, and played a pipe with seven reeds. Ever-lecherous, he had numerous love affairs with the nymphs especially Echo, Syrinx, and Pithys. Regarded as a high god."

PARAPSYCHOLOGY: The study of occult phenomena such as telepathy, clairvoyance, precognition and psychokenesis.

PEGAMANCY: Divination by observing spring water or bubbling fountains.

PENTACLE, PENTAGRAM: A five-pointed star; with one point up, it signifies deity, or rule of nature by mind. With two points up, represents Satan; "pentacle" may also refer to a talisman.

PHILOSOPHER'S STONE: A psychic substance used in Alchemy.

PHRENOLOGY: Divination from interpreting head formations of bumps on the head.

PHYLLORHODOMANCY: A means of divination that comes from Ancient greece; a person slaps rose petals against his hand, and the success of a venture is judged by the loudness of the sound.

PHYSIOGNAMY: Analysis of a person's character through observation of a person's features or physical characteristics.

POLTERGEIST: "Rattling Ghost," a ghost that tends to throw or break objects or generally cause mischief; presence of a person who has strong mediumistic tendencies.

POWER OBJECT: An object with "witch power" placed in a subject or victim's vicinity to complete a spell.

PRECOGNITION: The psychic ability to see the future.

PREMONITION: A foreboding of the future.

PROPHECIES: Ability to foretell the future.

PROPHETS: Senior brothers and sisters.

PROVISIONAL MASTER: Lieutenants leaders.

PSYCHIC: Pertaining to phenomena which are supernatural, or perhaps actually demonic; or a person who has this power.

PSYCHIC SURGERY: Surgery by a medium having no ordinary medical knowledge, while in a trance.

PSYCHOGRAPHY: A form of mysterious writing, usually of a divinatory type.

PSYCHOMETRY: The gaining of impressions from a physical object, usually having to do with the owner or the object's history.

PUNK ROCK: Punk rock began in England as a revolt against the economic education and political system. Shabby clothes, spiked hair, mowhawk hair cuts, shaved heads, and outlandish make-up represented the British youth rebellion against the status-quo. When punk came to America, the issued faded, but the anti-establishment statement was the same. Whatever society cherishes—religion, law, tradition—punkers denigrate. Punkers want to do anything they want to be, angry and alienated. Kids who follow punk rock groups view themselves as society's victims. Punkers ultimate goal is to live recklessly and to die young and fast. The punk rock dance, called the slam dance, involves slamming into someone else, kicking them and punching them. Many punkers seem bent on self-destruction, and it's not unusual for them to wound themselves with razor blades, knives, cigarettes or cigarette lighters. (Quotes by Darlyne Pettinicchio, probation officer from Orange County, Calif. Director of the Back in Control Center, news article, *The Press Enterprise,* Riverside, Calif., May 7, 1986). Note: While punk is not typically occult, one should remember that adolescents involved in this type of negative, violent activity sometimes become involved with occult groups.

PYROMANCY: Divination by fire, usually involving powdered substances thrown in.

READINGS: Information or revelations gotten during a seance.

REPURCUSSION: Injuries received by a projected form that appear on someone's physical body.

RESPONDERS: At rituals he states natures of Lucifer and Christ.

RHABDOMANCY: Divination by means of a rod or stick; the probably forerunner of the diving rod.

RHAPSODOMANCY: Opening a book, usually poetry, and reading words or passages at random, looking for omens.

RIGHT HAND PATH: In mysticism and occultism, the esoteric path associated with spiritual illumination and positive aspiration. It is the path of light as distinct from the so-called left-hand path of darkness which equates with evil, bestiality, and black magic.

RITUAL: Tool to focus individual power of group members on a common concern or object.

ROSE CROSS: A golden cross with a rose at its center, the emblem of the esoteric order of the Rosicrucians.

RUNES: From the German "raunen" meaning a secret or mystery; occult symbols that are known in many areas of Northern Europe. [Note: Runes are used for magick. We are seeing them in the United States in certain incidents occurring which involve ritualistic crime.]

SABBAT: Seasonal assembly of witches in honor of the Archfiend.

SACRAL: Pertaining to sacred rites or observances.

SACRAMENTAL: Consecrated.

SACRAMENTARIAN: A person who regards the Sacraments as merely visible symbols.

SACRIFICE: An offering made to a deity, often upon an altar. Sacrifices are performed ritually to placate a god and to offer blood—which is symbolic of the life-force and invariably associated with fertility. Some magicians believe that the ritual slaughter of a sacrificial animal releases life energy, which can be tapped magically and used to attune the magician to the god invoked in ritual.

SACRILEGE: Misuse, theft, desecration or profanation of anything consecrated.

SACROSANCT: Sacred and inviolable.

SADISM: Sexual satisfaction with the infliction of pain on others.

SADISTIC: Deliberately cruel.

SALAMANDER: An elemental who lives in fire.

SACRIFIST: Presiding priest—represents Christ.

SANCTUM: Main ritual room.

SATAN: Apollyon (the Destroyer); Archfiend, Antichrist; Tchort (Russian); Dev (Persian); Beherit (Syriac); Pucca (Welsh); Asmodeus, Belial; Apollyan (Biblical); Sheitan (Arabic); Set (Egyptian); Oyama (Japanese) Asmodeus, the adversary; Behemoth, Diabolus; Demon; Belial, Mehpistopheles; Old Horned One; Delil; Mulciber, Pentamorph; Lucifer, Grand Master. Principal infernal spirits, Lucifer (emperior); Beelzebub (Prime Minister); and Astorath (grand duke).

SATANIC: Pertaining to or suggestive of satan or evil; profoundly cruel.

SATANIC MASS: In Satanism, a blasphemous ritual that parodies the Christian Mass, invokes the powers of darkness, and sometimes employs the use of a naked woman as an altar.

SATANISM: The worship of Satan.

SCIOMANCY: Various forms of divination involving direct communication with spirits.

SEAL: A demon's summoning diagram or signature.

SEAL OF SOLOMON: A hexagram consisting of two interlocking triangles, one facing up and the other down.

SEANCE: A ritual by which a medium calls upon the supposed spirits of the dead.

SEEING: The ability to hold the item of another and see events or know facts about that person.

SEMEL: A likeness or image.

SEPHIROTH: The occult satanic tree of life one side negative, one positive, one side masculine, one feminine, one side severe, one merciful; the tree has ten steps one must pass through in order to achieve priesthood in satanic religion.

SERPENT: Serpent w/horns is symbolic of the demons.

SERVERS: Ritual assistants.

SERVITOR: A familiar.

SET: Egyptian name for Satan, in 1975 Michael Aquino established the temple of set church religion in the United States.

SHADE: The supposed spirit of a dead person.

SHADOWS, BOOK OF: In witchcraft, the personal book of spells, rituals, and folklore a witch compiles after being initiated into the coven. The Book of Shadows is kept secret and, traditionally, is destroyed when the witch dies.

SHAMAN: A witch or "medicine man."

SHAMAYIM: A Hebrew phrase that means "viewers of the heavens."

SHEBISIM: The only occurrence in the Old Testament is translated "caul" or "head-bank," but its use in the other literature indicates a possible translation as "sun-pendant," which would make sense here.

SHIGGUTS: An abomination or a detestable thing.

SHRINE: Ritual table.

SIDEROMANCY: Divining by observing the forms made by burning straws with a hot iron.

SIGIL: A "symbolic signature" inscribed on a talisman.

SILVER: The preferred metal to be used in occult objects and jewelry.

SKULL: Human or animal used in rites.

SKYCLAD: Nude.

SOLOMON: Legendary King of Israel. He was claimed to be the author of several magical grimoires including the Key of Solomon and the Lesser Key of Solomon.

SOLSTICE: Either of two times of the year when the sun has no apparent northward or southward motion. Summer solstice is approximately June 22 and Winter Solstice is approximately December 22.

SOOTHSAYER: A medium.

SORCERER (S): A wizard, witch or magician; a practitioner of black magic.

SORCERY: Magic, usually of the black variety.

SORILEGE: Casting lots hoping to find a good omen.

SPELL: An incantation designed to bring about magic.

SPIRITS: Discarnate entities, often the spirits of ancestors, who are believed to influence the world of the living.

SPIRITISM: Worship of or communication with the supposed spirits of the dead. The Bible seems to indicate that these spirits are demons in disguise.

SPONDOMANCY: Finding omens in soot or cinders.

STARS: Spiritual wisdom and development.

ST. JOHN'S EYE: The midsummer witch celebration. [June 23]

STICHOMANCY: A form of Rhapsodomancy.

STOLISOMANCY: Observing oddities in a person's dress for omens.

STOLICTES: The neophyte grade of the Hermetic Order of the Golden Dawn.

SUCCUBUS [succubi]: A female demon that copulates with human males.

SUPERIORS: Junior mothers and fathers.

SYCOMANCY: Divination by writing possible responses to questions on tree leaves, and observing which one dries the fastest; a modern equivalent is to put responses on pieces of paper, roll them up, and place them in a strainer above a steaming pot to see which opens first.

SYLPH: An elemental who lives in air.

TALISMAN: An object believed to hold magical powers.

TAROT CARDS: Cards used as a means of divination.

TELEKINESIS: Movement of objects by occult power.

TELEPATHY: Mind-to-mind communication.

TEPHRAMANCY: Divination by looking for messages in ashes, often burned tree bark.

THEOSOPHY: Literally "Wisdom of God"; a religion incorporating some Christian concepts along with reincarnation, karma, and spiritistic practices.

THE WAY: Bringing about social change with three (3) million people by 1990. They allegedly claim they will be in the White House. The Way appears to try to infiltrate law enforcement. They have a military group.

TRANSCENDENTAL MEDITATION: The Novice receives a Mantra—a special sound which he must keep secret. During meditation (which lasts for twenty minutes, twice each day), one must simply repeat the mantra mentally while ignoring all other thoughts. Regular meditation is supposed to let the mind descend to the deepest level of consciousness. The meditator experiences full relaxation, renewed energy and creativity, and a sense of well being. TM [Transcendental Meditation] is a religious system. The use of Mantras comes directly from the Hindu Yoga tradition and the "deepest level of consciousness" of which Maharishi speaks seems to be identical with the ground of being, I.E. Brahman. For these reasons Maharishi can be considered a Guru. Those followers who discount his religious role are misguided at best."

TRANSVECTION: Levitation, or the projection of a wraith form.

TRINITY "OCCULT STYLE": The triangle is the symbol of manifestation. It is here that the spirit will appear. A magician will do well to study the symbolism of the triangle and of the number three. Among other things, the triangle represents the trinity, the triple nature of our word (mental, psychic, and physical), and the electromagnetic dynamism of the universe.

TRUMPET SPEAKING: Musical notes supposedly made by spirits through a special trumpet during a seance.

UNDINE: An elemental who lives in water.

UROBOROS: A serpent depicted as eating his own tail; the symbol being used to show the unity of the sacrificer and the one sacrificed.

VAMPIRE: According to legend, one who rises from the grave by night to consume the blood of persons.

VAUDERIE, VAULDERIE: The witches' Sabbat.

VENFICA: A witch who uses poisons and philters.

VIBRATIONS: A magical aura or atmosphere.

VOODOO: Use of spell, sorcery, potions and fetishes to control the actions of others or outcome of events.

VOW: An earnest promise or pledge that binds one to perform a specific act or behave in a certain manner.

WALPURGIS-NIGHT: The eve of May Day, believed in medieval Europe to be the occasion of a witch's sabbath. An episode or situation having the quality of nightmarish wildness associated with this sabbat. (April 30).

WAND: Made of ash, willow or hazel usually 21 inches long plain or decorated priapic wand has an 8 or 9 inch phallus on one end.

WARLOCK: Originally meaning "one who breaks faith." It is more often used by non-witches to refer to a male witch.

WATCHER: A familiar acting as a guardian.

WATER: Symbolized Christ.

WAXING MOON: Changing Moor.

WEREWOLF: According to legend, a person who has been turned or turns himself into a wolf-like creature.

WHITE MAGIC: Magic that is helpful or beneficial; the Bible makes no such distinction, and neither do most dedicated occultists.

WICCA: An Old English word from which we get the word "witch."

WITCH: One who practices magic.

WITCHCRAFT: The practice of sorcery or magic.

WITCHES' SABBATH: Meeting of a witches' coven held in order to perform magical rites and ceremonies. A large number of witches and warlocks who would gather around a bonfire or cauldron, light black candles, and perform sacrifices. The Sabbath would culminate in a sexual orgy.

WITNESS: Student minister.

WIZARD: "Wise One"; male witch.

WRAITH: A projected astral body or mobile form of witch power.

XYLOMANCY: Divination using pieces of wood, either by interpreting their shape or noting the order in which they burn in a fire.

YAHWEH (sect): Allegedly black Hebrew Israelite. Originally headquartered in Miami and have an alleged branch in Tampa. It appears that their philosophy is a black supremacy philosophy. Their mode of dress is Biblical garb. [They have been identified in other areas of the United States].

YULE: Midwinter witch festival.

ZODIAC: The pattern of stars and planets used in astrology.

ZOMBIE: A corpse that moves and acts as if it were alive; or a person completely controlled by a magician.

Glossary References

1. W.A.T.C.H. Network, P.O. Box 12638, El Paso, Tx. 79913.
2. The Dictionary of Mysticism and the Occult, by Nevill Drury, Harper & Row, copyright 1985.
3. Mike Warnke Ministries, P.O. Box 1075, Danville, Ky. 40422.
4. Sandi Gallant, San Francisco Police Department, Intelligence.
5. Sgt. Hyatt, Polk County Sheriff's Dept., Florida
6. The Back in Control Center, The Punk Rock and Heavy Metal Handbook, by Darlyne R. Pettinicchio, 1234 W. Chapman, Suite 303, Orange, CA 92668.
7. Det. Sherry Poole, Lafayette Parish Sheriff's Department, 316 W. Main Street, Lafayette, LA.
8. Life Forces, A Contemporary Guide to the Cult and Occult, by Louis Stewart, Andrews and McMeel, Inc., copyright 1980.

BIBLIOGRAPHY

Adler, Margot, *Drawing Down the Moon*, (New York: Beacon Press, 1986)

Blum, Ralph, *The Book of Runes*, (New York: Oracle Books, St. Martin's Press, 1932)

Buckland, Raymond, *Complete Book of Witchcraft*, (St. Paul, Mn.: Llewellyn Publications, 1987)

Buckland, Raymond, *Practical Candleburning Rituals*, (St. Paul, Mn.: Llewellyn Publications, 1984)

Buckland, Raymond, *Practical Color Magick*, (St. Paul, Mn.: Llewellyn Publications, 1983)

Budge, E.A. Wallis, *The Egyptian Book of the Dead*, (New York: Dover Publications, 1967)

Call, Max, *Hand of Death*, (Lafayette, La.: Prescott Press, Inc., 1985)

Cavendish, Richard, *The Black Arts*, (New York: G.P. Putnam's Sons, 1967)

Cumbey, Constance, *The Hidden Dangers of the Rainbow* (Lafayette, La.: Huntington House, Inc., 1983)

Daraul, Akkon, *A History of Secret Societies*, (Secaucus, N.J.: Citadel Press, 1961)

Dey, Charmaine, *The Magic Candle*, (Bronx, N.Y.: Original Publications-Division of Jamil Product Corp., 1982)

Drury, Nevill, *Dictionary of Mysticism and the Occult*, (San Francisco, Ca.: Harper and Row Publishers, 1985)

Frost, Gavin and Yvonne, *The Magic Power of Witchcraft*, (West Nyack, N.Y.: Parker Publishing Co., Inc., 1976)

Frost, Gavin and Yvonne, *A Witch's Grimoire of Ancient Omens, Portents, Talismans, Amulets and Charms*, (West Nyack, N.Y.: Parker Publishing Co., Inc., 1979)

Gore, Tipper, *Raising PG Kids in an X-Rated Society*, (Nashville, Tn.: Abington Press, 1987)

Gygax, Gary, *Advanced D & D Dungeon Master's Guide*, (Lake Geneva, Wi.: TSR Games, Distributed in the U.S. and Canada by Random House, 1977, 1978)

Gygax, Gary, *Advanced D & D Players Handbook*, (Lake Geneva, Wi.: TSR Games, Distributed in the U.S. and Canada by Random House, 1978)

Gygax, Gary, Official Advanced D & D Monster Manual II, (Lake Geneva, Wi.: TSR Games, Distributed in the U.S. and Canada by Random House, 1983)

Gygax, Gary, *Official Advanced D & D Oriental Adventures*, (Lake Geneva, Wi.: TSR Games, Distributed in the U.S. and Canada by Random House, 1985)

Holmes, J. Eric, *Fantasy Role-Playing Games*, (New York: Hippocrene Books, 1981)

Hoyt, Karen, *The New Age Rage*, (Old Tappan, N.J.: Fleming H. Revell Company, 1987)

Hunt, Dave and T.A. McMahon, *America, the Sorcerer's New Apprentice, The Rise of New Age Shamanism*, (Eugene, Oregon: Harvest House Publishers, 1988)

LaVey, Anton, *The Satanic Bible*, (New York: Avon Books, 1969)

LaVey, Anton, *The Satanic Rituals*, (New York: Avon Books, 1972)

Line, David and Julia, *Fortune-Telling by Runes* (Wellingborough, Northamptonshire: The Aquarian Press, 1984)

Livingston, Ian, *Dicing With Dragons*, (New York: The New American Library, Inc., 1983)

Logan, Daniel, *America Bewitched: The Rise of Black Magic and Spiritism*, (New York: William Morrow and Co., Inc., 1974)

Lyons, Arthur, *Satan Wants You*, (New York: The Mysterious Press, 1988)

Malbrough, Ray T., *Charms, Spells and Formulas*, (St. Paul, Mn.: Llewellyn's Publications, 1987)

Maron, Kevin, *Ritual Abuse*, (Toronto, Canada: Seal Books, McClelland-Bantam, Inc., 1988)

Matriciana, Caryl, *Gods of the New Age*, (Eugene, Oregon: Harvest House Publishers, 1985)

The Devil's Web

Matriciana, Caryl, *Gods of the New Age* (videotape), (Rivershield Film Ltd. Productions, Huntington Beach, Ca.)

Pazder, Lawrence, M.D., and Smith, Michelle, *Michelle Remembers*, (New York: Congdon and Lattes, Inc., 1980)

Robbins, Rossell Hope, *The Encyclopedia of Witchcraft and Demonology*, (New York: Bonanza Books-Crown Publishers, 1959)

Scott, Sir Walter, *Demonology and Witchcraft*, (New York: Bell Publishing Co., copyright MCMLXX)

Seligmann, Kurt, *The History of Magic and the Occult*, (New York: Harmony Books, 1948)

Simon, *The Necronomicon*, (New York: Avon Books, a division of The Hearst Corp., 1977)

Slater, Herman, *Magickal Formulary Spellbook, Book II*, (New York: Magickal Childe Publishing, Inc.)

Smyth, Frank, *Modern Witchcraft*, (Printed in the U.S.: Castlebooks by Ottenheimer Publishers, Inc., 1975)

Suter, Paul, *HM A-Z: The Ultimate Heavy Metal Encyclopedia*, (London/New York/ Sydney/Cologne: Omnibus Press, 1985)

Stewart, Louis, *Life Forces: A Contemporary Guide to the Cult and Occult*, (New York: Andrews and McMeel, Inc., A Universal Press Syndicate Company, 1950)

Terry, Maury, *The Ultimate Evil*, (Garden City, N.Y.: Dolphin Books, Doubleday and Company, Inc., 1987)

Ward, James M. with Kuntz, Robert J., *Advanced D & D, Deities and Demigods Cyclopedia of Gods and Heroes from Myth and Legend*, (Lake Geneva, Wi.: TSR Games, Distributed in the U.S. and Canada by Random House, 1980)

Wedeck, Harry E., *A Treasury of Witchcraft*, (Secaucus, N.J.: Citadel Press, 1961)

Wippler, Migene Gonzalez, *The Santeria Experience*, (Bronx, New York: Original Publications, 1982)

Wooden, Kenneth, *The Children of Jonestown*, (New York: McGraw-Hill Book Co., 1981)

Wooden, Kenneth, and Kunhardt, Peter W., Producers, "The Devil Worshipers," on "20/20," May 16, 1985)

Zolar, *Encyclopedia of Ancient and Forbidden Knowledge*, (New York: Arco Publishing, Inc., 1984)

CARE FOR THE FAMILY

There are times when being a parent is the most difficult and loneliest task in the world and it may be that reading this book has brought you face to face with particular issues with which you may need help.

CARE for the FAMILY is part of the work of CARE Trust and has been set up to provide advice, help and encouragement to individuals and families in need. It is based in the UK and works very closely with Dr James Dobson and the ministry of Focus on the Family in the USA. If you need help or advice please write to: CARE for the FAMILY, 59 Wellfield Road, Roath Park, CARDIFF CF2 3PA.